The Progressive Mind 1890-1917

Revised Edition

DAVID W. NOBLE

University of Minnesota
Minneapolis, Minnesota

Burgess Publishing Company
Minneapolis, Minnesota

Cover art and design: Cherie Wyman, Wyman Graphics

Copyright © 1981 by Burgess Publishing Company
Printed in the United States of America
Library of Congress Catalog Number 80-70301
ISBN 0-8087-1441-4

Burgess Publishing Company
7108 Ohms Lane
Minneapolis, Minnesota 55435

J I H G F E D C B

To the Memory of Carl Becker

Contents

Contents

Preface to the Revised Edition

When I was writing this book at the end of the 1960s, I was not aware of the extent to which what I call the new industrial, urban, and overseas frontiers expressed by *The Progressive Mind, 1890-1917* were revitalized in the theories of modernization expounded by many social scientists between 1960 and 1970. After the serious questions raised about these new frontiers first in the crisis of 1919 and then again in the crisis of 1929, there were significant explorations of decentralized alternatives to those frontiers throughout the 1920s and 1930s. World War II renewed centralized expansion without, however, reestablishing an explicit philosophy of progress. But, by 1960, President John F. Kennedy was calling for a New Frontier which seemed very similar to the frontiers envisioned by Theodore Roosevelt and Woodrow Wilson. And economists such as Walt Whitman Rostow, in *The Stages of Economic Growth*, once more saw inevitable progress or modernization as had the progressive economists of 1914. But the failure of these prophecies of progressive modernization to explain the faltering American economy during the 1970s as well as worldwide economic and social instability throughout this decade has made possible another reconsideration of decentralization and rootedness in the current ecological movement. A reexamination of the commitments to the industrial, urban, and overseas frontiers in the Progressive Era with their implicit assumptions of endless and inexpensive energy, therefore, can provide perspective on the deep confusions about energy and growth which characterize our intellectual life as we go into the 1980s.

In many respects, therefore, I see the crisis of the Progressive Mind at the end of World War I being repeated at the end of the war in Vietnam. Progressive intellectuals at the beginning of the 1960s related President Kennedy's call for a New Frontier to a vision of a worldwide frontier modeled after the patterns of the United States, a vision similar to that of Woodrow Wilson. And they saw in President Lyndon Johnson's call for a Great Society the renewal of the vision of an urban frontier linked with an industrial frontier, a vision held by so many American intellectuals in 1914. As we begin the 1980s, many Americans seem to feel, after the unexpected frustrations of the late 1960s and 1970s, the need to create a vision of the future which does not rest on the Progressive beliefs in an industrial, urban, and overseas frontier.

This edition, then, reprints the book as it was published in 1970 with the single major addition of a chapter which explores the ideas of three women, Jane Addams, Charlotte Perkins Gilman, and Mary Parker Follett, who were important exponents of the idea of progress in the two decades before World War I.

Minneapolis, Minnesota   David W. Noble
Summer, 1980

Preface to the First Edition

This study assumes that every community has an identity of ideas and values which defines the forms of its economic, social, and political life. And it further assumes that the collective identity held by the dominant group of nineteenth-century, middle-class Americans was in severe crisis by 1890. All of the accepted forms of society were being called into question. The central focus of this book, therefore, is an analysis of the attempt of this middle-class group to resolve its identity crisis and reachieve a sense of vitality, a vision of a future that promised fulfillment rather than despair; a future in which new forms of order would emerge out of chaos. In making this emphasis, I have neglected necessarily those thinkers who are outside the dominant group. This book is not the history of ideas in America, 1890–1917, but of a particular cluster of ideas. I have not dealt, therefore, with a figure like William James in philosophy, who proposed an alternative to the progressive outlook, or with novelists like Stephen Crane or Theodore Dreiser, or with a poet like Edward Arlington Robinson, or other artists who stood outside the progressive synthesis. I have not considered those political, economic, or social radicals who also proposed alternatives to progressivism.

To a considerable extent my analysis of progressivism concurs with the overview of American history established by William Appleman Williams in his book, *The Contours of American History* (1961). I agree with him that the dominant imagination in America has been one that attempts to escape from the problem of community. I see the progressives searching for a new frontier force in industrialism that would allow for that continuous economic expansion which would guarantee constant social mobility. Such expansion and mobility would make unnecessary a confrontation with the problem of justice as a system of positive relationships between individuals. On the surface progressivism was a rejection of nineteenth-century competitive individualism in favor of an ideal of community. But most American progressives defined that ideal community as so spontaneous and natural that the individual would not have to sacrifice any of his autonomy and independence through participation in group endeavor. And the ideal community was defined in those same terms of constant expansion and mobility which avoided the need to define the meaning of justice.

In this respect I see American history as operating within the rhythms of western civilization. It was the international middle class of western Europe and the United States which was committed in the eighteenth and nineteenth centuries to stepping out of time into space as spaciousness; out of community into autonomy for the individual. The closing down of space for European and American expansion at the end of the nineteenth century resulted in a common identity crisis in Europe and America which can be seen by comparing a book like Leo Marx's *The Machine in the Garden* with George Mosse's *The Crisis of German Ideology*. Both explore the intellectual crisis of national communities, the United States and Germany, faced with growing internal complexity and without the promise of new internal frontiers that might provide mobility for the individual. Or, another comparison can be made between Walter LaFeber's *The New Empire, An Interpretation of American Expansion, 1860–1898* and Bernard Semmel's *Imperialism and Social Reform, English Social-Imperial Thought, 1895–1914,* in which the closing of internal frontiers is linked with the thrust of overseas expansion.

Another major parallel can be drawn between the themes described by Morton G. White in his *Social Thought in America: The Revolt against Formalism* and H. Stuart Hughes' *Consciousness and Society: The Reorientation of European Social Thought, 1890–1930.* Both are describing the attempt of American and European thinkers at the end of the nineteenth century to escape from a rigid philosophical system that seemed sterile and decadent. By rejecting the concept of static form, these Americans and Europeans hoped to create an intellectual atmosphere of choice and possibility and innovation. And the collapse of American middle-class progressivism in 1919 coincided with the failure of the European middle class to find creative patterns of revitalization as alternatives to the cultural values which had led to the suicidal self-destruction of World War I. From 1919 on, theories of revitalization in America and Europe would pass into the hands of radicals on the right or on the left as the American and European middle class tried to return to normalcy through nostalgia for a nineteenth-century paradise; a contrived and cultivated nostalgia which must deny that this class had faced any identity crisis in the gay nineties.

Minneapolis, Minnesota
Summer, 1969

David W. Noble

Chapter I

The Crisis of 1890: Rural Stability versus Industrial Change

The intellectual history of the United States between 1890 and 1917 is best understood as the expression of a profound cultural crisis caused by the rapid urbanization and industrialization of the nation during the nineteenth century. Until the 1890s most Americans had tried to ignore the continuous trend away from the agricultural society of the late eighteenth century. The people of the United States were unwilling to face this emerging new reality because it threatened the identity which the Founding Fathers had given to their revolutionary Republic as a chosen nation, saved from the terror of history just because it was agricultural.

For leaders like John Adams, Benjamin Franklin, George Washington, and Thomas Jefferson, the United States of America was the first modern nation to have completely freed itself from the heritage of medieval civilization. They accepted the premises of the Reformation and Renaissance that the medieval period was a dark age because it was an artificial culture, artfully contrived by priests and feudal aristocrats. They shared the Reformation and Renaissance attitude that the greatest human sin was the cultural creativity committed by medieval men and that the greatest human virtue was the imitation of God's law or natural law to which modern men had committed themselves.

These leaders of the American Revolution saw the years after 1500 as a period of purge of the artificial patterns of the Dark Ages, patterns created through the conspiracy of evil men. And they saw the English colonies in North America as the first place where European men had escaped completely from the artificial and profane human patterns of the Middle Ages to achieve unity with God's natural and sacred order.

Describing their revolution of 1776 as an attempt to preserve this natural order from George III's conspiracy to force vestiges of medievalism on the New World, the leaders of the American Revolution further argued that Europeans could never escape the heritage of the Dark Ages in Europe. Only by coming from the Old World to the New World could the European escape the corruption of historical culture and achieve harmony with God's natural order. It was providential that a virgin continent had been hidden from mankind until that moment when men realized their mistake in choosing artificial culture over a natural order.

The Founding Fathers believed that a natural order could prevail only in the New World because they defined natural man as a property owner, and only in the New World did the expanse of virgin land offer the possibility that every immigrant would be a property holder. The ownership of property made a man independent; it made unnecessary the artificial cultural patterns of dependence and lordship which had existed and would continue to exist in Europe where the population was large and land was scarce.

Hoping with Jefferson that the acquisition of the land stretching from the Appalachian boundary of 1789 to the Pacific Ocean would long preserve the United States from a population density like that of Europe, the founders of the nation saw cultural creativity as the greatest danger to their virtuous Republic. These eighteenth-century men did not define man as a culture-building animal. For them the creation of culture was an evil and conspiratorial act. The growth of cultural complexity during the Middle Ages was unnatural and sinful. Historical change was good only when it was a purge, destroying artificial complexity and restoring natural simplicity. That was progress. But the appearance of new patterns of social relations must be defined as decadence.

Arguing that their revolution had not created anything new but had preserved a God-given natural simplicity, arguing that the Constitution of 1789 embodied and imitated eternal natural principles, the Founding Fathers taught the citizens of the new nation that they were a chosen people, having a special covenant with God. As long as Americans continued to imitate the natural principles of 1789, they would be delivered from the terror of historical change, from the chaos of cultural conflict which characterized Europe. Americans, if they did not commit the sin of cultural creativity, would live in timeless harmony for all eternity.

But Americans, like all men, were culture-building animals, and they engaged in tremendous cultural creativity between 1790 and 1890. Americans were part of the international middle class of western civilization which had believed, during the seventeenth and eighteenth centuries, that a dedication to economic activity, to scientific research, and to technological innovation would destroy medieval cultural complexity and help mankind restore natural simplicity. If natural simplicity was defined, however, as the autonomy of the property-holding individual, symbolized by the yeoman farmer, how could the economic, scientific, and technological growth of the nineteenth century that developed industrialism be defined as progressive? For industrialism was characterized by the factory where workers came in groups, workers who did not own the factories, workers who were dependent upon those who did own them. Further, industrialism caused the growth of cities, cities that Thomas Jefferson had called sores on the body-politic, cities that fitted the Founding Fathers' definition of artificial European society with its complex patterns of dependence and lordship. Finally, industrialism, by the 1870s and 1880s, had brought into existence an artificial institution, the corporation, which threatened to become the dominant factor in the economy.

Until the 1880s most Americans had been so preoccupied with ridding the nation of the institution of slavery and the southern aristocracy, which parasitically, in feudal fashion, exploited slave labor, that they ignored the growth of the factory, the city, and the corporation. Until the 1880s most Americans could define national history as progress in the sense that the destruction of slavery and the slavocracy was a purge, eliminating cultural complexity and restoring natural simplicity.

Recognition of the presence of the factory, the city, and the corporation came as a terrible shock, therefore, in the 1880s, attended by the fear that the nation had broken its covenant with God by indulging in the sin of cultural creativity. Throughout the entire national culture in the 1880s there appeared expressions of the fear that the nation had begun the downward path of cultural decadence. Nowhere was this fear stronger, however, than in the Midwest and South, where the identification with the agricultural base of the national covenant was strongest. Here was the stronghold of the yeoman farmer, the most authentic American, and here the battle had to be waged against the forces of the factory, the city, and the corporation which threatened to drive these chosen people from their harmony with natural virtue into the disharmony of cultural complexity.

Ignatius Donnelly was one of the most important critics who represented and expressed these fears which ultimately found political expression in the Populist Party of the 1890s. Born in Philadelphia, Donnelly had come to the territory of Minnesota just before the Civil War to find fame and fortune. While fortune always escaped him, he did find immediate fame as a leader of the Republican Party during and after the war. Like so many Americans, Donnelly interpreted the war as the final fulfillment of a classless democracy of free and equal producers, and he was horrified as he watched his Republican Party, the instrument which had purged feudal aristocracy from the land, become the vehicle for the expansion of what he saw as a new corporate feudal aristocracy. Desperately he tried to educate the people of Minnesota in his election campaigns to this danger, but they refused to believe that businessmen, the traditional antithesis of medieval civilization, could represent a feudalistic threat to American democracy. More and more Donnelly was driven into his study to write books which might reach and alert a nationwide audience to the impending national catastrophe.

In 1882 and 1883 he wrote two books, *Atlantis* and *Ragnarok*, to discredit the way in which Darwinian evolutionary theory was being used by the apologists for corporate enterprise, who justified the new forms of capitalism by defining the corporation as an expression of natural law. These apologists had begun to explain the disharmonies of nineteenth-century capitalism through a criticism of the eighteenth-century concept of the Newtonian world machine. Nature, English economists began to argue in the early nineteenth century, was, upon closer observation, not static after all. And, therefore, when modern man had escaped from the disharmonious institutions of the Middle Ages, he had not returned to a peaceable kingdom. Man had escaped from the chaos of manmade traditions and institutions. But now he was in organic unity with a dynamic, evolutionary, progressive physical nature which had to purge man of his continuing biological weaknesses before he was capable of living in peace. Competition, survival of the fittest, was the purifying method of nature. And competition, survival of the fittest, was the method of capitalism. The disharmony of capitalism, therefore, was natural and progressive in contrast to the disharmony of medievalism, which was unnatural and regressive. Accepting this analogy between capitalism and physical nature, William Graham Sumner, an American professor of economics, wrote that new forms of capitalistic enterprise, such as corporations, were functional to this progressive process of evolution.

Donnelly refused to accept the idea of evolution, even as he refused to accept the business corporation, as natural. In *Atlantis* and *Ragnarok* he insisted that evidence of physical changes in earth structure and evidence of biological species which had died out could be explained in terms of natural catastrophes such as earthquakes, floods, and collisions with comets. These natural catastrophes, he continued, coincided with the destruction of past civilizations. They represented God's punishment of man's sinfulness.

Atlantis, he wrote, had been an early civilization which had endured for many generations in peace and plenty. Its people were happy because they lived simply and in harmony with God's creation. They did not create artificial institutions and traditions. They were innocent children obeying God's will. However, the people gradually came to deny this God-given world; they became discontented with this authentic environment and through their imagination constructed an artificial one. In this stage of sinful creativity, of cultural decadence, "skepticism becomes the synonym for intelligence; men no longer repeat; they doubt; they dissect; they sneer; they reject; they invent."

Donnelly warned that America, like ancient Atlantis, was moving away from the God-given simplicity of the Jeffersonian Republic and engaging in the unforgivable sin of social creativity; then, "if 'sensual sins grow large'; if 'brother spoils brother'; if Sodom and Gomorrah came again—who can say that God may not bring out of the depths of space a rejuvenating comet?" But, Donnelly declared in the 1880s, there was still time for Americans to repent, to stop building artificial institutions, and to regain their childlike innocence. "Take your mind off your bricks and mortar," he implored, "and put out your tentacles toward the great spiritual world around you . . . open communications with God . . . put your intellect to work to increase the productive capacity of Nature, that plenty and happiness, light and hope, may dwell in every heart, and the Catacombs be closed forever . . . and from such a world God will fend off comets with His great right arm."

By 1890 Donnelly's fears and frustrations had increased to the point where he could visualize the possibility of national suicide without the necessity of divine vengeance. His novel, *Caesar's Column*, portrays an America in 1988 on the verge of self-destruction because it has not acted in 1888 to preserve its cultural innocence. Traditionally, Americans have contrasted their virtuous natural simplicity with the corrupt complexity of Europe. But in 1988 Donnelly brings a visitor, Gabriel Weltstein, from the nation of Uganda, an oasis of arcadian purity in Africa, to view in amazement the cultural complexity of the United States which has continued to build diverse forms of economic, social, and political institutions. "What an infinite thing is man," the naive visitor from Uganda exclaims, "as revealed in the tremendous civilization he has built up! These swarming, laborious, all-capable ants seem great enough to attack heaven itself if they could but find a resting place for their ladders. Who can fix a limit to the intelligence or achievements of our species."

Donnelly presents a vision of an America which has constructed between 1880 and 1980 a new tower of Babel, a huge, artificial pattern which suggests order but which under close scrutiny is the embodiment of chaos itself. Paralleling Marx's analysis of the internal contradictions in capitalism, Donnelly prophesies the concentration of wealth in the hands of a small oligarchy, characterized by a "blind adoration of wealth and a heartless contempt of humanity." These new feudal lords rationalize their vicious exploitation of the masses through the theology of a religion of science closely related to the Social Darwinism that Donnelly hated, a theology which teaches that "the plan of Nature necessarily involves cruelty, suffering, injustice, destruction, death." Surrounded by armies who function as a police force to protect its property, the oligarchy seems invulnerable. But the impoverished, brutalized common people are organizing in small cells of a Brotherhood of Destruction and soon will rise up to destroy this corrupt, parasitical aristocracy. Here, Donnelly warned his readers, is the American future if the classless democracy of free and equal producers is replaced by the European model of class divisions. For, he wrote, "There is no bigotry so blind or intense as that of caste; and long established wrongs are only to be rooted out by fire and sword. . . . The upper classes might reform the world, but they will not; the lower classes would, but they cannot; and . . . these latter have settled down into a sullen and unanimous conviction that the only remedy is worldwide destruction." When America destroys itself in this orgy of class warfare, Gabriel withdraws to Uganda to warn against the retribution which accompanies the sin of cultural creativity. All contact with the outside world is broken off and "the government . . . stops every hole of opportunity; crushes down every instinct of cruelty and selfishness. And the wolves have disappeared; and our little world is a garden of peace and beauty, musical with laughter . . . and mankind moves with linked hands through happy lives . . . and God smiles down upon them from his throne beyond the stars."

For Donnelly the great serpent that had slithered into the American garden was finance capitalism which tempted men to surrender their roles as honest producers and to enter into the artificial and parasitical world of usury. As the productive people of the 1820s had found a hero in Andrew Jackson, a valiant knight who would destroy this serpent when it took the form of the Second Bank of the United States, so Donnelly hoped for the appearance of such a hero in his own time. As a campaign document for populism in 1892, he published *The Golden Bottle*, a fantasy in which all of his hopes for national salvation were embodied.

Out of the heart of America, Kansas, comes a hero of the people, Ephraim Benezet. Ephraim understands the sufferings of the people because he too has suffered. His family has been impoverished by the plottings of bankers. But Ephraim discovers a magic bottle which converts iron into gold. This enables him to destroy the control of the economy by the finance capitalists, restore the prosperity of the farmers, and stop their forced exodus into the cities where the once innocent young men become paupers and the young women prostitutes.

As Ephraim escapes assassination and thwarts the scheme of the eastern bankers to foment civil war, he recognizes his responsibility to preserve the national covenant which has made the United States a chosen nation. "Is not our Republic, resting on the broad base of popular support, a mountain, culminating in the sharp crest of authority? And had not the American Republic been built without hands, save only by the hands of the Almighty? It was not made. It grew inevitably out of its surroundings ... its principals were here before the colonists left their ships."

Ephraim, like Jackson, has purged the money-changers from the Jeffersonian temple and restored its purity. But, unlike Jackson, Ephraim cannot keep America isolated from a corrupt Europe. Relative peace had characterized the Old World during the nineteenth century because the United States served as a safety valve for its surplus population. When Ephraim closes off immigration so that "by wise laws and just conditions" he can "lift up the toilers of the country to the level of the middle classes," the European nations, under the conspiratorial rule of an alliance of capitalists and feudal lords, declare war on the United States. Ephraim then leads an army of the American people to Europe to make the world safe for democracy by destroying the artificial aristocracies and liberating the common people to live in timeless harmony with God's natural design.

Donnelly was invited to write that part of the Populist platform at Omaha in 1892 which explained why this people's party was in rebellion against the existing Republican and Democratic parties. For Donnelly the two old parties had become tools in the hands of the capitalist conspiracy and the professional politicians were unconcerned with the needs of the people. Unlike these parties, which were artificial institutions, the Populists were the spontaneous expression of the will of the people, dedicated to restoring the classless society of free and equal producers which had characterized the Republic of 1789.

In the platform Donnelly wrote that the nation was threatened with the creation of "two great classes—tramps and millionaires," that the nation was "rapidly degenerating into European conditions." And so, Donnelly concluded, "We seek to restore the government of the Republic to the hands of 'the plain people' with which it originated. We assert our purpose to be identical with the purposes of the National Constitution."

But the Populists, if they were to recapitulate the victory of Jacksonian democracy, had to modify the Jacksonian dedication to laissez-faire. They had to call for intervention in the economy by the government to regulate the corporations and to aid the farmers. They had to call for the control of the currency by the national government in order to destroy the power of the finance capitalists. In demanding the use of government planning to preserve the national covenant with nature, the Populists became vulnerable to the accusation that they, themselves, were un-American; that it was they who were destroying the national covenant by advocating artificial patterns of government activity; that it was they who were importing European artfulness to destroy American artlessness. It was the Populist party, the defenders of laissez-faire thundered, which was the serpent threatening the purity and innocence of the American garden.

The 1890s witnessed a terrible ideological division within the American people. In direct contrast to Ignatius Donnelly stood William Graham Sumner who believed with all his heart and mind that the business and industrial corporation was natural and no threat to the American covenant, but that political parties were unnatural and a direct threat to American harmony with nature. Raised within a tradition of orthodox theology, Sumner had been ordained a minister, but quickly came to reject traditional theology as irrelevant mystery. In 1872 he became a professor of sociology and political science at Yale. He had dedicated himself to the faith that a rational understanding of natural law and obedience to that law would guarantee national salvation. Such an understanding, he asserted, buttressed the middle-class doctrine of secular calling as the major means to salvation. Always Sumner would believe that "the only two things which really tell on the welfare of man on earth are hard work and self-denial" and that "the savings bank depositor is a hero of civilization."

The America of Jackson and Lincoln had believed that this doctrine of work would create a nation of free and equal producers. And Donnelly in 1890 could only believe that a conspiracy operating through artificial institutions was destroying social equality and creating an un-American class hierarchy. But Sumner accepted the growing inequality of wealth as natural. "Let it be understood," he wrote, "that we cannot go outside of this alternative: liberty, inequality, survival of the fittest; not—liberty, equality, survival of the unfittest. The former carries society forward and favors all its best members; the latter carries society downwards and favors all its worst members. . . . Society needs first of all to be freed from these meddlers—that is, to be left alone. Here we are, then, once more back to the old doctrine—*Laissez-faire.*"

Like Donnelly, Sumner was a self-conscious patriot warning his country not to slip from its chosen status as a nation in harmony with natural law back into the corrupting environment of manmade social, economic, and political patterns. Like Donnelly, Sumner saw a powerful conspiracy at work to submerge the United States under a wave of European historical institutions and traditions. "We have been borrowing old world fashions and traditions," Sumner warned, "all through our history, instead of standing firmly by the political and social philosophy of which we are the standard-bearers."

For Sumner, as for the Populists, America was the nation in which middle-class progress had first succeeded in its pilgrimage away from medieval civilization and toward nature. "It is the glory of the United States, and its calling in history, that it shows what the power of personal liberty is—what self-reliance, energy, enterprise, hard sense men can develop when they have room and liberty and when they are emancipated from the burden of traditions and faiths which are nothing but the accumulated follies and blunders of a hundred generations of 'statesmen.'" He, too, believed that the Reformation had begun this process of progress away from historical patterns toward natural ones. Europeans landing in the New World suddenly found themselves able to act according to reason and not tradition. Applying advanced European technology to the vast resources of the western continent, they had created a physical utopia in which starvation and disease were absent for the first time in history.

An economic and social democracy was the gift of New World resources and European technology to the first Americans. "In a new country with unlimited land, the substantial equality of the people in property, culture, and social position is inevitable." Fortuitous circumstance and not self-conscious choice determined the condition of man. "We are the children of the society in which we were born. It makes us. We are the products of the civilization of our generation." Geography and technology had determined that Americans were a chosen people, free from the terrible class conflicts of Europe which Donnelly had warned must not be allowed to occur here. And Sumner agreed with Donnelly that it would be catastrophic to destroy American individualism through the importation of class conflict.

But Sumner saw this threat coming from a very different direction than Donnelly did. Sumner did not agree with Donnelly that Americans were perfect secular saints, able and willing to live in harmony with a natural Eden. Instead Sumner warned, "The truth is that cupidity, selfishness, envy, malice, lust, vindictiveness, are constant vices of human nature." As a result of these personal weaknesses, "history is only a tiresome repetition of one story. Persons and classes have sought to win possession of the power of the State in order to live luxuriously out of the earnings of others." All political philosophy, Sumner admonished, is only the rationalization of the self-interest of these competing groups. In America, however, because of the great wealth taken from the land by advanced technology, men had been materially satisfied without attempting to rob one another through the use of the government. Unfortunately, however, Americans did not recognize that their democracy was produced by impersonal economic factors. Under Jefferson and Jackson they came to believe that democracy was a function of politics. They borrowed from Europe the idea that forms of government and the activity of political parties could operate independently of economic conditions. They were seduced into the belief that politicians could artfully regulate the economy to fulfill political or moral values.

And now Americans like the Populists were arguing the need to use the government to control or destroy the corporations in the name of the value of Jeffersonian and Jacksonian political equality. The only thing these foolish men could accomplish, Sumner declared, was to destroy the economic prosperity which saved Americans from the bloody class warfare of Europe. The corporation, he admonished, was not artificial but natural. "In human society, in its lower forms, organization has always produced itself spontaneously and automatically and has, therefore, just suited itself to the case. . . . In civilized society, organization is equally spontaneous and automatic." Rapid population growth, Sumner continued, made necessary a continuous growth of technological efficiency in exploiting natural resources if class warfare was to be avoided. Only the corporation was capable of such progress. And human organization depended upon leadership from exceptional individuals; it depended upon "the transcendent importance of competent management. . . . Those men nowadays who can foresee the next steps to be taken to advance on this line are the great generals of the modern industrial army.... If we should set a limit to the accumulation of wealth ... it would be like killing off our generals in war."

For Sumner the Populists were attempting to destroy the freedom of personal competition which produced the natural aristocracy that guided the corporation. It was the Populists who threatened to place the individual once again within the artificial institutional and traditional structures which had blocked progress during the Dark Ages. In attempting to subordinate the individual to political demands, the Populists were forgetting that it was because of the modern doctrine of economic individualism that "men have been emancipated from tradition, authority, caste, superstition, and to a certain extent from prejudices and delusions."

Sumner saw himself and other social scientists explicitly serving as defenders of the natural aristocracy of corporation directors. The social scientists must educate the public to the realities of experience. They must educate the public to recognize that man had only two choices: to live in harmony with natural reality or to live in disharmony in an artificial world of political theory and theological moralism constructed by imagination. "On every ground," he wrote, "and at every point the domain of social science must be defended against the alleged authority of ethical dicta." Social scientists must persuade the public that the corporation and the natural aristocracy which guided it were a healthy adjustment to the natural environment, but that political democracy, with its emphasis on equality, was a denial of that environment, and that such a denial of reality would deliver mankind back into the chaos which had characterized medieval civilization. Sumner admitted that the United States of 1890 was not perfect because vestiges of European civilization had accidently been brought to the New World. But the social scientist could teach the public what was natural and what was unnatural in the status quo: "We have inherited a vast number of social ills which never came from Nature. They are the complicated products of all the tinkering, muddling, and blundering of social doctors in the past.... The greatest reforms which could now be accomplished would consist in undoing the work of statesmen in the past, and the greatest difficulty in the way of reform is to find out how to undo their work without injury to what is natural and sound." Again, however, Sumner reassured his generation that social scientists could make this distinction and bring the nation "back to normal health and activity."

The ideological impasse between the views of Donnelly and Sumner was expressed in the presidential election of 1896. A rebellion against the leadership of President Grover Cleveland, who was committed to laissez-faire and the gold standard, brought about the nomination of William Jennings Bryan as the presidential candidate of the Democratic Party. Stressing the importance of using silver as the basis for national currency in order to inflate farm prices and lower interest rates, Bryan was also sympathetic enough toward other Populist causes to win the support of the Populist Party. Bryan presented himself to the national voters as a representative hero of the West and South, of rural America, of those natural regions which still preserved the simplicity and virtue of the arcadian Republic of 1789.

In his great "Cross of Gold" speech at the Democratic convention, which had driven the delegates into a frenzy of hysterical support, Bryan defined his role as a defender of rural innocence against the aggressive, rapacious finance capitalists of the urban East. His listeners knew that Bryan was attempting to defend sacred Americanism against profane un-Americanism, to defend productive yeomen against parasitical aliens. In their innocence these true American people had retreated from their attackers until their backs were against the abyss and they could retreat no more. At such a moment the innocents must fight to preserve their virtue. "We have petitioned," Bryan thundered, "and our petitions have been scorned; we have entreated, and our entreaties have been disregarded; we have begged, and they have mocked when our calamity came. We beg no longer; we entreat no more; we petition no more. We defy them!"

The alien parasites, charged Bryan, failed to recognize their own dependence upon the agricultural producers. They rejected the democratic idea "that if you legislate to make the masses prosperous, their prosperity will find its way up through every class which rests upon them." They did not recognize that "their cities rest upon our broad and fertile prairies. Burn down your cities and leave our farms, and your cities will spring up again as if by magic; but destroy our farms and the grass will grow in the streets of every city in the country." Bryan linked the un-American finance capitalists with England. They expressed alien values in arguing that the

United States must have a gold standard because England had one. But why, Bryan demanded, was it not possible that "instead of having a gold standard because England has, we will restore bimetallism, and then let England have bimetallism because the United States has it"? America would triumph against England, the American producer would be victorious against the un-American parasite, New World innocence would not be destroyed by Old World corruption, the forces of light would defeat the forces of darkness—this was the political-religious framework within which Bryan promised salvation. "Having behind us the producing masses of this nation . . . we will answer their demand for a gold standard by saying to them: You shall not press down upon the brow of labor this crown of thorns, you shall not crucify mankind upon a cross of gold."

Like Ignatius Donnelly, Bryan wanted a politics of salvation which would purge the nation of alien corruption and restore the sacred Republic of 1789. But the Republicans, whom Bryan defined as spokesmen for un-American doctrines, as traitors who were importing Old World patterns into the American garden of Eden, defined their role as defenders of the national covenant against the Democrats, whom the Republicans described as the real un-Americans.

It followed, in the logic of the editorials of the Republican newspapers in 1896, that Bryan and the Democrats, like the Populists of 1892, wanted to make the national government an artful manipulator of the economy and society. They wanted to destroy the God-given natural law of laissez-faire. Bryan's Democratic Party wanted to import European communism and anarchism; it wanted to destroy the property of the honest industrial producers; it wanted to establish a conspiratorial, parasitical elite as an anti-Christ ruling class. For these newspapers 1896 was indeed Armageddon, and political victory for the Republicans would mean national salvation and the preservation of American innocence from corrupting Old World ideologies. Hysterical editorials declared the profane nature of the Democratic conspiracy.

The *Philadelphia Press* declared:

The Jacobins are in full control at Chicago. No large political movement in America has ever before spawned such hideous and repulsive vipers. This riotous platform . . . rests upon the four corner stones of organized repudiation, deliberate confiscation, chartered Communism, and enthroned anarchy.

And the *New York Tribune* added:

The wretched, rattle-pated boy [Bryan] posing in vapid vanity and mouthing resounding rottenness was not the real leader of that league of hell. He was only a puppet in the blood-imbued hands of Altgeld, the anarchist, and Debs, the revolutionist. . . . But he was a willing puppet, Bryan was, willing and eager. Not one of his masters was more apt than he at lies and forgeries and blasphemies, and all the nameless inequities of that campaign against the Ten Commandments. . . . [The Democratic platform was] the hysterical declaration of a reckless and lawless crusade of sectional animosity and class antagonism . . . no wild-eyed and rattle-brained horde of the red flag ever proclaimed a fiercer defiance of law, precedent, order, and government.

For those who marched with the Democrats to Armageddon in 1896 and, like Donnelly, had defined Bryan as a hero, "raised up by Providence to save the country from sinking into Old World conditions," the victory of the Republicans was crushing. Evil had vanquished virtue and what hope was left. "Alas and alack," Donnelly wrote, "it seems useless to contest against the money power. Every election marks another step downward into the abyss from which there will be no return save by fire and sword."

For the victorious Republicans, however, 1896 could not be defined as the victory of the forces of light. Almost half the American nation had voted for Bryan and "atheistic communism." The country was not purged of evil. For the moment the Republic had been defended successfully but the enemy remained, strong and poised for another attack.

Unable as yet to find a formula which linked industrialism to progress, the purging of the complex, and the restoration of simplicity, most Americans in 1896 remained trapped by the fear that their nation was becoming decadent and was moving toward cultural complexity. It is possible, therefore, that a major reason for the development, in 1895 to 1898, of public pressure to go to war to free Cuba from Spain was that such a conflict offered Americans a chance to escape from their fear of moral decay and to restore their identity as a progressive nation dedicated to the victory of natural simplicity. The existence of rebellion in Cuba seemed to permit Americans a chance to return to a happier time in the past when middle-class Protestantism had decisively defeated medieval Catholicism to begin the upward spiral of modern progress.

American historians, like Bancroft, Prescott, Motley, and Parkman, writing between 1830 and 1890, had defined the United States as God's chosen nation in which the progressive forces of Protestantism had reached final and perfect culmination. For these historians, who served as political philosophers and secular theologians for the national culture, it had been the destiny of the Reformation to begin to free the individual from the tyranny of medieval monarchies which in turn were rooted in the ultimate tyranny of the Church of Rome.

They described the Roman Catholic Church as the anti-Christ which taught men to turn away from God. This "Holy Mother Church," they wrote, "linked in sordid wedlock to governments and thrones, numbered among her servants a host of the worldly and the proud, whose service of God was but the service of themselves." When England became Protestant, it was inevitable that she should smash Spanish power in 1588, because "whoever wishes to be made well-acquainted with the morbid anatomy of governments, whoever wishes to know how great states may be made feeble and wretched, should study the history of Spain." Spain, in contrast to England, lacked the vigor of free individuals fighting for God's purposes. Spain had only unfree citizens, fettered by monarchical absolutism and clerical despotism, who were motivated by material greed. By 1600 England had effectively destroyed Spain as a major power, and the historical drama of Protestant progress became England's conflict with Catholic France for the control of North America.

For these historians progress from medieval tyranny to Protestant liberty was inexorable and the victory for "English Protestantism and popular liberty" was predestined by God. With France's surrender of her New World power in 1763, medieval Catholicism had symbolically lost its power to profane the virgin land of the western hemisphere. And the United States, the heir of the Protestant Reformation, was the fulfillment of God's plan to build a refuge for Protestants in the New World. As medievalism continued to wither away in the Old World, it was assumed that it must wither away in the New. And, as fulfillment of the prophecy, in 1895 Catholic Spain retained only the island of Cuba from all her vast empire of 1600.

Now the Cubans were in revolt against Spanish misrule, against this anachronism of the feudal past, this last corrupting vestige of the Roman anti-Christ within the purity of the western hemisphere. Americans, the citizens of the United States, could understand the horror of this tyranny because it was unnatural, a perversion of the spontaneous virtue of nature which God had willed for the New World. The American historian Parkman wrote:

Nature had given [priests] all the passions of a vigorous manhood, and religion had crushed them, curbed them, or tamed them to do her work.... And while he, the priest, yields reverence and obedience to the Superior, in whom he sees the representative of the Deity, it behooves him, in his degree to require obedience from those whom he imagines that God has confided to his guidance. His conscience, then, acts in perfect accord with the love of power innate in the human heart.... The instinct of domination is a weed that grows rank in the shadow of the temple, climbs over it, possesses it, covers its ruin, and feeds on its decay. The unchecked sway of priests has always been the most mischievous of tyrannies.

Americans expected, then, the atrocity stories in their newspapers which chronicled the murder, rape, and arson committed by the Spanish troops as they attempted to suppress the rebellion. They awaited confirmation of nameless tortures, of hideous bestiality. And they demanded that their government drive the Spanish anti-Christ from the New World. No real danger, no great effort would be needed to accomplish this task. Decadent Spain had been destroyed by progressive England in 1588, and every newspaper calling for the use of force argued that it would take only from "ninety minutes to ninety days" to end this last monument of feudalism in the hemisphere of freedom.

But if Americans did purge the New World of medievalism, they would demonstrate their continued harmony with God's plan of progress from the historical complexity of the Middle Ages to the natural simplicity of modern civilization. They would prove to God that they had not renounced the covenant in which they had promised to refrain from building cultural complexity in order to live in timeless harmony with nature. No wonder newspaper editorials at the beginning of 1898 thundered that "the people want no disgraceful negotiations with Spain. Should the President plunge the administration into that morass, he and his party would be swept out of power in 1900 by a fine burst of popular indignation. An administration which stains the national honor will never be forgiven." The outline of the melodrama emerging in the editorials was the need for Americans to liberate Cuba from Spanish rule, to drive Spain out of the western hemisphere. To engage in diplomatic negotiations with a nation both corrupt and powerless would rob the United States of the possibility of acting as a Saint George destroying the dragon. President McKinley and his advisors, chiefly from the business community, had engaged in diplomatic activity and had hoped to bring about a negotiated settlement which would give Cuba autonomy within the Spanish Empire. But as the McKinley administration lost hope for significant concessions from Spain, it increasingly accepted the need to purge Spanish influence from the Americas. Finally on April 21, 1898, President McKinley asked Congress for the power to use the armed forces for this purge. Appended to his message to Congress was Spain's acquiescence on April 19 to his ultimatum that Spanish hostilities toward the rebels must cease immediately. McKinley had capitulated to the idea that Cuba must be freed by a purifying act of force and not by the corrupting entanglements of diplomatic negotiations.

Immediately Americans stressed the miraculous unity which this spiritual act of saving an innocent people from medieval oppression called forth. For Senator Chauncey Depew of New York: "We have witnessed the fiercest rivalry among the National Guard regiments to be called into service. The government has been overwhelmed with offers of volunteers. I venture to say that in no war and in no country until now have regiments and brigades petitioned to be sent to the front."

And for Bishop Ireland:

When America spoke there was no one in the land who was not an American. The laborer dropped his hammer, the farmer turned from his plough, the merchant forgot his counting-room, the millionaire closed the door of his mansion, and side by side, equal in their love of country and their resolve to serve her, they marched to danger and to death.... The President waved his wand; instantly armies and navies were created as by magic. Within a few weeks a quarter of a million men were formed into regiments and army corps; vessels of war and transport-ships covered the seas; and from one side of the globe to the other battles were fought, and victories were won. I know not of similar feats in history.

The meaning of the miracle of the victory of the United States over Spain was not to be understood, therefore, in military terms. The true miracle was the unification of a divided people. This new unity was a gift from God because the American people had turned away from their selfish interests, their petty political divisions, to serve God once again. The sound of American guns was "God's own trumpet-tones summoning His people out of their isolation." Other patriots agreed that "an all-ruling Providence directs the movements of humanity. What we witness is a momentous dispensation from the Master of men ... from time to time ... the dictates of religion impose war as righteous and obligatory." Still another patriot proclaimed: "We were driven into the war by the Spirit of the Lord."

It was clear that American entry into the war had delivered her citizens from the awful dilemma of whether McKinley or Bryan was the real preserver of the national covenant. Now there was no anguish. Medieval Spain was the devil and the American army was the heavenly host sent to fulfill God's plan to preserve the western hemisphere as a sacred space for Protestants. Glad tidings and rejoicings filled the press:

Our beloved country, human in the hour of triumph, gentle to the vanquished, grateful to the Lords of Hosts, a reunited nation forever, well may the people rejoice with the Royal Poet of Israel. "O Sing unto the Lord a new song for He hath done marvelous things; His right hand and His holy arm hath gotten Him the victory...." These American soldiers ... are the saints of liberty, the Church militant of freedom.... The soul of the United States is as white as the snow of the inaccessible peaks; as pure as the limpid mountain torrents; as serene as the eternal stars.

The "splendid little war" restored national optimism as the United States drove Spain out of the western hemisphere. But the peace brought apparent contradictions to this national crusade against colonialism. The United States immediately limited the sovereignty of Cuba by demanding naval bases on that island. And in the Caribbean the other Spanish-held island of Puerto Rico became the possession of a new American empire which stretched across the Pacific Ocean to incorporate the massive chain of the Philippine Islands ceded by Spain to the New World Republic. For many Americans, however, there was no real contradiction in the acquisition of empire in a war apparently fought against the idea of empire. If a major reason for the American declaration of war against Spain was an emotional crisis—the need to escape a sense of decline and decay, to escape from the chaos and conflict of the politics of social and economic discontent in the 1890s, the deliberate policy of the McKinley administration to acquire colonies in the Caribbean and the Pacific can be understood as another expression of the need to find new frontiers of opportunity to renew the national sense of progress and expansion.

In the 1880s major theologians like Josiah Strong were writing that the frontier of economic and social opportunity was closing within the continental boundaries of the United States. "When the supply [of western land] is exhausted," Strong warned, "we shall enter upon a new era, and shall more rapidly approximate European conditions of life. . . . We are the chosen people but we can no longer drift with safety to our destiny. We are shut up to a perilous alternative." Strong predicted an America with a rapidly growing population and a rapidly growing industrial plant. But, he argued, without a western frontier to absorb this population and this production, people and material goods would pile up one upon another until the nation would suffocate. Expansion overseas was the only healthy outlet for this human and mechanical energy. Thus, the American Anglo-Saxon Protestant must go forth and use his energy to Christianize the inferior colored races. Fortunately, Strong continued, "Commerce follows the missionary. A Christian civilization performs the miracle of the loaves and fishes, and feeds its thousands in a desert." America's industrial overproduction would follow its human overproduction into underdeveloped areas and provide economic abundance as America's missionaries provided spiritual and political abundance for the savages of the world.

Strong's extremely popular writings were echoed by men like Senator Beveridge, who declared, "God has not been preparing the English-speaking and Teutonic peoples for a thousand years for nothing but vain and idle self-contemplation and self-admiration. No! He has made us the master organizers of the world to establish system where chaos reigns. He has made us adepts in government that we may administer government among savages and servile peoples." And Henry Watterson, nationally renowned editor, agreed that expansion was necessary for national salvation:

From a nation of shopkeepers we became a nation of warriors. We escape the menace and peril of socialism and agrarianism, as England escaped them, by a policy of colonization and conquest. From a provincial huddle of petty sovereignties held together by a rope of sand, we rise to the dignity and prowess of an imperial republic incomparably greater than Rome. It is true that we exchange domestic danger for foreign dangers; but in every direction we multiply the opportunities of the people. We risk Caesarism, certainly; but even Caesarism is preferable to anarchism. . . . Already the young manhood of the country is as a goodly brand snatched from the burning, and given a perspective replete with noble deeds and elevating ideas.

Young intellectuals like Theodore Roosevelt, Brooks Adams, and Henry Cabot Lodge were persuaded by 1890 of the need for empire if America was to achieve both psychic and economic health in the future. And while Roosevelt and Lodge carried their ideas into politics, the writings of their friend, the naval officer Alfred Thayer Mahan, popularized them among the military elite. Increasingly these ideas of the need for empire and economic expansion overseas found approval among the business community. When the National Association of Manufacturers was founded in 1895, its leaders proclaimed that the expansion of foreign markets was essential to ending the economic depression that had begun in 1893.

In 1898 President McKinley and his advisors were well-acquainted with the thinking of men like Strong and Mahan and the thinking of the National Association of Manufacturers. The administration was ready to acquire Puerto Rico and build strategic bases in Cuba to control the access routes to Latin America and its vast untapped resources and markets; these bases would also control the isthmus of Panama, where American strategists planned to build an interocean canal. This canal would facilitate trade to Asia where even greater potential resources and markets awaited. To exploit this economic treasure, the McKinley administration was prepared to add the Philippines to Hawaii as American-controlled stepping stones to the infinite markets of China.

Committed to the idea of progress from the closed, limited, and decadent medieval world toward limitless opportunity for the middle-class individual, America was in ideological and spiritual crisis in the 1890s as it became apparent that the expanse of western lands, which Jefferson had promised would last a thousand years as both a spiritual and economic safety valve, had been exhausted a mere century after the founding of the Republic. By 1898 the concept of a new frontier of overseas expansion had become a significant part of the American imagination. But the appearance at the beginning of the twentieth century of a progressive movement, with its renewed optimism for the future, depended upon the redefinition of industrialism from a force creating complexity to that of a new frontier force leading from complexity to simplicity.

Chapter II

Turner and Beard:
The Historians View
the Frontier and Industrialism

The writings of the two most important historians of the progressive era, Frederick Jackson Turner and Charles Beard, illuminate the crisis of national identity and the major solution to that crisis which allowed many Americans to regain confidence that progress, not decadence, lay in the nation's future at the beginning of the twentieth century.

In 1893 a world's fair was held at Chicago to celebrate the four hundredth anniversary of the discovery of America. One of the ironies of this Columbian Exposition was the talk given by the young historian from Wisconsin, Turner. His address was entitled, "The Significance of the Frontier in American History." He spoke to a newly-formed professional group, the American Historical Association, that represented the massive revolution in American higher education in which provincial colleges were becoming huge universities geared to provide trained personnel for the vast urban-industrial complex of the twentieth century. This audience of a new professional association meeting in the setting of the new city of Chicago, which had changed from a village to a metropolis of a million in a single generation, provided dramatic emphasis for the central concern of Turner's paper. He called attention to the report of the census of 1890, which proclaimed the end of a frontier line, the disappearance of any significant area of unsettled land.

At first glance Turner's essay was not a Jeremiad like the writings of Donnelly. He did not suggest that an alien conspiracy was threatening to destroy the Republic of virtuous yeomen established by the Founding Fathers. Instead, Turner accepted the idea of evolution as the great scientific truth and argued that, as there was biological evolution, so there was social evolution. All societies, he wrote, evolve through similar stages, and, because European men stepped out of a complex civilization when they crossed the Atlantic, they reverted to primitive communities in the New World. These pioneering societies had then become more complex until now, at the end of the nineteenth century, they were approaching the level of European civilization once more. For Turner, "The United States lies like a huge page in the history of society. Line by line, as we read this continental page from West to East, we find the record of social evolution."

But Turner's scholarly paper did contain the terrible fears shared by Donnelly and Bryan and by Josiah Strong, Captain Mahan, and Theodore Roosevelt. Like these men, Turner feared that if America had reached a high level of civilization, then it must go into a stage of cultural decay. The individual, no longer able to act with the vitality of the pioneer, would be trapped by the increasing web of imprisoning institutions and traditions. America would slip back into the darkness which had characterized medieval civilization. Turner reminded his listeners, therefore, of the spiritual salvation, the rebirth experienced when Europeans escaped Old World civilized decadence to find spiritual refuge in the New World:

Into this vast shaggy continent of ours poured the first feeble tide of European men . . . and this great American West took them to her bosom, taught them a new way of looking upon the destiny of the common man . . . and even as society on her eastern border grew to resemble the Old World in its social form and its industry, ever, as it began to lose faith in the ideal of democracy, she opened new provinces, and dowered new democracies in her most distant domains with her material treasure and with the ennobling influence that the fierce love of freedom . . . furnished to the pioneer.

Like the Founding Fathers, Turner believed that the continued existence of that virgin land would provide the experience of rebirth for subsequent generations. As long as physical nature remained as a reservoir of spiritual innocence, a spiritual landbank, America could be defined as a sacred New World and not as part of the profane Old World. But now, after 1890, that religious experience of rebirth and renewal was no longer possible and a new nation was taking shape, new but ˙old, new but artificial and complex:

> The transformations through which the United States is passing in our own day are so profound, so far-reaching that it is hardly an exaggeration to say that we are witnessing the birth of a new nation in America. . . . The familiar facts of the massing of population in the cities and the contemporaneous increase of urban power, and of the massing of capital and production in fewer and vastly greater industrial units, especially attest the revolution.

Nostalgic for the frontier, Turner did most of his historical writing about the first half of the nineteenth century when he believed that the still existing virgin land had provided the spiritual strength for Jacksonian democracy's victory over the encroaching European-type complexity which overwhelmed the eastern seaboard by the end of the eighteenth century. The triumph of Jacksonian democracy, he wrote,

> meant that an agricultural society, strongest in areas of rural isolation rather than in the areas of greater density of population and of greater wealth, had triumphed, for the time, over the conservative, industrial, commercial, and manufacturing society of the New England type. It meant that a new aggressive, expansive democracy, emphasizing human rights and individuals, as against the old established order which emphasized vested rights and corporate action, had come into control.

In 1828 the pure force of physical nature had defeated the corrupt force of civilization. Democracy had defeated aristocracy. America had defeated Europe. Like Donnelly and the Populists, Turner in the 1890s wanted to believe that this political victory could be recapitulated, that the religious ritual of purification could be repeated. He described the Populists as the heirs of Jackson who saw that the forces of complexity, defeated in 1828, had reappeared and once more threatened the definition of the Americans as a chosen people with a special covenant with physical nature. The Populists saw, he declared, "the sharp contrast between their traditional idea of America, as the land of opportunity, the land of the self-made man, free from class distinctions and from the power of wealth, and the existing America, so unlike the earlier ideal." They saw, he continued, that "under the forms of the American democracy ... there [is] in reality evolving such a concentration of economic and social power in the hands of a comparatively few men as may make political democracy an appearance rather than a reality."

For Turner, however, the tragedy was that 1828 could not be repeated. The Jacksonians had achieved a political victory over the eastern aristocracy because they had not used institutional power to defeat the establishment. The Jacksonians won because they represented the spontaneous strength of nature, while their enemy could call only upon the artificial strength of manmade economic and political structures. Now in the 1890s, for Turner who had declared that "American democracy was born of no theorist's dream. ... It came stark and strong and full of life out of the American forest and it gained new strength each time it touched a new frontier," the corollary was that "the free lands are gone. The material forces that gave vitality to Western democracy are passing away."

While Turner did not agree with William Graham Sumner that the Jacksonians were guilty of using artificial political means to legislate equality, he was forced reluctantly to agree that the Populists were guilty of that charge. For Turner, as for Sumner, men could not legislate their social patterns. These were imposed on man by an external reality. Until the middle of the nineteenth century that reality had been nature; now, however, the laws of social evolution had moved Americans away from this state of primitive nature back toward a complex civilization. And there was nothing Americans could do about it. The Populists thought they could destroy this complexity because it was artificial and conspiratorial. But it was not. We must learn from German scholars, Turner wrote, "that the state is not in reality governed by laws of man's devising, but is part of the moral order of the universe, ruled by cosmic force from above." We must accept "the doctrine of Herder. Society grows.... Society is an organism."

All Turner could offer his readers, then, was stoic acceptance that the Eden of the 1830s was gone forever. "Never again," Turner commented, "can such an opportunity come to the sons of men. It was unique." At best, he hoped that the ideals of Jacksonian democracy could be temporarily prolonged in the midwestern universities and that briefly the academic communities could stave off the Europeanization of American society as it more and more approached Donnelly's prophecy of two warring classes of the rich and poor. For a moment in time these democratic educational centers could serve as "bulwarks against both the passionate impulses of the mob and the sinister designs of those who would subordinate public welfare to private greed," but ultimately the doom of Donnelly's 1988 must come.

At the same time that Turner was sharing in the general intellectual despair of the 1890s, a young student from the Midwest, Charles Beard, was traveling and studying in Europe, to discover for himself whether the end of the physical frontier did indeed spell the death of American democracy or whether industrialism might be interpreted as a greater and stronger frontier force than physical nature itself, a frontier force that destroyed cultural complexity and led to natural simplicity. His European experiences in the 1890s prepared Beard to become the most important historian of the years 1900 to 1917, and to become a prophet of the progressive moment when Americans escaped the feeling of aging and decadence and regained the sense of youthful vigor.

The great vision that Beard had seen in Europe was that industrialization was destroying institutions and traditions which had persisted from the Dark Ages. The great frontier of opportunity which had broken the imprisoning patterns of the past and made the individual mobile was not the discovery of a new continent but the discovery of a new method to extract wealth from nature. Beard declared:

Man, who through the long centuries had toiled with his hands, aided by crude implements, to wrest a pitiful subsistence from nature, suddenly discovered that the blind forces against which he had been struggling could be chained to do his work. . . . Suddenly, almost like a thunderbolt from a clear sky, were ushered in the storm and stress of the Industrial Revolution. The mechanical inventions of the centuries were eclipsed in less than one hundred years.

To save the idea of progress defined as the escape of mankind from cultural complexity to natural simplicity, Beard had to destroy the view of American history held by Donnelly and Turner and to modify the view held by Sumner. He rejected Donnelly and Turner's view that America had stripped itself of European cultural patterns and had become a pure state of nature which began decaying in the late nineteenth century. But he would also deny Sumner's view that industrialism necessitated the growth of a natural aristocracy of business leaders or that evolution must proceed through the mechanisms of competition.

For Beard, nineteenth-century America, like nineteenth-century England, had suffered initially from the social chaos which had attended the beginning of industrialism. This chaos was temporary because the law of history was progress which first brought "the substitution of intelligence for precedent" and then the substitution of "organization for chaos and anarchy." If Americans, appalled by the "chaos and anarchy" brought by industrialism in the years between 1865 and 1900, would look to England where industrialism had begun and had become mature, they would see the inevitable growth of a new harmonious order of industrial democracy. "Within the last one hundred years, the world has witnessed a silent revolution in English politics, which has resulted in the vesting of power in the hands of the people."

Beard agreed with Sumner that the corporation was a necessary institution to keep the industrial revolution from stagnating, but he believed that the corporation leaders were neither scientific nor rational. They were robber barons concerned with selfish, not public interest. However, the laws of progress would bring the people, dedicated to productivity, not profit, into control of the corporation. "Just as the political history of the past one hundred years has centered in political democracy, so the industrial history ... has centered in Industrial Democracy." There seems "to be but little doubt that the trusts are merely pointing the way to higher forms of industrial methods in which the people, instead of a few capitalists, will reap the benefits."

This was the message of his book, *The Industrial Revolution*, published in 1901. But Beard discovered that most of the professional historians and political scientists took the position that their scholarship, to be objective, had to be neutral. This pose, Beard believed, led them to be apologists for the status quo that was corrupt politically and economically because it was dominated by selfish men dedicated to preserving chaos and anarchy for personal profit. The intellectual who defended this status quo, Beard argued, necessarily became a prophet of gloom who, like Frederick Jackson Turner, argued the inevitability of the destruction of American democracy.

But, Beard declared, it was inevitable that industrialism would produce a greater democracy in America than ever existed before. It was unscientific, therefore, for scholars to defend the status quo. To be truly objective, they would have to demonstrate those factors which would inexorably bring about a cooperative democracy. Beard called for a "new history," written to explain the progressive forces at work in America in the first decade of the twentieth century. In 1907 he collaborated with James Harvey Robinson, his colleague at Columbia University, in a pioneering essay for this "new history" entitled *The Development of Modern Europe.*

The key to the new history, Beard and Robinson wrote, was its search of the past to explain the problems of contemporary society. Twentieth-century America, they continued, began in the eighteenth century when both the industrial revolution and the intellectual revolution of Enlightenment occurred. This progress, they wrote, was caused by the rebellion of the productive middle class against the improvident peasantry, aristocracy, monarchy and, above all, against the Roman Catholic Church of the Middle Ages. They found their greatest heroes among the scientists of the eighteenth century, who urged "that man was by nature good; that he should freely use his own God-given reason; that he was capable of becoming increasingly wise by a study of nature's laws, and that he could indefinitely better his own condition and that of his fellows if he would but free himself from the shackles of error and supersition."

Economic productivity and philosophical enlightenment provided the base for the growth of political, social, and economic democracy in Europe throughout the nineteenth century. The spread of education, the use of the popular press, and the emancipation of women made possible the creation of a unified and intelligent people who were able to govern themselves. It was true, the authors admitted, that industrialism had created some temporary economic hardships and, as a result, there had arisen the doctrines of Karl Marx, who challenged the idea of peaceful progress. But the American historians rejected the necessity of violent revolution. "It is clear...

that the evils of our present organization are being more and more generally understood, and there is hope that many shocking inequalities may gradually be done away with."

Beard's great enthusiasm for progress, his sense of its inevitable triumph, is nowhere more clearly stated than in his lecture of 1908 entitled "Politics." Here he called attention to the new synthesis of political science with history, sociology, and economics in which "solid foundations are being laid in reality in place of the shifting sands of speculation. We are getting away from metaphysics, from artificialities, to find the whole man participating in the work of government." Accepting Turner's use of the concept of social evolution, but without Turner's nostalgia for a lost American paradise, Beard asserted that political scientists were learning that "man is infinite in variety and capacity" and that political history was not a decline from a state of nature, but an upward movement out of "a dim and dateless past . . . into an illimitable future, which many of us believe will not be hideous and mean, but beautiful and magnificent."

The pattern of ideas that enabled Beard to be optimistic about the future was becoming clear. He did not define a golden age of American democracy during the age of Jackson as had Turner. For Beard the great age of democracy was just ahead. He did not have to describe the nineteenth century as a decline from the state of nature established by the Founding Fathers into a state of decadence. He described the entire nineteenth century as being dominated by an artificial culture, given institutional form by the makers of the Constitution, which was to be stripped away by the force of industrialism. He did not describe economic laissez-faire as a natural American frontier doctrine, but as an unnatural English ideology.

If history is progress, Beard continued, then the nineteenth-century political scientists who argued that the forms of nineteenth-century law and economics were unchangeable must be mistaken. The absolute claims for freedom of contract and private property must be modified. Men would never achieve pure communism, he wrote, but neither could they live by pure laissez-faire. Let us then, he declared, escape from the class bias which makes us too defensive about contracts and property and see the facts as they really are.

We must remember, he continued, that the essence of political life is sovereignty. In the history of western civilization there had been a trend to take sovereignty from the king and place it with the people. And yet in the United States of America, he declared, we had not had "a democratic constitution but an aristocratic one, which balanced one group against another; it was inefficient for positive action ... and characterized by that irresponsibility which power inevitably engenders." Compare this, he urged, with an ideal democratic society, "where the rule of the majority is frankly recognized (a condition of affairs gravely feared by the framers of our Constitution), government tends toward a type, unified in internal structure, emancipated from formal limitations, and charged with direct responsibility to the source of power."

Since the trend of history was toward democracy, Beard declared, since one could see the evolution of such political sovereignty of the people under the impact of industrialism, the United States, also experiencing the industrial revolution, must inevitably develop a democratic constitution, one which escaped from the aristocratic concept of checks and balances and frankly recognized the rule of the majority. Forward-looking political scientists, Beard pointed out, like Woodrow Wilson, Henry Jones Ford, and Frank Goodnow "have conclusively shown the unreality of the doctrine of divided powers, and the positive fashion in which our democratic political society seeks through extra-legal party organization to overcome the friction of a disjointed machine."

In this analysis Beard expressed one of the dominant themes in the political theory of the progressive movement. Like Herbert Croly, the most important political theorist of progressivism, whose books *The Promise of American Life* and *Progressive Democracy* also argued the undemocratic nature of the Constitution, Beard was rewriting American history so that the national identity as a democracy of free and equal producers lay in the future and not in the past. He stressed the undemocratic nature of the Republic of 1789 and the aristocratic quality of its leaders. Americans, he argued, must reject an undemocratic political system based on eighteenth-century English aristocratic principles. To find the key to their coming democracy, they must look to nineteenth-century England where, in response to industrialism, modern democratic patterns of popular sovereignty had appeared in the freedom of Parliament from the checks of a supreme court, a written constitution, or an executive veto.

Beard chose to end his lecture with a dramatic affirmation to his listeners that American industrial democracy was part of a world-wide pattern: A "new division of political research may be denominated world politics. . . . The shuttle of trade and intercourse flies ever faster and it may be weaving the web for a world state. It may be that steam and electricity are to achieve . . . that unity of mankind which rests on the expansion of a common consciousness of rights and wrongs through the extension of identical modes of economic activity."

Pointing toward an imminent international millennium, Beard was asking Americans to participate in the shaping of a world made safe for democracy. Like most other American intellectuals, he did not argue that democracy could be artificially constructed. Like them, he expressed a horror at artful human activities which were contrary to the dominant natural economic forces. Like them, he did not define man as a culture-building animal. He too believed that those men who created culture were evil and conspiratorial.

In 1912 Beard published a savage criticism of the plutocratic status quo entitled *The Supreme Court and the Constitution*, which linked the present aristocracy with the makers of the Constitution. He bitterly criticized contemporary political scientists who argued that the current Supreme Court, in its conservative attack on progressive social and economic legislation, was breaking from the tradition of the Founding Fathers, who had not intended to block the will of the people through the aristocratic power of judicial review. But Beard insisted that the Federalists had "regarded it as their chief duty, in drafting the new Constitution, to find a way of preventing the renewal of what they deemed legislative tyranny!" Assuming the existence of a natural, spontaneous democracy under the Articles of Confederation, Beard drove home the exploitive conspiracy of the Founding Fathers: "Judicial control was really a new and radical departure . . . which did not spring from Anglo-Saxon 'ideas' but from the practical necessity of creating a foil for the rights of property against belligerent democracy." This was the thesis that Beard was to expand in his most important book, *An Economic Interpretation of the Constitution*.

In his book *Contemporary American History, 1877–1913*, published in 1914, he asked Americans to disassociate themselves from this artificial status quo and to achieve harmony with natural economic forces. We had become an industrial nation during these years since 1877, he wrote, but we had not adjusted our social and political, economic and legal thought to the facts of industrialism. This necessary change was made difficult by the fact that, when the industrial revolution came to America from England, it brought with it the eighteenth-century English economic theory of laissez-faire, which made impossible any real adjustment to the social and economic problems caused by industrialism. Harmful in England, this fallacious economic philosophy was disastrous in America because here the Supreme Court could enforce this vicious theory; worse still the Court had acquired a potent new weapon to protect property from democracy in the clause in the Fourteenth Amendment to the Constitution which denied to the states power over property.

Until 1896, he continued, the people had almost passively accepted the terrible problems of capitalism. Giant corporations, governed by aristocratic elites, spawned an industrial proletariat. The American people had been complacent and passive in the face of this alien conquest because they had been taught that European patterns could not cross the Atlantic. That had been true of the dying medieval culture. It was not true, however, of vital, growing industrialism, which had spread to the United States and was spreading throughout the entire world. But while the first impact of industrialism was chaotic, its ultimate consequence must be the destruction of the aristocracy established by the Founding Fathers and its replacement by the kind of industrial democracy already growing in England. Ultimately it would destroy aristocracies throughout the entire world.

In the election of 1896 Beard found evidence of a turning point in American history. The people were at last aroused to both the dangers and potentialities of the industrial revolution. Now the people were striking down the power of the robber barons and their mercenaries, the professional politicians, by establishing direct methods of expressing their will. Direct elections, the initiative, the referendum, the recall, the popular election of United States senators, the income tax would all humble the un-American aristocracy. This popular revolution was bringing a new emphasis on social and economic legislation that would check the growth of an American proletariat and lift the depressed masses back into the ranks of the people. Beard rejoiced that American provincialism was ending, that "it was apparent from an examination of the legislation of the first decade of the twentieth century that [the United

States] were well in the paths of nations like Germany, England, and Australia."

The omnipotent people, breaking through the unreal patterns of nineteenth-century finance capitalism to build a democracy that was in harmony with the reality of industrialism, had found in Theodore Roosevelt a representative hero to give focus to this purge of the profane. According to Beard, Roosevelt understood that industrialism had created a national economy which required control by the national government. He wanted a new democracy that was neither anarchic capitalism nor tyrannous socialism; he wanted a return to the middle way of the people; a philosophy of flexible utilitarianism which aimed at strengthening the democratic community. With deepest admiration Beard quoted Roosevelt's formulation of this new democracy:

> The New Nationalism . . . puts the national need before sectional or personal advantages. It is impatient of the utter confusion that results from local legislatures attempting to treat national issues as local issues. It is still more impatient of the impotence which springs from over-division of government powers, the impotence which makes it possible for local selfishness or for legal cunning, hired by wealthy special interests, to bring national activities to a deadlock. This New Nationalism regards the executive power as the steward of the public welfare. It demands of the judiciary that it shall be interested primarily in human welfare rather than in property, just as it demands that the representative body shall represent all the people.

Governed from the beginning of its history by a conspiratorial aristocracy committed to introducing parasitical English finance capitalism, the American nation had never had a covenant with nature; it had never been pure and innocent; it would find such purity and innocence only in the future when the productive force of industrialism destroyed the nonproductive robber barons. There were no past heroes to mourn, only spokesmen for the future, like Theodore Roosevelt. In 1915 Beard published *The Economic Origins of Jeffersonian Democracy* as his final argument against the Populist hope for a purge of urban-industrial complexity which would restore the virtue of Jefferson's America. In 1912 Beard had bitterly attacked the nostalgia of Woodrow Wilson's "New Freedom" which had harked back to Jefferson's national covenant. But, Beard wrote,

"Agrarian democracy," is as fallacious "as the equally unreal and unattainable democracy of small business" that "is Wilson's goal." Bitterly, Beard asked, "Today nearly half of us belong to the 'mobs of the great cities'—sores on the body politic. What message has the sage of Monticello for us?" Beard harshly separated Jefferson from "the people." Jefferson and his fellow republican leaders were farmers, but unlike "the people," they formed "an aristocracy of slave-owning planters." They took power away from Hamilton, not because of their commitment to democracy, but to defend their own selfish, materialistic, and aristocratic interests. Here were no champions of innocence but only another group of parasitical aristocrats.

In 1915 Beard was pleading with Americans to concentrate on industrial America and to reject laissez-faire. "The purpose of government," he wrote in a series of textbooks on state and city government, "is to do those things which cannot be done well or justly by individuals working alone, and to regulate the doings of private persons in such a manner as to improve the general standard of life, labor, and education. The very essence of government, according to the democratic ideal, is cooperation or union of effort for the common good." By 1917 Beard believed that he was participating in the first stages of a new democracy made possible by the industrial frontier. In the United States, indeed across the face of the entire world, industrialism was smashing the institutional and traditional vestiges of historical civilization. People everywhere were being emancipated from the slavery of history to live in the freedom of natural harmony. The victory of women in the United States, he declared, in winning the right to vote was "not ... a temporary episode of current politics, but ... a part of an age-long battle of the common mass of people upward from serfdom to freedom." The only dark cloud on the horizon was World War I. And Beard found that it had a most significant silver lining.

For Beard the industrial frontier in Germany had inexplicably failed to destroy the German aristocracy and its feudal institutions. The reality of German life was industrialism, and political and social patterns must ultimately adjust to that economic reality; political and social democracy must develop wherever industrialism became established because that was the logic of this productive system. Soon Germany must become a democracy. But in the meantime its feudal aristocrats, like cornered rats, would fight to save themselves from extermination. Desperately they would strike out at the nations which had already become democracies, hoping against hope that they might defeat the inexorable forces of progress and drive mankind back into the Dark Ages. This aggressive war, caused by the German elite, Beard declared, was the last stand of medieval power against the complete victory of democracy.

Sounding remarkably like Donnelly in 1892, Beard justified the use of force in 1917 to defend innocence and to defeat evil at the great battle which would determine the future of mankind. For Beard, who came to Armageddon knowing that American soldiers were only accelerating the inevitable victory of industrialism, this was the ultimate triumph of democracy:

> For more than two hundred years, a great ideal has been taking form and spreading throughout the earth: governments must derive their powers from the consent of the governed. . . . The democratic principle has been compelled to battle every step of the long way from despotism to liberty against the ancient doctrine that government belongs by divine right to kings whom it is the duty of the people to obey in all things.

In Germany alone, of all the industrial nations, this medieval doctrine persisted and conspired to defeat democracy. The aggressive German aristocracy, proclaimed Beard, had forced war upon the peaceful United States. The American people resisted this brutal attack by expressing the power of their general will through the representative hero, Woodrow Wilson. But Wilson was the representative hero of all the democratic peoples of the world, including the German people. Wilson waged war only against the Kaiser and his war machine. He fought to liberate the German people from their tyrannical leaders. He would welcome them as equals in the concert of democratic nations who would compose a league to preserve peace. Wilson's views reflected

> the slowly-maturing opinion of the masses of the people everywhere in the earth . . . those who have faith will believe that a real change has come in the long course of history and that the years, 1917–1918, as surely as the age of the American and French Revolutions, will mark the opening of a new epoch in the rise of government by the people and in the growth of a concert among the nations.

Chapter III

Harmony through
Technological Order:
Taylor, Ford, and Veblen

In presenting technology as a frontier force capable of liberating mankind from the irrational complexities of civilization and fulfilling the progressive prophecy that a harmonious natural simplicity was the final earthly paradise, Beard was representative of the most significant theme of optimism which appeared in America at the beginning of the twentieth century. Large numbers of Americans escaped the growing sense of despair and decadence in the 1880s and 1890s by defining the machine process as one which purged complexity. For these men the factory became a temple, a sacred space, in which citizens could be freed from the doubts and uncertainties of their secular lives, to achieve salvation through unity with the absolute rationality of the machine.

Frederick Winslow Taylor was born into the middle-class aristocracy of the east coast. Like his contemporaries Theodore Roosevelt, Henry Cabot Lodge, and Henry and Brooks Adams, he was obsessed by a sense of the decadence of his class. His father, who used his leisure to write poetry, seemed symbolic, in the eyes of the young Taylor, of the inability of this aristocracy to engage any longer in vigorous and productive work. In rebelling against his family, Taylor developed psychosomatic trouble with his eyes so that he could not be sent to college to be further corrupted by bookish culture. Instead he asked to be allowed to work as an apprentice in family-controlled industrial enterprises. Here Taylor could go through the ritual of becoming a self-made man, of escaping the effete culture of his family. Here also, confronted by the discipline of the machine, he found that relief from thinking and imagination from which, as a troubled adolescent, he had asked a doctor to save him. And in 1895 when he read his paper, "A Piece-Rote System, Being a Step toward a Partial Solution of the Labor Problem," to the American Society of Mechanical Engineers, Taylor began to acquire a reputation as the leader of the cult of efficiency which was such an important part of the progressive imagination. By 1911 a Taylor Society was formed to further his hope that a science of management would be developed which would be as precise and exact as any physical science, built on the same methods of experiment, measurement, and generalization. It was Taylor's prophecy that the discovery of these laws of management would allow factories to be run with total mathematical objectivity and without any human emotion, with total and timeless harmony.

For Taylor factories ultimately must be run by scientifically trained engineers and not by irrational businessmen:

> The shop (indeed, the whole works) should be managed, not by the manager, superintendent, or foreman, but by the planning department. The daily routine of running the entire works should be carried on by the various functional elements of this department, so that ... the works could run smoothly even if the manager, superintendent, and their assistants outside the planning room were all to be away for a month at a time.

Some of Taylor's disciples carried this logic further in creating the organization, "The New Machine," in 1916 with the hope of ending irrationality in politics by replacing the professional politicians with scientific and objective bureaucrats. For political theorists like Herbert Croly and Walter Lippmann, who established the *New Republic* magazine in 1914, nonpartisan politics guided by specialists was the logical political organization for a united and harmonious people. If there was a single public, why should there be political parties to create artificial divisions and conflicts? If there was a single public welfare, why shouldn't it find efficient expression through the guidance of men trained to solve specific problems? Professors of political science like Charles Beard and Frank Goodnow cooperated with the National Voter's League and the Bureau of Municipal Research in New York City to help educate the people to the need to break from traditional, corrupt politics to a new and pure politics guided by selfless experts.

Another major spokesman for technology as a "New Messiah" was Henry Ford. Unlike Taylor, Ford was one of the numberless farm boys from the Midwest who had come to the city because it had displaced the land as the frontier of economic opportunity. But Ford was so indoctrinated by the arcadian tradition that his reaction to the city was one of intense hatred. For him the city was artificial and, therefore, evil; the countryside was natural and, therefore, good. Like so many of his generation, however, Ford believed that industrialism was destroying the city and was making it possible for everyone to live in the country. Ford, then, like Taylor, believed that he was living through a period of intense national purification, another Reformation, in which the corrupt and decadent leadership of a parasitical eastern aristocracy would be rejected in the name of a new class of producers who had returned to the ancient faith that one best served God through his secular calling.

Leaving his family's farm in Michigan, Ford had come into Detroit to work as a mechanic. Soon he was fascinated by the efforts of this carriage-making center to develop horseless carriages powered by the internal combustion engine invented in Europe and pioneered in Europe as the basis for a new vehicle, the automobile. In the 1890s Ford made a car of his own which showed little originality. By 1902 he had built a successful racing model which brought him the attention of men with capital to invest in the infant but rapidly growing industry of auto-making.

This outside capital made possible the formation of the Ford Motor Company in 1903, which competed unsuccessfully for several years in the market for luxury cars. Then in 1908 Ford brought out the inexpensive Model T, tough, compact, light, with a high chassis that was ideal for the poor roads of the day. Overwhelmed by orders, the Ford company produced ten thousand cars in 1909. A major new plant at Highland Park outside Detroit began to experiment in lining up the machinery used in assembly to create a stationary production line, and by 1913 the time needed to build a car had been cut to twelve hours and twenty-eight minutes. Ford then accepted the plans of his engineers for a moving assembly line with an endless-chain overhead conveyor, and the time to produce a single auto was cut to ninety-three minutes by the end of 1914. In that year Ford doubled his wages to five dollars a day and in the next two years cut his labor turnover by 90 per cent. His companies' profits increased from $30 million after taxes in 1914 to $60 million after taxes in 1916.

A major reason for this pay raise was the need to reduce the disturbing rate of labor turnover caused by the dislike of the workers for the great increase of work pressure that had come with the assembly line. Until the new high wage scale, workers had rebelled against the speed-up of production which had forced them to work at a much faster pace to adjust to the tempo of the assembly line.

As Ford moved so dramatically to create factories that literally stretched for miles, he was not troubled by the idea that he was creating something artificial and complex. Indeed, like Taylor, he invested his factories with the theological power to purge the artificial and the complex and to restore the natural and the simple.

For Ford the homestead farm of the nineteenth-century yeoman had been almost a utopia because the farmer had been independent, free from exploitation by parasitical urban classes, free to work in harmony with nature, free to be a producer as God had intended man to be productive. But Ford did not really mourn the passing of the rural homestead. It had not been perfect. It had demanded a cruelly long day of drudgery which Ford had hated as a boy. The factory still provided the opportunity for productive work, but the machine could take upon itself the heaviest burden of physical exertion. More important, however, for Ford was the fact that rural America had always been infected by cities, and American farmers, like those of the Old World, did not have the means to destroy the city. Like Beard, Ford believed that the frontier of physical nature in the New World had allowed an agricultural democracy to develop in the seventeenth and eighteenth centuries. There had been a democratic people but always they had lacked freedom from economic, social, and political control by a European-oriented aristocracy. Always, as towns turned into cities on the east coast, this elite exploited the common man.

Until the advent of the machine process, there was no hope of ending this dualism of people and aristocracy, no hope for that earthly paradise from which all parasites would be purged. Until the twentieth century the city, the evil city, always qualified the possibility of an earthly garden. As Ford wrote:

There is something about a city of a million people which is untamed and threatening. Thirty miles away, happy and contented villages read of the ravings of the city. A city is really a helpless mass. Everything it uses is carried to it. The city cannot feed, clothe, warm or house itself. City conditions of work and living are so unnatural that instincts sometimes rebel against their unnaturalness.

When Ford called the machine the "New Messiah," he indeed visualized it as bringing the millennium. In the first place he defined the machine as natural in its productivity, "an elemental force, blindly creative, like nature." And in the second place Ford designed his factories to blend in organic harmony with physical nature. As he boasted of one of his plants, "We have dammed the river, the dam also serves as a bridge for the ... railway ... and a road for the public—all in one construction. We are going to make our glass at this point. The damming of the river gives sufficient water for the floating to us of most of our raw material. It also gives us our power through a hydro-electric plant." Finally, and most important for Ford, because his factory was outside the city, his workers, riding in the cars produced by the factory, "will have plots of ground or farms as well as their jobs in the factory, and these can be scattered over fifteen or twenty miles surrounding—for of course nowadays the workingman can come to the shop in an automobile." For Ford then, "The ultimate solution will be the abandonment of the city. ... we shall solve the city problem by leaving the city."

By 1914 Ford had escaped the fear of the future which had haunted Donnelly. Where Donnelly could only resort to the magic of the "Golden Bottle" to destroy the power of the finance capitalists and to save the purity of farm boys and girls from the sinful enticements of the city, Ford was certain that the machine, especially his people's car, was eliminating both the city and its parasitical aristocracy.

Ford defined himself as a producer, and desperately wanted his factories and those of all other producers free from disruptive raids by the robber barons of Wall Street. As Taylor had seen the factory as the means of his personal salvation from the decadence of his family, Ford saw it as the means of freeing those large numbers of Americans who had been corrupted by the effete eastern aristocracy.

Ford postulated that the factory would force the workers out of unnatural habits of pleasure and leisure and bring them back into harmony with their natural instinct for work. "The natural thing to do is to work—to recognize that prosperity and happiness can be obtained only through honest effort. Human ills flow largely from attempting to escape the natural course. . . . the day's work is a great thing—a very great thing! . . . Work is our sanity, our self-respect, our salvation."

The Puritan logic of the machine which would suppress the temptations to unnatural leisure and artificial pleasure was its emphasis on efficiency and, for Ford, "the net result is the reduction of the necessity for thought on the part of the worker and the reduction of his movements to a minimum." Efficiency for Ford was goodness, truth, and beauty; it was God's will. "The most beautiful things in the world are those from which all excess . . . has been eliminated." We must "cut out useless parts and simplify necessary ones."

Between 1900 and 1914 he shared the mounting optimism of so many Americans that something like the millennium was approaching. And following the logic of Beard's definition of technology as an international frontier force, Ford, like Beard, expected the millennium to be worldwide; he expected technology to make the world safe for producers everywhere, safe from the medieval aristocracies which had exploited them through history from their dens of urban iniquity.

When Ford was approached, therefore, by a group of idealists in 1915 to help bring the war in Europe to a quick conclusion, he accepted the challenge with enthusiasm. He believed that the international conflict, like the chaos in America, was caused by those in Europe who were comparable to the "absentee owners and the parasites of Wall Street." And for Ford professional soldiers in America or Europe were equally "lazy or crazy." "Do you want to know the cause of war?" Ford asked. "It is capitalism, greed, the dirty hunger for dollars. Take away the capitalist and you will sweep war from the earth."

When the "Peace Ship" financed by Ford, which sailed in 1915 to Europe to call the productive soldiers out of the trenches through peaceful rebellion against their parasitical officers, failed to end the war, Ford began that retreat from Armageddon which marked the disillusionment of so many of the progressive era. Having divided the world between the artless producers and the artful parasites and having prophesied that the machine was going to purge the parasites and make the world safe for the producers, Ford had to admit by 1919 that the conspiratorial power of the parasites was stronger than he had believed. Ford entered the 1920s convinced that this conspiracy, which kept the world in unnatural chaos, was dominated by Jews. And in the early twenties he offered himself to his nation as a possible presidential candidate who could save America from this international Zionist plot to continue to impose artificial and corrupt urban civilization upon the simple and honest productive folk of field and factory.

Taylor and Ford, like Beard, had escaped from Donnelly and Turner's pessimistic view that it was only the existence of the vast expanse of virgin land which had allowed European immigrants to escape medieval civilization. For those who linked freedom to an arcadian environment, it was obvious that freedom, the culmination of progress from cultural complexity to natural simplicity, had reached its high point in the early nineteenth century and was now in decline. But Beard, Taylor, and Ford had a revised theory of progress which held that freedom from cultural complexity had not yet reached its culmination because such progress was dependent, not upon physical nature, but upon technology. These men were achieving a new sense of optimism, of destiny, of an impending millennium by Americanizing Marx, by fitting the Marxist theory of progress into a middle-class framework.

Turner's view that progress, the liberating of the individual from coercive institutions and traditions, culminated with the election of Jackson to the presidency in 1828 coincided with the view of the great economists of early nineteenth-century England that at last mankind was accepting the natural laws of the science of economy, the laws of the free competition of the marketplace, the laws of laissez-faire. By the 1850s, however, Karl Marx had begun a massive attack on the naturalness of the middle-class society. The middle class, he declared, had not fulfilled its promise to free mankind from medieval institutions and traditions to live in natural harmony. Instead, Marx insisted that the middle class had merely replaced the medieval establishment with one of its own. Its political state, its social hierarchy, its coercive economic system were as artificial and therefore as corrupt as those of the Dark Ages. It would be the proletariat, Marx continued, not the middle class, which would purge civilization and restore a natural and harmonious order. And the victory of the workers was inevitable because it was the logic of the great impersonal force of industrialism to destroy the bourgeois parasite and to elevate the productive workers who were in harmony with this new economic system.

Beard, Taylor, Ford, and other major spokesmen for progressivism in 1900, however, described most Americans as middle-class producers who were being exploited by a small group of parastical finance capitalists. For these progressive Americans, the logic of industrialism would purge the parasitical aristocracy and liberate the productive middle class. Implicit for men like Beard, Taylor, and Ford was the vision of the progressive era as a new Reformation, in which a decadent medieval establishment which created conflict and chaos through its artificial institutions was being purged by the new technology. The American philosophers of the progressive movement vigorously denied any debt to Marx, however, as they also vigorously insisted that the American reformation would proceed through peaceful means, unlike Marx's prophecy of bloody class warfare. This viewpoint became explicit in the writings of Thorstein Veblen.

Leaving the farm home of his Norwegian immigrant family in Minnesota, Veblen had come east to participate in the academic revolution which witnessed the emergence of the modern university with its specialized graduate training. Veblen was to use the prestige of the Ph.D. he took in philosophy at Yale, and a second Ph.D. in economics at Cornell, to undermine the commitment of so much of the academic establishment to laissez-faire economics.

The economists who defended the status quo in 1890, like William Graham Sumner, defined themselves as protectors of the successful Puritan revolution, begun with the Reformation, that had liberated the individual from the feudal institutions and traditions through which a parasitical nobility and priestly class had exploited the common people. Ultimately, this progressive revolution had reached fulfillment when it was understood that economic law must imitate physical law. And so, since the distinct atoms of the physical universe were held in constant harmony with one another by the law of gravity, it followed that each individual operating as an atom of economic self-interest would necessarily work in harmony and not in conflict with other individuals. Into this world of natural order there had come by 1850 the dragon of chaos, Marxist socialism, which was trying to seduce men away from this sacred imitation of natural law back into an artful, chaotic, manmade society. For the economists loyal to classical capitalist economic doctrine, this was indeed the doctrine of the devil as it attempted to substitute the transitory and human for the eternal and divine.

Veblen began a frontal attack in the 1890s on this theory of history. First in a series of scholarly articles directed at the economics profession and then in his book, *The Theory of the Leisure Class*, directed at a broad audience, Veblen argued that there had been no successful Puritan revolution. There was no natural harmony to be defended. Medievalism still existed and progress from cultural complexity to natural simplicity was still to be fulfilled. And if medievalism had not been destroyed, then it followed logically that the economists who were defending the status quo were also defending medievalism. And if this were true, then professional economists were not modern scientists dealing with objective truth; they were a priestly class rationalizing the parastical privilege of an exploitive feudal aristocracy.

Veblen began his proof that the laissez-faire economists were committed to traditional religious mystery by asking his readers to consider the attitude of these so-called scientists toward values. Men like Sumner had announced that all social sciences must be purged of values and must express nothing but facts. But in his article, "Why Is Economics Not an Evolutionary Science," Veblen analyzed the ways in which values, moral commitments, and theological assumptions were central to the writings of those economists who were defenders of laissez-faire capitalism. Accuracy and observation, objectivity and induction were their watchwords. But without exception, Veblen argued, they placed their information within a pattern of assumed metaphysical principles; their facts were subordinated to the mystery of a spiritual truth. These economists shared, therefore, the irrational faith of the Dark Ages that nature acted as if it had animistic qualities.

Veblen then declared himself to be the first truly scientific economist. Analyzing the great English capitalist economists—Adam Smith, John Stuart Mill, Marshall, and Cairnes—he dismissed them all as mystics. And then he also dismissed Marx as a mystic. Marx's philosophy, Veblen asserted, was a house of cards constructed of pure irrelevancies because it rested on two metaphysical traditions,

English capitalism and Hegelian romanticism. Veblen, therefore, presented himself to his readers as the only economist whom they could trust. He would function as a scholarly muckraker who would persuade his readers that they had been the victims of a vast conspiracy which had falsified the records of history and had so deluded the people that they believed that medieval civilization had been destroyed by the Reformation. He alone would deal with the facts and nothing but the facts.

These facts, said Veblen, revealed that the culture of the Dark Ages still survived and provided the values for the aristocracy which dominated the United States economically, politically, socially, and intellectually. Veblen began his education of the American public with the definition of this aristocracy as a leisure class with roots deep in the past. This class, he wrote, "emerged gradually during the transition from primitive savagery to barbarism . . . during the transition from a peaceable to a consistently warlike habit of life." This class, he continued, despised peaceful productivity and industry and loved warlike exploitation. Here in America, as in western Europe, the extremely warlike stage of barbarism had given way to a quasi-peaceable stage "whose characteristic feature is a formal observance of peace and order" but which "still has too much of coercion and class antagonism to be called peaceable." This was "the age of status."

But while Americans might be dismayed to discover that they had a feudal class, Veblen gave the reassurance that "the best development" of the leisure class "lies in the past rather than in the present." The basic economic pattern today, he declared, was rational industrial productivity which was completely contradictory to the parasitical values of conspicuous consumption and waste which characterized the modern leisure class. And this evolutionary economic force must ultimately destroy this obsolete culture because "the evolution of society is substantially a process of mental adaptation on the part of individuals under the stress of circumstances which will no longer tolerate habits of thought formed under and conforming to a different set of circumstances in the past." For Veblen it was the workers who most strongly expressed the values of industrial productivity, and the leisure class which necessarily was most insulated from them. But there was no doubt, he asserted, that ultimately industrialism would destroy the culture of the leisure class.

Veblen was certain of the victory of the producers over the parasites because he believed that man was instinctively a producer and became a parasite only through historical conditioning. "The barbarian culture," Veblen wrote, "has been neither protracted enough nor invariable enough in character to give an extreme fixity of type." There was, he insisted, an original biological nature of man, peaceful and productive. Industrialism was, of course, fast freeing the productive workers from intellectual bondage to the barbarian values of status:

> These habits... begin to lose their coercive force for the community... so soon as the habit of minds... due to the predatory discipline cease to be in fairly close accord with the later-developed economic situation. This is evident in the case of the industrious classes of modern communities; for them the leisure class scheme of life has lost much of its binding force, especially as regards the elements of status.

Having attempted in *The Theory of the Leisure Class* to persuade Americans that they still lived within a medieval environment, Veblen then proceeded in his next book, *The Theory of Business Enterprise,* to explain how the people had been misled in believing that medievalism had been destroyed centuries before. This book also expanded on the hopeful aspect of industrialism as the force that must inevitably accomplish the final destruction of medievalism.

To liberate themselves from the parasitical control of the feudal aristocracy, Veblen related, the seventeenth-century middle-class reformers had developed a theory of private property as a "Natural Right." The great spokesman of this philosophy, John Locke, was wrong in assuming that in the state of nature private property had existed. Locke and his followers could be sympathized with, however, Veblen declared, because they wanted to help men to be productive and constructive and they hoped to accomplish this by protecting the property of the productive individual from the feudal robber barons. And this system had worked not too badly until the end of the eighteenth century because the majority of the capitalist property owners fulfilled Locke's description of private property as that with which a man mixed his labor.

But by the beginning of the nineteenth century individualistic production gave way to the mass production of the age of industrialism. And Locke's definition of property no longer applied. The men who worked in the factories did not own the means of production. By law individual capitalists owned the factories and the machines. But factory production, Veblen declared, depended upon the cooperation of the entire community and in fact, then, the machines belonged to all the people. This was the terrible irony of the present situation. The middle class, attempting to escape the parasitical medieval aristocracy, had created a new parasitical class —that of the finance capitalists. The finance capitalists were in a strategic position to sabotage the machine because they hid behind the courts which sustained the fiction that the Lockean definition of private property was the reality of the economy in 1900. Seventeenth-century Englishmen had placed private property within the protection of impersonal law to protect it from the barbaric feudal lords whose values were meaningless warfare.

Now the factories, however, were legally owned by the finance capitalists who lived in an unreal, irrational, artificial world with the predatory values of the feudal past expressed in the modern form of a desire for profits. Their economic world was that of paper money and abstract credit which had no functional relationship to the concrete facts of productive wealth. And they made their profits by sabotaging the productive economy to create fluctuations which worked to their personal gain. These raids were comparable to those of the feudal barons on the shipping which passed their castles.

These modern parasites posed a direct threat to the harmony implicit in the logic of the machine because they knew how to use the continued commitment of Americans to private property as natural and sacred in order to protect and further their disruptive schemes. But Veblen promised that the machine would defeat this artful vestige of medievalism. The machine represented timeless and eternal truth while the finance capitalists represented ephemeral historical institutions and values.

> The ultimate ground of validity for the thinking of the business classes is the natural rights ground of property—a conventional, anthropomorphic fact having an institutional validity, rather than a matter-of-fact validity such as can be formulated in terms of material cause and effect; while the classes engaged in the machine industry are habitually occupied with matters of causal sequence, which do not lend themselves to statement in anthropomorphic terms of natural rights.

The images which Veblen used to describe the factory were similar to those that Turner had used to describe physical nature. For Veblen the factory provided the frontier experience which allowed the men who entered its door to be reborn, to step out of artificial culture into harmony with the organic. While the finance capitalists, with their lawyers and judges, tried to interpret "new facts in terms of accredited precedents, rather than . . . in the matter-of-fact light of new phenomena," the machine had liberated the masses from bondage to tradition, and the legal structure of absolute property rights was being questioned by the juries who "speak for the untrained sympathies of the vulgar." The masses no longer took their values from civilization but from the machine, and "what the discipline of the machine industry inculcates, therefore, in the habits of life and of thought of the workman, is regularity of sequence and mechanical precision. . . . Mechanically speaking, the machine is not his to do with it as his fancy may suggest. His place is to take thought of the machine and its work in terms given him by the process that is going forward."

The working majority involved in the productive work of the factories was leading the way, therefore, to an adjustment of society to its economic basis. There was no way that finance capitalism could halt this trend, because its profits came from the productivity of the machine. If the finance capitalists destroyed the machine, society would revert directly to the medieval past and the old feudal aristocracy would destroy the financiers. On the other hand, if the bankers continued to accept the machine, they must also accept their own rapid destruction, because the machine was undermining the institution of private property. "Broadly, the machine discipline acts to disintegrate the institutional heritage of all degrees of antiquity. . . . It thereby cuts away that ground of law and order on which business enterprise is founded." The machine would guarantee that there would be no more ephemeral historical values because "the mechanically trained classes, trained to matter-of-fact habits of thought, show a notable lack of spontaneity in the construction of new myths or conventions as well as in the reconstruction of the old."

A third book, *The Instinct of Workmanship,* was now written to explain the tragic fall of man from the state of nature and his restoration to that prehistorical harmony by means of the machine which would not allow the fall to occur again. The original savage Eden, Veblen wrote, was

characterized by considerable group solidarity within a relatively small group, living very near the soil, and unremittingly dependent for their daily life on the workmanlike efficiency of all the members of the group. The prime requisite for survival under the conditions would be a propensity unselfishly and impersonally to make the most of all the material means at hand and a penchant for turning all resources of knowledge and materials to account to sustain the life of the group.

Veblen was teaching his final lesson to his fellow Americans. They had prized productivity and hated parasites; they had prized peace and hated war; they had prized common sense and hated the artificial. But they had believed that these good traits were to be found in a retreat from medievalism to a state of nature characterized by private property held by the self-reliant individual. But, declared Veblen, there was no private property in the state of nature. Natural man instinctively was part of the interdependent group; he was not an isolated individual. Natural man had the instinct of workmanship that led him to high material productivity; the instinct of parental bent which was broader than family feeling and led to a general humanitarian concern for the welfare of the whole community; and the instinct of idle curiosity which was the basis of all matter-of-fact knowledge leading to scientific progress.

Why then had men fallen from this natural harmony into the unnatural disharmony of history? For Veblen the flaw was in man himself. Man had the capacity for imaginative flights of fancy. Out of his imagination man constructed the evil artificial structure of profane institutions and traditions that imprisoned him and thwarted his productive instincts which should have kept him in harmony with nature. This was the fatal flaw in mankind—imagination.

The sacred temple of the machine, the factory, was now, however, providing the discipline which forced men to think only in matter-of-fact terms. Imagination was brought under control and repressed. The fruitful instincts were liberated and man could live perpetually in harmony with these primitive instincts because the machine would never again allow imagination to create that false, artificial, and profane world of timeful history.

When World War I began in 1914, Veblen was ready to interpret this tragic event in terms which paralleled Charles Beard's. This was a moment of necessary suffering which would speed the industrial millennium. His book *Imperial Germany and the Industrial Revolution* applied his philosophical formulas to that unhappy nation. Veblen argued that industrialism had appeared first in England because that nation was less burdened by medieval civilization than its continental neighbors. Englishmen had remained closer to their original primitive natures and were attuned to this new economic system which repeated the peaceful and productive principles of the savage Eden. Germany was in direct contrast to England. More than almost any European group, the Germans had remained the prisoners of medievalism. Veblen hastened to stress that racially the Germans were no different from Englishmen; the mass of Germans were genetically linked to the innate peacefulness of prehistoric man. It was not the German people who had chosen war but only their feudal lords.

Again Veblen emphasized that it was because of the primitive, productive instincts of savage prehistory that the German people had turned so enthusiastically to industrialism when it crossed the channel from England. The fundamental biological impulse of the Germans which linked them to all of mankind was that "of workmanship and fecundity rather than of dynastic power, statecraft, priestcraft, or artistic achievement." Veblen's premise, therefore, was that the feudal war lords of Germany were unnatural, an artificial social aristocracy holding "irresponsible authority," and he reminded his readers that "the scheme of institutions in force in any given community ... being of the nature of habit, is necessarily unstable ... whereas the type of any given racial stock is stable." Warlike Germany was ephemeral; peaceful Germany was immutable.

It was Prussia, the most feudal and least industrial of all the German states, which had dominated the unification of the nation and which had begun the policy of an aggressive predatory imperialism that had forced Europe into war in 1914. The violent, selfish, brutal Prussian aristocrats were attempting to destroy the peaceful, productive English commonwealth from which industrialism was spreading to undermine feudalism throughout the entire world. This war, for Veblen as for Beard, could be described, therefore, as Armageddon. Imperial Germany was the last great stronghold of medievalism and there was no way for its parasitical war lords to win this struggle because, to achieve the military might to defeat England, they had been forced to create a modern army dependent upon the productivity of industrialism. "The Imperial State [is] unable to get along without the machine industry, and, also, in the long run, unable to get along with it; since this industrial system in the long run undermines the foundation of the State." Veblen also had a final ironic bit of good news. It would be the German officers who would suffer the greatest casualties. Their death would immediately eliminate the evil aristocracy which suppressed the virtuous German people. The war must speed the inevitable victory of industrialism over feudalism.

Chapter IV

The Social Nature
of the Natural Man:
Dewey, Cooley, and Rauschenbusch

The two major aspects of the progressive outlook were muckraking and education. Muckraking revealed the unnatural and undemocratic quality of the establishment. Education revealed the natural and democratic reality toward which the American public should make progress. Perhaps it was inevitable, therefore, that the single most important philosopher of progressivism was John Dewey, the greatest spokesman for progressive education.

Born in Vermont in 1859, Dewey in the 1880s, had become a severe critic of the nineteenth-century tradition of individualism. In graduate school at Johns Hopkins he eagerly embraced the neo-Hegelianism of the English philosopher, Thomas Hill Green, who was bitterly critical of the metaphysics of empiricism which were being used to justify laissez-faire capitalism. This philosophical position assumed individual motivation came from a hedonistic calculus of pleasure and pain. But Dewey, following Green, argued that man by nature was social and altruistic, not antisocial and selfish. He contended that personality developed through social communication. "In social feeling," he wrote, "we merge our private life in the wider life of the community, and, in so doing, immensely transcend self and realize our being in its widest way."

Into the 1890s Dewey defined himself as a philosophical idealist and a theist. History, he believed, symbolized the unfolding of God's will. The ultimate reality was spiritual. The material world was an expression of God's spiritual purpose. In establishing spirit as the ultimate reality, Dewey had created a standard by which he could challenge the status quo. English and American defenders of competitive capitalism, like Spencer and Sumner, argued that man had no freedom but to obey the major law of nature, evolution, and to submit to its mechanism of ruthless competition. Until the end of the 1890s Dewey insisted, however, that man owed obedience to the higher, spiritual law of brotherly love. But by the end of that decade Dewey had made a radical shift to accept the physical world as the only reality and evolution as the major natural law. This meant that Dewey also had found the general formula discovered by so many of his intellectual contemporaries of the progressive movement that allowed them to turn evolution against the laissez-faire position of the Spencers and the Sumners. The first element in this formula was to deny that capitalism was natural. For Dewey recent anthropology had demonstrated that primitive man, natural man, lived in a cooperative, tribal situation. Private property and competition were not aspects of the prehistorical, precivilized state of nature. It followed, Dewey argued, that nineteenth-century capitalism was a historical institution. It had emerged in time; it would disappear in time. This, he argued, was certainly the message of evolution. Change was constant. And the nineteenth-century establishment must change. It was the law of nature, and Dewey could happily proclaim: "We must follow the order of nature, not the order of convention."

Dewey, who had damned empiricism and called for the transcendence of the material world in order to challenge the establishment, was now in a position to define himself as a philosopher against abstract philosophy, as an empiricist who adjusted to the facts of experience. "Metaphysical philosophy," Dewey declared, "bound the once erect form of human endeavor and progress to the chariot wheels of cosmology and theology." By redefining the competitive establishment as transcendental and not empirical, he could now argue that social cooperation was the reality to which man should conform.

Once, Dewey began, man lived in a primitive society of organic harmony with nature. Primitive man used his intelligence to solve his needs for food, clothing, and shelter. His ideas were functional. They facilitated his necessary actions to adjust to his environment. They provided him with means of hunting and agriculture that were in perfect unity with his goal of survival. In the beginning, then, thinking was a natural response to the authentic problem that man, as a biological organism, faced in the survival of his species. And this thinking was social because primitive man lived in tribal groups. Man was by instinct gregarious and altruistic. Dewey, like Veblen, was reminding his fellow Americans that their Puritan ancestors were supposed to have rejected the complex metaphysics and theology of medieval civilization that had been used to rationalize the power of the parasitical feudal aristocracy and priesthood by which they had exploited the productive masses. He was reminding them that their capitalist ancestors had promised to return to a simple natural state where every man could be a free and equal producer. But, like Veblen, it was his intention to demonstrate the continued existence of this complexity of metaphysics and theology by revealing that the productive people had not freed themselves from an exploitive aristocracy. America in 1900 had a leisure class and, like all leisure classes in the past, it used artificial metaphysics and theology to justify its nonfunctional, destructive role. This class insisted that present social patterns represented eternal and immutable philosophical and theological truths. It argued that the present establishment was timeless and changeless.

For Dewey the explanation for the existence of this false and artful tradition of metaphysics and theology was to be found in the experience of men in ancient Greece. Through the use of imagination mankind had moved away from the spontaneous community of the tribe to create complex and artificial institutions in which people no longer lived in cooperation but in competition, no longer in classless solidarity but in class divisions. Then, in the time of Socrates, Plato, and Aristotle, these institutions began to decay, as all institutions inevitably must. The response of the Greek philosophers was not to understand that intelligence must be used as a tool to help man adjust to the natural environment. Instead, they postulated that intelligence was the means by which man transcended the flux of life to find timeless and immutable ideal types. And they argued that only a leisured aristocracy was in a position to isolate itself from the profane, changeful situation in which the common man lived in order to contemplate and appreciate eternal patterns. This emphasis in classical civilization on an aristocratic, philosophical elite as the guardians of passive truth that had no place in the active life of the average man became, in the Middle Ages, a sanction for the feudal aristocracy and priesthood to remove themselves from productive activity and to exploit the people because, supposedly, these parasites were the defenders of timeless political and theological truth. "The defining characteristic of medievalism," Dewey continued, "in State and in Church, in political and spiritual life, is that truth presents itself to the individual only through the medium of organized authority."

But in 1900, Dewey declared, we found in America a ruling class that still attempted to tell the people what the truth was. We found that clergymen, social scientists, professional philosophers, speaking for this upper class, told the people that they must accept the status quo because it embodied immutable truth. And they defended themselves from attack by arguing that, because they were specially educated into tradition, they could understand truth better than the people who had no time for leisured and bookish study.

But, Dewey promised, as Americans began the twentieth century, they were witnessing the culmination of a revolt against classical and medieval civilization that had been gaining momentum since the Renaissance and Reformation. The key to this long progressive revolution was the contrast between the appearance of a productive economy within medieval civilization and the feudal ideal of parasitical leisure.

> The substitution of moving commerce for fixed custom meant a view of wants as the dynamics of social progress, not as the pathology of private greed.... The conception of a social harmony of interests in which the achievement of each individual of his own freedom should contribute to a like perfecting of the powers of all through a fraternally organized society is the permanent contribution of the industrial movement to morals.

From 1600 to the present the common man, broken loose from loyalty to medieval institutions and metaphysics, had been attempting to live by the ideal that "science, art, religion, political life, must all be made over on the basis of recognizing the claims of the individual." The new philosophical movement for which he spoke, Dewey affirmed, "is simply the coming to consciousness of this claim of the individual to be able to discover and verify truth for himself, and thereby not only direct his own conduct, but become the influential and decisive factor in the organization of life itself."

Again Dewey agreed with Veblen that this revolution had not yet reached fulfillment because, rebelling against an artificial society, modern men had not recognized that the individual was a free and responsible member of a natural society. Rebelling against the traditions and institutions, metaphysics and theology of an artificial community, they had failed to recognize that the scientific method provided a foundation for democratic social agreement. Instead, modern man had committed himself to the false ideal of the self-sufficient individual.

Dewey saw his role in 1900 as one of accelerating the revolution away from medievalism and civilization by making Americans conscious of the forces of industrialism and science which were returning them to the happy condition of primitive man. Industrialism had given them a sense of history as change and progress. Science could provide an understanding of why they should accept change and progress as the only reality and why they should strip themselves of all vestiges of the tradition that had taught them that thought and action existed in separate realms.

Primitive man had thought only in conjunction with his productive actions. The men of classical and medieval civilization had argued that, since action took place in the environment of profane change, thought must dwell in the realm of transcendent, eternal verities. Now, as industrialism encouraged modern man to be proud of his productive activity, science was demonstrating that change was natural, and thought, if it was not to be irrelevant, must relate itself to this real world of change.

From 1900 to 1917 Dewey became an enthusiastic popularizer of Darwin because Dewey affirmed that "in laying hands upon the sacred ark of absolute permanence, in treating the forms that had been regarded as types of fixity and perfection as originating and passing away, *The Origin of Species* introduced a mode of thinking that in the end was bound to transform the logic of knowledge, and hence the treatment of morals, politics, and religion."

In the fashion of Veblen, Dewey was appealing to men to forswear the dangers of imagination which seduced them into believing in castles in the air. The only safe use for intelligence was to be functional to the biological problem of the species in gaining the food, clothing, and shelter necessary for survival. For Dewey the new philosophy, purged of concern for metaphysics and theology, would "forswear inquiry after absolute origins and absolute finalities in order to explore specific values and the specific conditions." Repressing curiosity about the past or concern for the future, Dewey affirmed that "philosophy must become a method of locating and interpreting the more serious of the conflicts that occur in life, and a method of projecting ways of dealing with them."

Rejecting the need for metaphysical or theological speculation about value and meaning, Dewey, like Veblen, proposed that authentic values were given in the natural instincts of man. Part of nature, man was naturally productive. Part of nature, man was naturally cooperative with the fellow members of his biological species. Part of nature, man was naturally curious, in a scientific way, to understand himself and his environment. For Dewey, like Veblen, man had fallen from the state of nature into the hell of civilization because man had created false values for himself. Now industry and science were suppressing this imaginative and evil creativity and restoring man to the natural good. "We are," Dewey asserted, "happy to absolve ourselves from the responsibility of creating the goods that life provides. But we cannot . . . absolve ourselves from responsibility for maintaining and extending those goods when they have happened. . . . We have to act in order to keep secure amid the moving flux of circumstances some . . . precious good that nature has bestowed."

For Dewey there was no uncertainty, no doubt, no debate about ultimate values. They were given in nature as productivity, scientific inquiry, and democracy. "Democracy," he wrote, "the crucial expression of modern life, is not so much an addition to the scientific and industrial tendencies as it is the perception of their social or spiritual meaning." Those meanings, of course, were cooperation in productivity and cooperation in adjustment to the environment. Dewey's famous commitment to a philosophy of pragmatism is not, therefore, a commitment to relativism about values.

Dewey liked to call his variety of pragmatism, instrumentalism. "The holding an end in view," he declared, "and selecting and organizing out of the natural flux, on the basis of this end, conditions that are means (for its fulfillment) is intelligence." Ideas, then, are instruments to further the cooperative and productive adjustment of society to the environment. And one must pragmatically test the truth of an idea by testing it in action. If it works, it is true;

if it does not, it is false. Absolute about ends, Dewey formulated a theory of relative truth for the means of fulfilling those naturally given ends. Here, "truth is an experienced relation of things, and it has no meaning outside of such relation." In this relative area of means, Dewey proclaimed the great usefulness of the scientific method. He described this method as the formation of a hypothesis for the solution of a problem and the test of the hypothesis in action where its validity could be ascertained through public observation. Men were to be open and critical in their use of the scientific method for the testing of the means to achieve their goals. They were to acknowledge that there was no absolute truth but only relative truth in this area of means. But Dewey, speaking about industrialism, science, and democracy, insisted that "modern life involves the deification of the here and now." There was to be no critical testing of values.

While all of the spokesmen for progressivism—economists, sociologists, historians, political scientists—were engaged in the attempt to educate the public to the continued existence of medieval philosophical and social patterns and to the social and altruistic qualities of the natural man, Dewey gained special fame through his philosophy of progressive education in which he defined the progressive school as an auxiliary frontier force that would free the child from the falsehoods of establishment traditions and institutions and help the child reestablish the strengths of his fruitful and cooperative instincts.

The strategy in Dewey's approach to education as to philosophy was to insist that a revolution in this area of self-conscious human effort was not to be a creative revolution; men were not to construct an artificial and artful institution which would inculcate artificial and artful traditions. Dewey described the current educational establishment as an artificial institution teaching artificial traditions. A revolution in education, like the revolution in philosophy, would purge the artful and restore the natural. And this restorative purge in education, as in philosophy, would only rationalize and accelerate the great revolutionary purge of industrialism which was undermining the centuries of parasitical civilization and returning man to his nature role as honest producer. For Dewey industrialism had ushered in a democracy of free and equal producers and education must express this reality of democratic productivity. "Our social life," Dewey wrote, "has undergone a thorough and radical change."

Never in history has there been "a revolution . . . so rapid, so extensive, so complete. . . . If our education is to have any meaning for life, it must pass through an equally complete transformation."

Refusing any longer to speak of a transcendent God, Dewey ascribed ultimate value to the natural order of democratic productivity. Educational reform was, nevertheless, for Dewey a religious crusade to destroy the profane institutions and traditions which for so long had separated mankind from the reality of its true identity as a cooperative producer by teaching the heresy of individual selfishness and competition. "I believe," Dewey proclaimed, "that all education proceeds by the participation of the individual in the social consciousness of the race." "I believe," he continued, "that the only true education comes through the stimulation of the child's powers by the demands of the social situation in which he finds himself. Through these demands he is stimulated to act as a member of a unity, to conceive of himself from the standpoint of the welfare of the group to which he belongs. I believe that the school should simplify existing social life; should reduce it . . . to an embryonic form." And finally Dewey declared, "I believe that every teacher should realize . . . that he is a social servant set apart for the maintenance of proper social order and the securing of the right social growth. I believe that in this way the teacher always is the prophet of the true God and the usherer in of the true kingdom of God."

At the beginning of the new century, Dewey wrote, the school was the most powerfully conservative institution in the country being used "to hamper the adequate realization of the democratic ideal." This was so because education has been built on the metaphysical principles that there were timeless truths which must be inculcated, and children, instead of being taught to relate fruitfully to their industrial environment, were indoctrinated with unreal and irrelevant principles that were supposed to represent eternal verities.

But, Dewey affirmed, the school could become the most radical of institutions if it were used to free children from this false philosophical tradition which has been used to buttress parasitical economic and social patterns as being themselves timeless and eternal. The school, he declared, could be the "chief agency for the accomplishment of this end." It should be "the office of the school to see to it that each individual gets an opportunity to escape from the limitations of the social group in which he was born, and to come into living contact with a broader environment."

The vicious aim of the educational traditions and institutions established by the parasitical aristocracies of historical civilizations had been to impose artificial patterns on children, to force them to adhere to unreal standards. "In education today," Dewey continued, "the currency of these externally imposed aims is responsible for the emphasis on the mechanical and slavish." But a true aim, he argued, "denotes the result of any natural process brought to consciousness. ... It signifies that an activity has become intelligent. A true aim is thus opposed at every point to an aim which is imposed upon a process of action from without." For Dewey this meant that "the first approach to any subject in school ... should be as unscholastic as possible." Children must not learn in the abstract; they must do. "All of us," he continued, "have callings, occupations—only the luxuriously idle and the submerged idle, only the leisure class of fashion and of pauperism violate this law." Children must be encouraged, then, to participate in the productive callings which they would pursue throughout their lives. We must, he affirmed, make "each one of our schools an embryonic community life, active with the types of occupations that reflect the life of the larger society."

The closest thing to abstract theory that Dewey would emphasize in the curriculum was to be science and history. But both of these were to be taught in a fashion that would help liberate the child from debilitating nineteenth-century aristocratic culture and encourage him to participate in the productive industrial democracy of the twentieth century. The essence of science was evolution and an understanding of evolution would lead to the child's "emancipation from local and temporary incidents of experience and the opening of intellectual vistas unobscured by the accidents of personal habit and predilection." The history taught would be economic and scientific. For Dewey, "economic history is more human, more democratic, and hence more liberalizing than political history" because political history recounted the irrelevant and unnatural patterns by which the parasitical elite had dominated the people, while economic and scientific history demonstrated the reality of man's progressive efforts to achieve a productive relationship with nature.

In 1915 Dewey published a book, *German Philosophy and Politics*, which dramatically reaffirmed the fascination of Germany for the progressive imagination. Accepting, like Veblen, industrialism as an international frontier force which would inevitably destroy all historical institutions and traditions with which it came in contact,

Dewey was forced to answer the question which troubled so many of his contemporaries—why the most rapidly industrializing nation in Europe was also the most medieval in its politics.

Dewey's answer was that German industrialization had taken place within an established social and political framework controlled by the ancient aristocracy. And this aristocracy had succeeded in keeping the population in bondage to archaic institutions by inculcating through the school system the false and harmful tradition of philosophical dualism. This had resulted in the paradox that, while the Germans were the "most technically pragmatic of all peoples in their actual conduct of affairs, there is no people so hostile to the spirit of a pragmatic philosophy."

For Dewey his exposure of the terrible tragedy that must come to a nation which held to an erroneous philosophy of life should serve as an object lesson to Americans and serve to speed their acceptance of pragmatism. "The witness of history," Dewey declared, "is that to think in general and abstract terms is dangerous; it elevates ideas beyond the situations in which they were born and charges them with we know not what menace to the future." What had happened in Germany, Dewey wrote, was that the aristocracy had created a very efficient system of public education which was used not to free the people so that they might live freely in productive harmony with industrialism but rather to discipline them so that they would accept passive subordination to the political and social power of the feudal elite.

The German upper classes were able to do this by teaching the people that there were two worlds—one of experience and one of ideas. And these two worlds expressed the division in the individual between lower and higher motives. The aristocracy then taught the people that their everyday experience was dominated by their lower, selfish motives, that it was "an expression of man's egoistic nature. . . . Its typical manifestation is in competitive economic struggle and in the struggle for honor and recognized social status." The only escape from this world of chaos, personal and social, was to the world of pure ideas and motives. The highly institutionalized school system controlled by the elite instructed the people that such an escape could come only through loyalty and obedience to the state. The state, in contrast to the economic world, represented the world of pure ideas and motives. The Germans were taught that "it is the duty of the State to intervene so that the struggle may contribute to the ideal ends which alone are universal." For Dewey, then, the artificial and parasitical pattern of "politics has been the controlling factor in the formation of philosophic ideas and in deciding upon their vogue" in Germany. In the United States, however, Dewey asserted, philosophic ideas were free to be shaped by the authentic and productive pattern of industrialism because the frontier had not allowed an aristocracy of the European type to become dominant. While Dewey acknowledged the existence of Americans loyal to "a priori philosophy" and "systematic absolutism," he found them limited to "narrow and professional circles" because "the American environment with its constant beginning over again and its comparative lack of a traditional background of law and social institutions, demands a philosophy of experiment."

Contrasting Germany and the United States, Dewey described Germany as the great contradiction, industrial yet feudal, while America was freely fulfilling the logic of industrialism to become a productive democracy. Looking toward the future, Dewey could predict conflict between the two nations. The German aristocracy was trying to suppress the logic of industrialism by preserving medievalism while Americans were trying to fulfill it by prophesying a worldwide revolution which would result in an international, industrial democracy. In 1917 Dewey urged American participation in a war against German leaders. His arguments were similar to those of Beard. Dewey defined two kinds of wars, just and unjust. Germany, he argued, had begun an unjust war by attempting through the use of violence to coerce its neighboring nations into subordination to its aristocratic leadership. Unjust wars, then, were characterized by the use of violence to impose artificial patterns on people for the purpose of parasitical exploitation. In contrast, a just war was marked by the use of force and not violence. Force, as opposed to violence, operated to free people from artificial patterns and from parasitical exploitation. Force operated to free people to live in productive harmony with a natural order.

Dewey, who had defined the school as an auxiliary force that would help free people to achieve harmony with the natural order of industrialism, now defined war as just such an auxiliary force. Not only would United States participation prevent the German aristocracy from imposing artificial and parasitical political patterns upon other nations, but, by destroying this vestige of feudalism in Germany, it would free the German people so that they might achieve democratic harmony with the industrial order which already existed in their nation. For Dewey 1917 marked the beginning of a world made safe for democracy.

A major key to the optimism expressed by historians like Beard, economists like Veblen, and philosophers like Dewey, was their certainty that the nineteenth century had been mistaken in its definition of the relationship between the individual and society. These progressives argued that many Americans were obsessed by the fear of cultural decadence and increasing social complexity because they had committed themselves to the belief that man in the state of nature was solitary and self-sufficient. Americans had seen history as the loss of this natural autonomy as men had come to live in complex civilizations until the discovery of the New World had given mankind a second chance to live in a natural state of individual self-sufficiency. But after 1800 the increase in population, its concentration in cities, its employment in factories demonstrated the inevitable return of the individual to a social context and the inevitable return, even in America, of the individual's bondage to unnatural social institutions and traditions.

Now, however, the progressives were arguing that the decline of nineteenth-century individualism was not a movement from the natural to the unnatural but actually the reverse of that; it was a movement from the unnatural to the natural. Man, for the progressives, was social by nature. Therefore, it had been unnatural for the nineteenth century to define the individual in antisocial terms. The key to progress, they argued, was not to liberate individuals from an unnatural society so that they might live as autonomous units. The key to progress was to liberate the individual from an unnatural society to live in a natural society. In the state of nature men had lived in spontaneous harmony with one another. But in historical civilizations they had been forced into disharmony by artificial institutions and traditions which had divided and confused them. And they had been led into further disharmony and confusion by the philosophy of self-sufficient individualism. But the progressives optimistically concluded that the logic of industrialism was both undermining the artificial institutions of historical civilization and the false doctrine of autonomous individualism and helping the individual understand his true nature of spontaneous, noninstitutionalized social unity and cooperation. Industrialism was returning man to the peaceful conditions of precivilization.

The success of the claims of the progressives to establish a new history, a new economics, a new political science, a new philosophy based upon the concept of a social individual rested finally, then, with the appearance of a new social psychology and a new sociology that could provide scientific sanction to that concept. The most important figure in the development of this progressive social psychology and sociology was Charles H. Cooley, a long-time professor of sociology at the University of Michigan.

Cooley's intellectual career illustrates and reinforces the pattern of rebellion and the search for a new philosophy of progress which characterized so many of his contemporaries like John Dewey. Born in Michigan into a family that traced itself far back into New England history, Cooley, as an adolescent, had a personal identity crisis which he could relate to the national identity crisis. Sickly, sensitive, shy, he felt overwhelmed by his father who was a successful jurist and legal philosopher. The older Cooley expounded a philosophy of law which he rooted in eternal and immutable natural principles. It was a philosophy of law which justified absolute property rights for the individual who had no responsibility for community welfare. The young Cooley was taught by his father that there could be no argument with these rational patterns. He was taught that a fact was a fact and could not be ignored by sentimentalists who objected to the harshness of property rights which denied either the need or the right of charity toward the nonproperty holder.

Rebelling against the rigid and harsh natural order that he had been taught to accept, Cooley, like Dewey, turned initially to a philosophy of spiritual transcendence in order to find the strength to refute his father's law. This he found first in Emerson, who reinforced the belief that the young Cooley had expressed in his journal: "A man does right as he follows his conscience." From Emerson he gained confidence in his belief that the external world with its established codes and institutions was not as powerful as the individual with his intuition and insight. "Man," Cooley recorded in his adolescent journal, "is the greatest thing in creation and it is part of his duty to recognize this fact in his every act." This meant that man had a freedom and creativity that placed him above control by judicial pronouncements which falsely attempted to rationalize the world and impose order upon it. Abstract reason is not the basis of philosophical principles, Cooley wrote. "Instinct is the foundation and only criterion for these."

As Cooley reached intellectual maturity, he had fashioned a philosophy that justified rebellion against his father and his father's world. Still outwardly diffident, Cooley was inwardly confident in his search for a new and better world. He was certain that "new thoughts are born, not found. They are born to those who follow the spirit utterly, and follow nothing else." He now had the confidence openly to criticize his father, who had failed to break from the materialistic forms of the establishment.

Having justified individual rebellion against the accepted social and intellectual patterns of the day, Cooley needed next to define the purpose of that rebellion against the legal individualism of his father. As he confided to his journal: "The ideal of my active life is to concern myself with work whose aim is goodness and equity and which has no aim that is selfish." Like Dewey in the 1880s, he came to define God as a spiritual force calling mankind away from materialistic selfishness toward spiritual cooperation. Progress was away from the fragmented and chaotic world of his father toward a unity of man with man and man with God. Increasingly his journal reveals this growing sense of religious identification. "I believe," Cooley wrote, "that a vague sense of the whole grows upon me—intangible, not to be scrutinized, yet deep and supporting."

Desiring social reform in the direction of greater social cooperation, Cooley decided to train in the new academic profession of sociology. But the specific goal for reform and the specific techniques for reform he was considering ran counter to the social science philosophy of the American graduate schools of the 1890s, dominated as they were by the rationalism of men like William Graham Sumner and Lester Frank Ward, who insisted that sociology was as precise and mechanical as physics because society was controlled by the same kind of predictable laws as was physical nature. Cooley, however, described his own vision of sociology in this way: "I would like to make a connecting link between science and poetry, to show the pressing facts of human life as members of an ideal and beautiful whole."

Cooley had to respect the great reforming sociologist of the 1880s, Lester Frank Ward, because Ward attacked those who, like Sumner, used sociology to defend the status quo. But Ward denied the basic spirituality of the human situation. "Society," wrote Cooley, "of course, is spiritual, but current philosophy does not see this, it sees only the shell." Emphasizing the external, he continued, thinkers like Ward had postulated the same kind of control of society by physical law as was found in the natural world, but Cooley asserted: "Exact prediction and mechanical control for the social world ... is a false ideal inconsiderately borrowed from the provinces of physical science. There is no real reason to think that this sort of prediction or control will ever be possible."

Ward had seen the fatal logical weakness in the conservatives like Sumner who appealed to Darwin but really relied upon Herbert Spencer. The gospel of Spencerian evolution was that man was part of physical evolution, controlled by natural law, and that morality must express whatever environment humanity found itself in because morality was adjustment to natural law. Spencer, however, asserted that evolution was progress, that natural law was carrying men ever upward. Ward had asked why man's reason, his scientific understanding, after discovering the pattern of evolutionary progress, should not, then, lift man out of the present into the future. He had asked why morality should not be defined as the effort to bring man into conformity with the inevitable future and not the outdated present.

Cooley, however, could not accept the evolutionary determinism of Ward which was based upon French rationalism and English empiricism. Instead, like Dewey in the 1880s, he looked to the German tradition of philosophical idealism for guidance. Cooley's greatest inspiration while he was in graduate school came from the writings of the German sociologist Albert Schaefle. For Cooley the German contribution to social knowledge was an understanding of the social environment of man. The German idealists affirmed that man was a social, not a biological, animal, and his crucial environment was not physical nature but society. It was society that made the human animal into a civilized man. It was on this necessary social nexus that ethics should rest: ethical behavior must contribute to the welfare of the group.

Looked at from this perspective, Spencer's sociology was lacking in human sympathy: it disregarded human personality; it had no insight into the human mind and soul; it was biological and individualistic when it should have been historical and social. In an essay "The Process of Social Change," published in the *Political Science Quarterly* in 1897, Cooley lashed out at Spencer's definition of evolution as the survival of the fittest. Man, he wrote, reared within society was cooperative. Man's natural energy was released not in physical competition but in social creativity. Progress was made not by the working of physical law upon society, but by the working of individuals within society. Human progress was not the negative elimination of the unfit; rather it was based on the positive ability of men to learn and grow so that all could share in the forward progress of society originated by a few exceptional individuals.

Cooley, like Dewey, was aware of the possibility that German idealism also could be used to defend the status quo. But Cooley shared with Dewey a rejection of the German emphasis on institutions as necessary expressions of spiritual unity. For Cooley, as for Dewey, the individual was not disciplined into social harmony by institutions. Rather Cooley concurred with Dewey's view that the individual was by nature totally social and that it had been artificial institutions which had fragmented this innate sociability.

This was the theme of his first major book, *Human Nature and the Social Order*. Here he firmly expressed the organic relation of individual to society and society to individual. "A separate individual is an abstraction unknown to experience, and so likewise is society when regarded as something apart from individuals. The real thing is Human Life, which may be considered either in an individual aspect or in a social." This did not mean, Cooley declared, that society was only the sum of its individuals; the basic reality of social life was the social process. Look at an infant, he continued; from its earliest days it exhibited sociability, and these impulses were brought into contact with other personalities through communication. Personality and the human mind were developed by a give-and-take process between the infant and the people in its environment. As these social tendencies were objectified through communication, the child came to have ideas about the people around him. These ideas, developed out of this reciprocal process, were not isolated phenomena but were part of a total web of associations, colored by emotion and sentiment. There was, then, no absolute separation of individuals from each other or from society because they were society, and this society was part of the thinker's mind. Reality, then, was social; it was the social process which connected the minds of men. For Cooley: "So far as the study of immediate social relations is concerned, the personal idea is the real person. That is to say, it is in this alone that one man exists for another, and acts directly upon his mind. My association with you evidently consists in the relation between my idea of you and the rest of my mind."

Given this mutual development of individual and society, there was no need to suppress inherent selfishness, which did not exist, or to encourage sociability, which did inherently exist. The normal individual acted both individually and socially. "In a truly organic life, the individual is self-conscious and devoted to his own work, but feels himself and that work as part of a large and joyous whole. He is self-assertive, just because he is conscious of being a thread in the great web of events."

Cooley, living in a confused and chaotic society, postulated an ideal, organic society which could be used as a standard to criticize the present and as a goal to approach in the future. The competitive capitalism of 1900, he wrote, obviously failed to produce normal, social individuals. It was a false system because it was built upon ephemeral, not eternal, values. Competitive capitalism claimed to be based upon a system of natural rights, but competitive individualism was not natural. There were, however, natural rights by which any historical establishment could be judged. "If it is true," he declared, "that human nature is developed in primary groups which are everywhere much the same, and that there also springs from these a common idealism which institutions strive to express, we have a ground for somewhat the same conclusions as came from a theory of natural freedom." Human nature, he went on, was social, but while the individual reflected that social environment of which he was a part, there was a form of universal society beneath the relative forms of any conventional culture; there was unity beneath the vast multiplicity of groups and institutions. This unity was in the form of universal traits that were found in the primary groups of all societies. Primary groups, he wrote, were

> those characterized by intimate face-to-face association and cooperation. They are primary in several senses, but chiefly in that they are fundamental in forming the social nature and ideals of the individual. . . . The most important spheres of this intimate association . . . are the family, the play-group of children and the neighborhood or community group of elders. These are practically universal, belonging to all times and all stages of development; and are accordingly a chief basis of what is universal in human nature and human ideals.

Cooley, like his fellow progressives, had found a normal, social man who had existed in the childhood of the race. Now he had to explain the fall from this original garden of Eden into the hell of history and then show how progress was returning man to his primitive harmony and happiness. Man was naturally good, he declared, and "We are so happily contrived that humanity can progress without a change in nature." Evil, therefore, was negative, the absence of good. Historical civilization had been characterized by this negative evil because populations had become too large to allow for the humanizing, socializing contact of the primary groups that characterized primitive society. In their place men were forced to substitute artificial institutions and traditions which unfortunately dehumanized and desocialized humanity. But now the industrial revolution had brought new techniques of communication and transportation which were restoring the possibility of the face-to-face contact of the primary groups on a universal level.

Cooley, like Dewey, could only express this miracle of emerging democratic unity in explicitly religious terms. "Modern communication fulfills one condition of the 'Kingdom of God on earth' by bringing all mankind into somewhat familiar intercourse." Knowing that, evil was to be defined as "negative rather than positive, as inertia and confusion and . . . selfishness is not something additional to ordinary human nature . . . but rather a lack." Cooley could offer this millennial assurance because "assuming that the human heart and conscience, restricted only by the difficulties of organization, is the arbiter of what institutions are to become, we may expect the facility of intercourse to be the starting-point of a new era of moral progress."

Many Americans by 1900 had come to believe that the political parties were artificial institutions which thwarted the will of the people and that the professional politicians were a parasitical aristocracy committed to personal and not democratic government. Throughout the nation there was pressure to reduce the importance of the party and the politician or even destroy them completely by giving public opinion freedom of expression through primaries, the initiative, and the referendum. Cooley's sociology, like Dewey's progressive education, provided intellectual support for this movement. Clearly Dewey hoped that progressive schools would help the people to express their will spontaneously without recourse to political institutions, parties, or politicians. And now Cooley through his sociological theory was arguing that America and the world stood on the threshold of an era of such perfect communication that the people could speak spontaneously with one voice.

Made up of perfectly communicating individuals, Cooley declared, society could act and think as one individual. The individual and society were largely creatures of sentiment and emotion; the central fact of human psychology was the urge to act. It was the common man who furnished the sentiments for which society must work. The function of leadership was to provide organization for the more or less chaotic impulse of the group. The mass provided the originality in the social process, and the leaders gave it effective and intelligent expression. When Cooley asked, "What are these ethical aims of society?" his answer was that of his progressive colleagues. They were "rational aims, representing the ideal of efficient total organization."

Cooley, then, was also a religious prophet of a new reformation that would end medieval chaos and provide organic order. The forces of light must conquer at Armageddon because "It is God that is working. Life is onward, glorious, transcendent. I am in it; a part of it." This end of historical chaos, for Cooley, was to be marked by the merger of "the idea of God and the social state . . . and thus patriotism and religion will reinforce each other—a new unity of Church and State." This perfect unity was to arrive through "the impressing of a unitary life upon the hearts of the people by tradition, poetry, music, architecture, national celebrations and memorials, and by a religion and a philosophy teaching the individual that he is a member of a glorious whole to which he owes devotion."

Throughout the nineteenth century the well-to-do had both denied and accepted the existence of poverty in the growing urban centers. Given the promise that America in 1800 represented the culmination of progress from the chaos of medieval civilization to the harmony of nature, the presence of people without adequate food or shelter was an embarrassing contradiction to the national identity as a restored garden of Eden. And until the end of the 1890s, it was obvious that most comfortable Americans did not want their complacency shattered by muckraking which documented the economic and social misery of so many human beings in the slums.

On the other hand, early nineteenth-century America was committed to an economic, social, and religious outlook of self-sufficient individualism which insisted that America was in a state of nature and not a historical civilization just because its citizens were free from restraints by institutions and traditions. Now each individual was personally responsible for his economic and social existence and for the salvation of his soul. Accepting social, economic, and theological laissez-faire, many Americans placed personal blame on those who failed to achieve economic and social security. This demonstrated a lack of character, moral weakness, even sinfulness. The formula that to be sinful was to be poor and to be poor was to be sinful became widely accepted.

This philosophy of individualism which denied any relationship between personality, character, and the social environment helped to persuade large numbers of Americans to accept the identity of Anglo-Saxon racism. The Anglo-Saxons, it was claimed, had had the biological strength of personality and character to reject the corrupting institutions and traditions of Europe and migrate to the New World to live as free men in harmony with nature. More and more frequently throughout the nineteenth century poverty was explained as moral weakness that reflected biological weakness. And the rationalization for withholding aid to the poor had become twofold. In theological terms the poor were being punished by God for their sins, and in biological terms they were being punished for their failure to embody the strength of the race. In either case these paupers were unclean and abnormal pariahs who must be segregated and allowed to perish in isolation from the good and normal people.

By 1890 this attitude toward the poor was being reinforced by the massive immigration of Slavs and Latins who were Catholics and Jews into the urban-industrial areas of the nation. Here were biologically inferior people of the Old World who had not had the strength of character to become Protestant, like the Anglo-Saxons, who had not had the strength of character to rebel against ancient and profane institutions and traditions. Obviously the pauperism of these degenerate and sinful immigrants was not the responsibility of the Anglo-Saxon Protestants who were the authentic Americans.

In 1890 the dominant groups in the North as in the South defined the fundamental national identity as white, Anglo-Saxon, Protestant. These northerners and southerners also held, as the legacy of Radical Reconstruction, the concept of second-class citizenship for those who did not fit this definition of racist democracy. Between 1890 and 1917 the foundation of a new sectional conflict between North and South was laid, therefore, as the South moved to destroy this concept of second-class citizenship and the North moved to strengthen it.

Given the logic of the theological and biological definition of pauperism, Anglo-Saxon leadership might have moved to establish barriers of legally enforced physical separation around the Jewish and Catholic ghettos and systematically to deny civil, political, and educational rights to these new immigrants. But the decision was reached among the ruling groups to encourage the Catholics and Jews in a second-class citizenship in which they would follow the political, economic, social, and intellectual leadership of the Anglo-Saxon first-class citizens. Unlike southerners during the progressive period, northern Anglo-Saxon leaders did believe that one could create a subordinate democracy within a dominant democracy.

This decision meant that a significant portion of the northern business community began to follow the intellectuals like Dewey and Cooley who were moving away from the racism that was overwhelmingly dominant in intellectual circles as elsewhere in the nation in 1890. The emphasis on environmentalism in the new sociology, social psychology, and educational theory was paralleled among business and political leaders. Added to the general need for a new definition of the nation in terms of urban-industrial cooperation was the fear of the business community that the new immigrants would not accept their poverty as the result of their own personal irresponsibility. By 1890 Marxism had become a widespread ideology throughout Europe, and Marx argued that the poverty of the industrial workers was the result of their exploitation by middle-class entrepreneurs. For Marx nineteenth-century capitalism did not operate according to the model of free and equal producers competing with each other but rather it operated with one class exploiting another. Competition and conflict, Marx argued, took place between classes and not individuals. If, then, the new immigrants were denied leadership by the Anglo-Saxons while white leaders in the South were isolating themselves from the Negro, would these northern urban ghetto dwellers develop their own leadership, Marxist leadership, and engage the old Americans in class warfare?

Perhaps from the perspective of business leaders, the new spokesmen for educational reform, like Dewey, were not mistaken when they argued that people were always shaped by their social en-

vironment. Progressive education promised to purge the child of excess social baggage from the past, the erroneous and harmful traditions which kept him from being a cooperative and productive
member of society. And clearly this concept of purging the child of
outdated ideas could be applied to the Marxist ideas brought from
Europe. Certainly the business community in the North accepted
a huge new burden of taxes in adding the high school to the gram-
mar school as part of the necessary public education of every child.
The high school, it was argued would socialize the child; it would
teach him citizenship and, through vocational training, fit him into
the expanding industrial frontier. Just when the white South was
denying the high school to the Negro, the Anglo-Saxon North made
certain that it was available to the children of the new immigrants,
because, as one leading educational reformer, Ellwood P. Cubberley,
wrote, the new immigrants are "illiterate, docile, lacking in self-
reliance and initiative, and not possessing the Anglo-Teutonic conceptions of law, order, and government; their coming has served
to dilute tremendously our national stock, and to corrupt our civic
life." Therefore, he continued, the task of education was to break
up their ghettos and "to assimilate and amalgamate these people
as a part of our American race, and to implant in their children . . .
the Anglo-Saxon conception of righteousness, law and order, and
popular government, and to awaken in them a reverence for our
democratic institutions and for those things in our national life
which we as a people hold to be of abiding worth."

From a dominant attitude in 1890 that criticism of the system
must be suppressed, large numbers of the middle class came, by
1900, to welcome such criticism. Suddenly, between 1900 and 1910,
men emerged who were popular middle-class heroes as muckrakers.
Lincoln Steffens became a household name through his exposures of
political corruption. Others like Jacob Riis and Robert Hunter became famous through their revelations of urban poverty. It is clear
that much of middle-class America shared the outlook of the middle-
class intellectuals who were creating new history, new political
science, new sociology, new economics, and new educational and
philosophical theory. America in 1900 was not old; it had not aged
or decayed since its birth as a natural democracy in 1789. Democratic America, an America free from medievalism, was yet to be
born. This was the moment of the triumph of progress, of a reformation and renaissance, of an enlightenment which would end the

long history of darkness and usher in an earthly paradise. The new immigrants, these Catholics and Jews, were not people who had rejected the opportunity to escape from medievalism in 1600; rather they were still prisoners of the medievalism that continued to ensnare even the American Anglo-Saxons down to the present. And the American Anglo-Saxons, in breaking the bonds of this feudal heritage, could also liberate the Catholic and Jewish immigrants in their midst, even as in 1917 the whole world might be purged of corrupt civilization and made safe for democracy.

Symbolic of the dramatic change in attitude toward the poor was the development of the settlement house. As long as the poor were defined as sinful and profane, they could not be helped by the middle class. But spreading from England to the United States was the idea of social Christianity, that salvation was not possible for the solitary individual but must be defined as salvation for the entire society. The poor were not personally sinful but were imprisoned by a sinful system which kept them from being productive and useful members of society. When in the 1890s middle-class Anglo-Saxon women like Jane Addams, Florence Kelley, and many others began to go into the slums and mingle with the inhabitants, most of whom were not Anglo-Saxons, it was a clear sign that these lower-class people were no longer defined as necessary corrupters of Anglo-Saxon innocence but as themselves innocent victims who could be redeemed by these angels of mercy. The logic of the settlement house was parallel to that of Dewey's progressive school or Cooley's primary group. Assuming a situation of social chaos, it offered itself as a model of social cooperation which would gradually be imitated until its kind of harmony became universal. Again emphasizing that the garden of democratic brotherhood had not been lost but rather was only now being approached, the social reformers emphasized the arguments of economists like Simon Patten that it was not until the advent of industrial productivity, which had vastly increased the wealth of mankind, that the abolition of poverty had become possible.

Up until 1890 there had been ministers like Washington Gladden who had criticized the economic system for causing the poverty of the workers, but these critics had not become leaders of major changes in their denominations. But by 1900 it was clear that something like a widespread conversion movement was taking place among Protestant denominations in the North and Midwest and that many ministers and parishioners were rejecting the individualistic emphasis of the nineteenth century in favor of a social gospel that absolved the poor of responsibility for their condition and instead blamed the system.

Faced with ghastly conditions in the city tenements, unemployment, low wages, a vicious child labor system, sickness, widespread alcoholism, gambling, and prostitution, the progressive prophets of the Social Gospel could ask for more detailed, factual studies of the illness of urban-industrial America because they were certain that, faced with the reality of a corrupt system, their parishioners would choose the right. Evil existed only because it was not recognized. And when evil was stripped of its mask of respectability—that it was the natural order of things—and was revealed as an artificial, alien, and parasitical growth, it would be easily removed from a society which was basically healthy. This was the message of Walter Rauschenbusch, a Baptist minister who became the most important theologian of the Social Gospel movement.

The starting point of Rauschenbusch's theology was the argument, common to his progressive contemporaries in the social sciences and arts, that Americans misunderstood the origin of their outlook of individualism, in this case individual salvation. Americans were mistaken in believing that an emphasis on personal rather than social salvation was a repudiation of medieval tradition in favor of a natural, primitive Christianity. For Rauschenbusch, primitive Christianity embodied the true nature of man, his social nature. It had been during the artificial civilizations of Rome and the Middle Ages that this truth had been obscured and mankind had been inculcated with the error of individual autonomy and the belief that salvation must be otherworldly.

Christianity and the Social Crisis was the title of Rauschenbusch's first book in 1907. This crisis, he wrote, was caused by the industrial revolution, which, in destroying the past, had brought mankind to a totally new era in history. And he insisted that this was not another of the major changes that had characterized past history. This was Armageddon, when men must either find complete salvation or pass completely into the hands of evil powers. Fortunately, Rauschenbusch affirmed, industrialism, which had brought on the crisis by destroying established institutions and traditions, had also constructed the foundations for a new and perfect community, a Heavenly City of God on Earth. The constructive elements of the present, its more sensitive means of communication and speeded transportation, blending peoples into one great friendly community, had been made clear by the economists, sociologists, and historians. But this peaceable kingdom could not be attained, he warned, if men did not commit themselves to a spiritual awakening which would free them from the selfish forces still in control of the industrial system. Only the enthusiasm born of a Christian revival could assure the birth of the new era. Only a renewed witness to Christ's teachings that men must have social justice would give them the strength to reject the temptations of the false creed that the individual must pursue his own self-interest. And this selfish creed had masqueraded as Christian doctrine in churches for centuries, making it more difficult to root out.

But make no mistake, Rauschenbusch continued, the essential purpose of Christianity always had been "to transform human society into the Kingdom of God by regenerating all human relations and reconstituting them in accordance with the will of God." Even before Christ's teaching, he continued, the Hebrew prophets had proclaimed the fundamental truth that religion must find expression in ethical conduct and that the perfection of ethical behavior in human society was the highest religious act. God had revealed himself in history, and the study of the historical roots of Christianity in the Old Testament would clarify God's message to man.

Mankind, Rauschenbusch declared, at the beginning of written history was a pure expression of God. The original family group was perfect in its brotherly love. The Hebrew tribes had lived in a primitive democracy without social class and with an equal distribution of property. But the Hebrews lived surrounded by peoples who had created complex and artificial societies in which injustice was the rule. And these societies warred upon one another and warred upon the Hebrews who prayed for deliverance of their nation from this chaos.

But, in its very emphasis on the Jewish group, Hebrew religion failed to express the truth of the fraternity of all men in the eyes of the Father; it was a narrow and nationalistic faith which erred in denying God to all men. In one sense, then, it was advantageous to the progress of understanding the true faith when the Jews were conquered by nonbelievers and the possibility of a national salvation in the midst of other sinful nations was destroyed. But the impossibility of a perfected Jewish community drove the Hebrew prophets to shift the goal of salvation from an immediate earthly future to a far-off dream. With the focus for immediate ethical reform removed, ceremonialism increased, and ritual became more important than practice.

This was the disastrous state of religious thought when God caused His son Jesus to be born into the world. Now Jesus explained the universal meaning of the fatherhood of God and the brotherhood of man—that love is the key to God's relation to all men and of each man to every other man. It was Jesus who transcended the Jewish national faith to make it universal while he, at the same time, retrieved it from otherworldly speculation to the business of worldly salvation for every member of the community.

It was Jesus, above all, who realized that this social salvation would be accomplished slowly and gradually until the eventual establishment of the Kingdom of God on earth. Jesus, according to Rauschenbusch, was the first evolutionist. Accordingly, Jesus was the constant attacker of all established law and religious ceremonialism. The institutions of any period expressed man's past progress, but it was his destiny to strive forward and upward and to make his institutions conform to the spiritual ideal which was his constant inspiration. The past, the orthodox, must always be superseded until the Kingdom was reached.

Mankind, however, had lost this message of Christian progress because the heritage of false ideas created in the past managed to obscure and pervert it. Out of the tradition of Jewish national defeat came the idea of millennialism, the hope of the immediate return of Christ. With it marched the equally vicious fallacy of otherworldliness, the belief that the Second Coming would deliver mankind into heaven. From Greek culture were added the debilitating doctrines of extreme individuality and hostility to government, and, worst of all, the lack of awareness that the family was the model of the perfect society in miniature. Slowly Christianity was twisted into a doctrine of asceticism which encouraged the individual to withdraw from any attempt to reform society and to prepare his soul for the next world.

But since men do live in this world, social institutions, even the Church, came to be controlled by non-Christians who continued the authoritarian traditions of the manmade civilizations of antiquity rather than the democracy of the family group created by God. This pagan aristocracy formed the established order in Europe and America at the beginning of the twentieth century, a pagan aristocracy which defended itself from reform by claiming to be a Christian establishment fulfilling God's will.

It was time, therefore, Rauschenbusch proclaimed, for an authentic Christian revival which would destroy this evil masquerade. And an analysis of recent history demonstrated, he continued, that the foundations for such a revival had already been constructed. "The sadness of the failure," he wrote, "is turned into brightest hopefulness if we note that all the causes which have hitherto neutralized the social efficiency of Christianity have strangely disappeared or weakened in modern life."

First the people were no longer ground under heel, but had risen through democracy to a commanding place in society and government. Democracy, with its fraternalism, was the secular parallel of the Christian doctrine of brotherly love. Democracy had opened the door for free discussion and criticism of the corrupt minority that tried to suppress progress. Based on faith in human ability in this world, democracy was turning men away from otherworldliness and was ending their distrust of government activity. Democracy was forcing men away from asceticism, ceremonialism, and dogmatism; democracy was committed to a faith in experimentation as the most efficient way of controlling the social and physical environment. And finally, democracy had the perfect tool for reform: social science which revealed the course of human progress.

Finally men had regained Christ's concept of evolution and history. They were coming to understand that there had been the false history created by man and the true history which was God's will. And they now had the analytical tools of social science to cut through the meaningless history of civilization to see the progressive evolution of God's history, the spread of the ancient Jewish pattern of social democracy to the entire world.

But again, Rauschenbusch warned, "We are standing at the turning of the ways. We are actors in a great historical drama. It rests upon us to decide if a new era is to dawn in the transformation of the world into the kingdom of God, or if Western civilization is to descend into the graveyard of dead civilizations."

There was crisis because the industrial revolution, which was the economic foundation for the growth of social and political democracy, had taken place within the framework of older traditions that were in a position to corrupt it. Coming out of the medieval past, when the people had been taught by the Church to take no responsible role in economics and politics, was the tradition of economic self-interest on the part of the social aristocracy, which used politics to support its exploitation of the people. This tradition was now in control of the new economic order and was determined to destroy its potential for universal fraternity and true Christianity. Since all men were prisoners of the false values taught by this aristocracy through its control of the churches, schools, newspapers, and political parties, they could only free themselves from its control through inspiration received from God. "No man can help the people until he is himself free from the spell which the present order has cast over our moral judgment. . . . The men of faith are the living spirits, the channels by which new truth and power from God enter humanity."

Like so many of his fellow progressives, Rauschenbusch's optimism increased during the years between 1900 and 1914. Like them he shared in the psychology of a coming millennium, and in 1912, when he published *Christianity and the Social Order,* he was much more certain that the crisis would be won by the forces of light. "When 'Christianity and the Social Crisis' was published in 1907," he wrote, "I thought I had said all that God had given me to say on our social problem. . . . But meanwhile the social awakening of our nation set in like an equinoctial gale." Spiritual regeneration had occurred in the hearts of the majority of Americans. "This," he proclaimed, "is religious energy, rising from the depth of that infinite spiritual life in which we all live and move and have our being. This is God."

The virtues of the family, Christian virtues of cooperation, love, and equality, had become established in the churches freed from medieval tyranny, in the schools freed from aristocratic pedantry, and in politics freed from class rule. Only in economics did the aristocratic anti-Christian values of selfishness and competitiveness prevail. But now this final citadel of evil was to be conquered by the ongoing religious revival. A cooperative commonwealth was to appear which would fulfill the message of Christianity that the social democracy of the primitive Hebrews was to become universal. Again, like his fellow progressives, Rauschenbusch had used the doctrine of progressive historical development to undermine the foundations of the status quo, but he shared with the other progressives the definition of evolutionary progress as a historical purge of manmade civilization with its artificial institutions and traditions so that man could return to the God-given reality of a natural social democracy.

Chapter V

Women for Progress and Progress for Women: Jane Addams, Charlotte Perkins Gilman, and Mary Parker Follett

Many cities doubled their populations between 1880 and 1890. Chicago's spectacular surge from 500,000 in 1880 to 1 million in 1890 to 2 million in 1910 came, as was the case with most northern and midwestern cities, from a wave of immigration from southern and eastern Europe. As 20 million immigrants, many of them Slavic and Italian peasants, came into American cities between 1890 and 1914 to add to the already strong Catholic presence of the earlier Irish immigration, the Protestant middle class feared that it had lost the ability to govern the nation's major cities. Already there were many cities that had fallen under the power of city bosses who had the support of the immigrant masses and who solidified their power by taking graft from the criminals who controlled prostitution and gambling. For the males of the white Protestant middle class who wanted to restore order to the cities, the energetic efforts of middle-class women to control liquor, prostitution, and crime were becoming welcome. This tentative cooperation between Anglo-American men and women which began to characterize middle-class efforts to reform the cities in the 1890s, however, followed several decades of increasing confusion and rising tension about the proper roles outside the home for respectable women.

Between the end of the Civil War in 1865 and the 1890s, the rigid separation of the home as the world of middle-class women and the marketplace as the world of middle-class men had begun to break down. The women of this period had been taught that there was a special purity about the home which was lacking in the marketplace. They had been taught that there was a sexual double standard: middle-class men could engage in sexual promiscuity in their lives outside the home while middle-class women remained sexually pure within the home. Now, after 1865, many middle-class women began to demand that the purity of their homes should become a redeeming influence in the corrupt marketplace world of their husbands.

These women insisted, for example, that prostitutes were created by a bad social environment. Up to this time, it was thought that prostitutes were fallen women who had chosen a life of sin because of their evil instincts. The new thinking of the middle-class women held that, if the purity of the middle-class home could be brought into the lives of lower-class women, prostitution would disappear and so would the double standard. While the major theologians of the Social Gospel movement were men, it is clear that the driving force to relate sinfulness to the social environment rather than to individual choice came from middle-class women in northern cities.

Widespread prostitution had followed the northern armies during the Civil War and many members of the medical profession recommended that prostitutes be placed under legal and medical supervision. Since this action would perpetrate prostitution and the double standard, middle-class women reformers opposed this. They immediately began to fight this recommendation by lobbying in state legislatures and Congress.

Two of the principal leaders in the crusade to abolish prostitution were Elizabeth Blackwell, one of the first American women to become a physician, and her sister, Antoinette Blackwell, the first woman ordained as a Protestant minister. They were able to win the support of other major women leaders, among them Susan B. Anthony and Frances Willard, the president of the Women's Christian Temperance Union (WCTU). This women's purity crusade had met with initial resistance, but gradually many middle-class men were coming to see that it coincided with their desire to bring order out of the urban chaos of the late nineteenth century.

In an interesting way, then, these middle-class men and women were searching simultaneously for a new identity as part of the public life of the developing urban frontier. The Republic of the Founding Fathers had been for men only and the loss of the agrarian foundation for the Republic had caused a cultural identity crisis for middle-class men, who began to create a new Republic based on the development of an industrial, urban, and overseas frontier. But, if men had to experience the anguish of rejecting an old identity while groping toward another pattern of meaning, so did the middle-class women who were rejecting their nineteenth-century segregation in a private home walled off from public life.

Three women who made the transition from the privacy of the home to the public arena and who became major theoreticians for the growing reform movement were Jane Addams, Charlotte Perkins Gilman, and Mary Parker Follett. Each represents a very different philosophy of progress and a very different relationship to the dominant male world. Jane Addams had important ties to the Social Gospel movement, but Hull House and other settlement houses provided middle-class women with an area of autonomous leadership in the battle to bring progress to the cities. Charlotte Perkins was creative and prolific in developing a critical analysis of the contradictions between what she saw as the logic of the progressive male world of industrial production and the reactionary female world of unproductive consumption. For Gilman, the liberation of women from the medieval home and their entry into the modern economy would also liberate men from the burden of living in a badly divided society where their wives and children were part of an alien culture. Mary Parker Follett, unlike Addams and Gilman, was primarily concerned with the same issues of social and political theory that were debated within the predominantly masculine intellectual community of the Progressive Era. Follett's writings were accepted by that community, and she survived into the 1920s better than most male progressives because she was respected by the intellectuals of that part of the business world which identified with Progressivism.

Jane Addams, born in northwestern Illinois in 1860, lost her mother when she was two. She was encouraged by her father, a successful businessman, to develop her mind and to look forward to a college education. Addams was one of the first generation of women college graduates. Almost half of these first women graduates chose not to marry. These women did not want to share the fate of their mothers. Addams became ill when she returned home after graduation, but she quickly recovered her health when she traveled again. She had to have a life away from home, but, for an educated and ambitious woman of the 1880s who chose not to marry, opportunities were limited. Women could not vote in national elections until 1920. Custom kept them from becoming executives in the developing corporations and government bureaucracies and made it almost impossible for them to enter the professions, such as medicine and law. Jane Addams was a victim of this social arrangement.

As a teenager, she had dreamed of public success. "Deeds make habits, habits make character, character makes destiny," she wrote in her diary. "Nothing is more certain than that improvement in human affairs is wholly the work of uncontented characters." In her restless search for a constructive role she could play in the improvement of human affairs, she traveled to Europe twice. During the second trip, she visited Toynbee Hall in London. There, in the 1880s, well-to-do young English men and women were choosing to live with the urban poor in an attempt to improve the lives of the underprivileged.

Addams immediately felt inspired and liberated by this English Christian Socialism. She had long wondered how a middle-class woman could engage in reform. "Our young people hear in every sermon, learn in their lessons, read in their very fiction of the great maladjustments, but no way is provided for them to help," she had lamented. "One is so overpowered by the misery and narrow lives of so large a number of city people, that the wonder is that conscientious people can let it alone."

Determined to begin a settlement house in Chicago, Addams and her friend Ellen Starr won widespread support from wealthy families and were able to move into an old mansion, Hull House, in a district that had become a slum densely populated by immigrants from Italy and eastern Europe. For Addams, this was a chance to live fully, because "there is nothing so fatal to life itself as the want of a proper outlet for active faculties." Here she had the opportunity to use her faculties in the service of others.

The six settlement houses in the country in 1891 exploded to more than a hundred by 1900. Middle-class women had created an institution which enabled them to provide leadership in public life. While some men participated in the founding of settlement houses, it was much more difficult for middle-class men in the United States than in England to share in this new institution. Men in America did not have the option open to Englishmen to avoid participation in the marketplace and in production. Social pressures defined as effeminate a man who spent his whole life in social service without the expectation of a good salary and the chance for professional advancement. Many men at the beginning of the 1890s shared Addams' belief that "the movement toward Christian Socialism is certainly becoming more general from the very stress of misery." They wrote about the misery and the coming of reform from within their positions in the church, academic, or business structures but felt they could not lead lives fully dedicated to the transformation of American society. In a sense, they envied and admired – almost to the point of worship – the freedom of women like Jane Addams to live among the poor and directly help transform their lives.

Henry Demarest Lloyd was a well-to-do, middle-class radical living in Chicago. During the 1880s and 1890s, he had become a national figure because of the success of his books analyzing the undemocratic concentration of economic and political power in such major corporations as Standard Oil. He began the pilgrimage of male reformers to Hull House to gain inspiration and wisdom from Addams, who quickly became known as "Saint Jane." Richard T. Ely, a professor of economics who became a spokesman for Christian Socialism while at Johns Hopkins University, regularly visited Addams when he transferred to the University of Wisconsin. He also invited Addams to lecture at the University. When the University of Chicago was founded in 1894, Albion Small, a reform-minded professor there and the editor of the *American Journal of Sociology*, encouraged Addams and her staff at Hull House to contribute a steady stream of articles to the journal. John Dewey joined the University of Chicago faculty and quickly became closely associated with Hull House. Dewey always affirmed that his theories of education were strongly influenced by that association. "I cannot tell you how much good I got from my stay at Hull House," he wrote to Addams, "my indebtedness to you for giving me an insight into matters there is great."

Addams had been baptized as a Christian when she returned from her conversion experience at Toynbee Hall in England and had begun Hull House as a form of lay ministry. By 1900, however, she no longer identified what she believed was the coming democratic transformation of America with the actions of the God of Christianity. As she entered the twentieth century, her views changed toward a secular religion that found hope in the laws of social evolution and in the democratic values of the people. Her new views were much closer to those of Dewey than to those of Rauschenbusch, and they paralleled the values of many of the men who were establishing the social sciences between 1880 and 1900. A number of these men had been Christian ministers or were inspired by Christianity to become reformers using the tools of social science to bring constructive change. By 1900, as they came to identify themselves as professional sociologists, economists, political scientists, historians, and philosophers, it seemed unprofessional to bring a traditional religious commitment to one's scholarship.

After 1900, more and more women in the settlement houses defined themselves as professional social workers. Addams cultivated a detached attitude. She came to see herself as a social scientist committed to "the application of knowledge to life." Encouraged by Ely, the Hull House staff, led by Florence Kelley, engaged in systematic, statistical studies of the neighborhood which were published as *Hull House Maps and Papers*. These studies were used by political reformers in their argument for better housing codes in Illinois cities and by spokesmen for tenement reform throughout the country.

Addams at Hull House was determined to liberate the new immigrants from their Old World culture. The purpose of her settlement house, like that of Dewey's school, was to free the immigrants and their children from unprogressive undemocratic traditions of the Old World and to bring them into American traditions of progress and democracy. When Addams spoke about "sordid and ignorant immigrants" and "the pathetic stupidity of agricultural people," she was talking about culture and not individuals. It was European customs that were "sordid and ignorant" and that created "the pathetic stupidity" of the newcomers to America. In her first book, *Democracy and Social Ethics* (1902), she celebrated the willingness of the middle-class Protestant reformer to see how the peasants from Europe had the potential to be constructive American citizens. "Formerly, when it was believed that poverty was synonymous with vice and laziness, and the prosperous man was the righteous man," she wrote, "charity was administered harshly with a good conscience, for the charitable agent really blamed the individual for his poverty." But now, Addams declared, reformers saw the poor as potential equals who should be given the chance to act like middle-class Americans.

For Addams, raising the new immigrant poor up to equal citizenship had the added importance of rescuing the middle class from its temptation to surrender its democratic ideals and to see itself as a privileged aristocracy dominating the urban poor. Writing for a middle-class audience, she reminded them that "the acceptance of democracy brings a certain life-giving power" and "we belong to the whole."

Like the male progressives, Addams was certain that the laws of social evolution were inevitably leading the United States toward a classless, middle-class democracy. The great problems, for her, were stemming from ignorance. The poor did not know how to act in a democratic and middle-class fashion and the middle class did not understand that the problem of the poor was ignorance rather than innate depravity. Addams repeated this message in her book of 1909, *The Spirit of Youth and the City Streets.* Concerned with juvenile delinquency, she described the corrupting influences of the city and the demoralizing impact of dead-end jobs for young people of the slums. Proving once more that social conditions, not innate depravity, was the major source of juvenile crime, she provided no proposals for structural changes in the economy. Like so many progressives, she had faith that the forces of evolution were overcoming urban problems. She returned to this kind of analysis in a book on prostitution, *A New Conscience and an Ancient Evil* (1912), and once again offered hope for the inevitable victory of progress.

In 1912, she broke from her long-held position of nonpartisanship to back Theodore Roosevelt as the presidential candidate of the newly formed Progressive Party. The high point of Addams' belief in progress, like so many of the male progressives, coincided with Roosevelt's candidacy. Suddenly, politics seemed to be transformed as part of that new world Addams had been confidently predicting for more than twenty years. Explaining why she had become active in the politics of the Progressive Party, she wrote, "When a great party pledges itself to the protection of children and the care of the aged, to the relief of overworked girls, to the safeguarding of burdened men, it is inevitable that it should appeal to women and should seek to draw upon the great reservoir of moral energy so long undesired and unutilized in practical politics."

Roosevelt welcomed Addams' support because she had become such a strong national leader of reform sentiment between 1890 and 1912. But the years between 1914 and 1917 largely destroyed her reputation and her influence. Unlike her friend, John Dewey, and other male progressives such as Thorstein Veblen and Charles Beard, Addams had become a pacifist after the Spanish-American war. And she could not believe, as they did, that American participation in World War I would speed the coming of the progressive millennium. She made a pilgrimage to the great Russian author, Leo Tolstoy, who had become a world leader of pacifist thought, and she won the admiration of the American philosopher, William James, for her book, *Newer Ideals of Peace* (1907). Here and in her autobiography, *Twenty Years at Hull House* (1910), she put forward her belief that the ability of the United States to blend immigrants from many different nations into harmonious unity would serve as a model for other countries to follow toward permanent world peace.

When war broke out in Europe, she was sure that it was because of a lack of true understanding between the leaders of the warring nations and a lack of communication between the leaders and the common people in each nation. She traveled to Europe in 1915 to enlighten the leaders who "were absorbed in preconceived judgments, and had become confused through the limitations imposed upon their sources of information." When her trip with other women leaders of the peace movement failed, she was ready to support the trip planned by Henry Ford in 1916 to once again appeal to the common sense of the European heads of state.

A significant peace movement had developed in the United States between 1900 and 1914, and, while it included many men, it was another area where middle-class women exerted their leadership. A Woman's Peace Party was formed in 1914 and Addams became its most important leader. She opposed the preparedness campaign of 1914 to 1916 and could not give her support to American military involvement in 1917. By 1916, she was being vilified by her former friend, Theodore Roosevelt, who was a leader in the call for military preparedness and involvement. Roosevelt tried to destroy her with articles calling her "poor bleeding Jane" and mocking her former support for him in 1912 with the epithet that she was now a "Bull Mouse." After 1917, the Justice Department put her under surveillance because of her pacifism. No longer the Saint Jane of 1912, she was denounced as a traitor to her nation. For male progressives, such as Dewey, Veblen, and Beard, who supported the war, hope for the progressive millennium was dashed in 1919. But, for Jane Addams, it was the years 1914-1917 which ended the Progressive Era and led her into the uncertain future of the 1920s.

Charlotte Perkins Gilman was also born in 1860. Her father was a member of the famous Beecher family of New England. Unlike Jane Addams' father, however, he deserted his wife and children. Raised among relatives, Charlotte never felt close to her mother. As a teen-ager, she felt fiercely independent and self-confident. "I did not do anything I thought wrong," she confided to her diary, "and did, at any cost, what I thought right."

Without the moral or financial support of a father, she could not afford a college education and never attained one. She married Charles Stetson soon after she turned twenty. After the birth of their daughter, however, she fell into a deep depression. Medical treatment failed and she decided that she could only regain her health by separating from her husband. She left him and went to California, where she supported herself and her child. Belatedly, she had decided that she could not surrender her independence to a traditional marriage.

Unlike Jane Addams and so many others who were of the first gen-eration of college-educated women and felt their only choice was inde-pendence or marriage, Gilman decided that there could be a new kind of marriage where married women were economically independent. When Jane Addams wrote that "without the advance and improvement of the whole," there was no hope for the improvement of "the moral or material individual condition" or of "social and individual salvation," she saw the problem of the whole as the reconciliation of different economic and ethnic groups. For Gilman, however, the crucial issue of the Progressive Era was the reconciliation of women and men in a harmonious whole.

In 1898, Gilman published *Woman and Economics,* a book whose message was that the division between the home as the world of women and the marketplace as the world of men must end. "Humanity means being together," she declared, "and our unutterably outgrown way of living keeps us apart." We must, she continued, "free our entire half of humanity from an artificial position."

Women and Economics made Gilman famous overnight. It was pub-lished in England and translated into seven languages. She was invited to lecture in England and on the continent. People clamored for her to amplify her message, and she poured out a series of books, *Concerning Children* (1900), *The Home* (1903), *Human Work* (1904), and *The Man-made World* (1911). In addition to writing this constant stream of books and lecturing throughout the United States and abroad, she published, edited, and wrote most of the material for a magazine, the *Forerunner.*

Gilman acknowledged that the inspiration for the vision expressed in *Women and Economics* and all her subsequent books came from the writings of Lester Frank Ward, who was a pioneer in the transition from amateur social philosophy to professional sociology. A government bureaucrat before his books won him a position as an academic sociologist, Ward developed an argument in the 1880s that the belief in a male-dominated evoluation – a view he called androcentric – was false. Instead he proposed a gynaecocentric theory of human evolution, one which declared, "The female sex is primary in point both of origin and of importance in the history and economy of organic life. And as life is the highest product of nature and human life the highest type of life, it follows that the grandest fact in nature is woman."

The drama in Jane Addams' view of the conflict between the forces of reaction and progress rested on the possible reversion of America to medieval darkness. This could happen not only because of the influx of immigrants who had peasant characteristics but also because the American middle class might take on the characteristics of a feudal aristocracy in relationship to that peasantry. The middle class might develop a life-style of frivolous and unproductive leisure supported by exploitation of the labor of the lower class. The progressive solution for Addams was to Americanize the immigrants, to bring them up to middle-class standards. The drama in Charlotte Perkins Gilman's version of this conflict between reactionary and progressive forces rested on her belief that middle-class women were forcibly kept within a reactionary life-style while middle-class men were encouraged to be progressive and forward looking.

For Gilman, such an intermingling of progressive and regressive cultural patterns was frustrating the evolutionary laws of nature which constantly pushed toward progress. Gilman associated industrialism with evolution and saw progress defined by an ever more rational society. "We have trained men in the large qualities of social usefulness," she declared. "Our men must live in the ethics of a civilized, free, industrial democratic age." But, every night when they returned home from this rational, democratic, industrial world, they entered their homes and immediately became feudal despots because "they were born and trained in the moral atmosphere of a primitive patriarchate."

Men had justified keeping women in the home because they said that women were biologically incapable of transcending the irrational qualities of the Dark Ages. Women, therefore, were to be judged by their irrational virtues of beauty and sexuality. Refusing to acknowledge the potential rationality of women, middle-class men regressed to medieval values themselves as they ruled their homes by the irrational means of brute force or encouraged their wives to engage in non-productive and irrational consumption. Why can't men see, Gilman pleaded, that, "as the priestess of the temple of consumption, as the limitless demander of things to use up, her economic influence is reactionary and injurious?"

Building irony upon irony, Gilman pointed out how apparently democratic and rational men, by becoming oriental despots at home with their "harems of one," doomed their sons to social stagnation because whatever progress they made in the work world was offset by a regressive experience at home. "Marry a civilized man to a primitive savage," she declared, "and their child will naturally have a dual nature."

Then Gilman offered the hope of a progressive millennium brought by the irresistible forces of impersonal economic evolution, a harmonious whole of happy, productive, and rational men, women, and children. "It is as natural for an industrial society to live in peace as for a hunting society to live in war," she proclaimed, "and this peace is not the result of heroic and self-sacrificing effort on the part of the industrial society. It is the necessity of their condition." At the moment, this peace was not the reality of everyday experience because of the cultural contradiction that women were not made virtuous by this industrial society but were made evil by the medieval home and were in a position to corrupt their husbands and children. "Not women, but the condition of women has always been a doorway of evil," she warned, "The sexuo-economic relation has barred her from the social activities in which, and in which alone, are developed the social virtues. She was not allowed to acquire the qualities needed in our racial advance."

The fulfillment of industrial harmony would come, Gilman declared, when all women worked outside the home. Living in large apartment buildings, families would have collective kitchens with professional cooks. Professionals would do the cleaning. And professionals would provide care for small children while mothers worked. "Where our progress hitherto has been warped and hindered by the retarding influence of surviving rudimentary forces," Gilman reassured her readers, "it will flow on smoothly and rapidly when both men and women stand equal in economic relations." With the entry of all women into the work force, the undemocratic experience of men as overlords and women as their vassals would finally end. "An economic democracy must rest on a free womanhood," Gilman concluded, "and a free womanhood inevitably leads to an economic democracy." It was a tribute to the progressive forces of evolution that they had brought humanity so close to the peaceable kingdom of industrial democracy while women and the men who dominated in the home still were chained to the Dark Ages. It was a tribute because men who had experienced most of the effects of modern progress were innately less progressive than women. "Social evil, warfare, and poverty are androcentric in nature," Gilman insisted, "while the distinctly feminine or maternal impulses are far more nearly in line with human progress than are those of the male."

For Gilman, however, there was no tension between these feminine characteristics and the rational productivity of industrialism. It was the man-made, androcentric world that defined sex as irrational, mysterious, and seductive. It was clear, however, Gilman declared, that "sex union is intended primarily for parentage and that we today are over-sexed and grossly over-indulgent." And she warned against contraception which for her "had come to be a free ticket for selfish and fruitless indulgence." True sex was rationally productive as industrialism was rationally productive.

The first progressive sociologists such as Lester Frank Ward had challenged the sociological conservatism of William Graham Sumner by introducing the concept of cultural lag. For Ward, the forces of evolution moved inevitably in a progressive direction. In the most fundamental sense, people had no free will but were carried along by the evolutionary process. On a secondary level, however, humans had the free will to create cultural patterns that brought them into adjustment to evolution at any given time. But, when evolution moved on, the existing culture became obsolete and had to be brought forward to reflect the next stage of evolution. Using this pattern, Gilman argued that industrial evolution had brought people into cities, where the work women had done on farms was now done by machines. Since there was almost no productive work to be done in the home, women increasingly were working outside the home. Gilman insisted that this evolutionary trend could not be stopped and that a new culture expressing this reality must be established. "This change is not a thing to prophesy and plead for," she affirmed, "it is a change already instituted. All we need do is to understand and help." It followed, for Gilman, that those who opposed these "slow friendly forces of social evolution" were unscientific and irrational. Only those aiding the liberation of women from the home to participate in industrial production could be called scientific and rational. Gilman did not think of herself as a prophet calling for religious conversion. Like Addams after 1900, she did not associate herself with any church. Her only authority, she claimed, was science. "The one real study which did appeal to me deeply was physics," she wrote. "Here was Law at last; not records of questionable truth or solemn tradition, but laws that could be counted on and Proved. That was my delight, to know surely."

By the end of World War I, however, Gilman's belief that a new world was emerging, one of "equality and mutual respect between parents; pure love, undefiled by self-interest on either side; a new grade of womanhood proved, strong, serene, independent; great mothers of great women and great men; a clean and healthful world with homes of quiet and content" seemed more a utopian vision than a scientifically demonstrable reality.

Mary Parker Follett was eight years younger than Jane Addams and Charlotte Perkins Gilman. Reaching intellectual maturity in the 1890's, she did not seem to share Addams' concern for finding a progressive role as a middle-class woman or Gilman's concern for finding a progressive role for all women. Rather Follett seemed confident of her ability to operate as an intellectual among intellectuals without concern for her identity as a woman. Her vision of progressive reform, therefore, was more ambitious than that of Addams and Gilman and so intensely optimistic that unlike the visions of most progressives, male or female, it survived into the 1920s. By 1920, Follett was one of the major political philosophers of progressivism and the one most friendly toward business corporations. It was her belief in corporations as a progressive force that helped her to be as confident about progress after 1920 as she had been before World War I.

Follett was born in Quincy, Massachusetts, was educated at Radcliffe College, and went to work in a neighborhood house in the Boston suburb of Roxbury. In 1891, however, she had traveled away from the Boston area. Like Addams, she made a pilgrimage to England to learn more about the efforts at urban reform being experimented with there. She also was interested in the theories of the English philosopher Thomas Hill Green, which were being used by English reformers to criticize the practices of competitive capitalism. Like so many male American progressives, Follett accepted Green's position that individuals are part of an encompassing whole.

But by 1900, as she began work to improve the quality of neighborhood life in Roxbury, Follett agreed with Jane Addams' statement that "the social organism has broken down in large districts of our great cities." Follett declared that "a free, full community life lived within the sustaining and nourishing power of the community bond is almost unknown now." Follett's life work was to help people create this community bond. Whereas Addams saw the problem of social reunification as primarily one of ending class conflict and Gilman saw the problem as primarily one of ending the division between men and women, Follett felt that all individuals, rich as well as poor, men as well as women, were separated from their true selves and needed to be brought into organic unity. Progress depended upon victory over the division within the individual.

Her vision began to take shape with the hope that a grass roots neighborhood association started in Roxbury would find thousands of parallels in neighborhoods across the country. Americans were being kept, she believed, from true "community bonds" by their erroneous philosophy of economic individualism and their equally false political philosophy that democracy meant counting individual votes and compromising conflicting interests. Follett was impatient with such progressive reforms as the direct election of senators, the primary, and the initiative, referendum, and recall. All were based, she believed, on a mechanical rather than an organic principle of political life and were expressed in political institutions which kept people divided from one another. Instead of a politics of competing individuals and groups, Follett offered a politics of organic wholeness. "We are lost, exiled, imprisoned," she insisted, "until we feel the joy of union."

Starting at the neighborhood level, she visualized the growth of a new nonpartisan politics of consensus rather than conflict and compromise. As people learned to feel themselves as part of the whole at the neighborhood level, they would then learn wholeness at the state and finally the national level.

Such an upward movement, for Follett, represented the forces of progressive evolution which are within each individual. "We are always reaching forth for union," she declared. "The spirit craves totality, this is the motion of social progress." Follett believed that the emergence of a "new psychology" could help people discover how to reach organic consensus. "This new psychology," she wrote, "gives understanding of collective activity, of the essential unity of man and the whole secret of progress." Solutions to the problems of moving from the false traditions of individualism and the reactionary institutions of political and economic life would come from the science of the new psychology which enabled reformers "to discover the law of the situation and to obey that."

In asking for "a scientific technique for evolving the will of the people" Follett by World War I saw more evidence that such scientific techniques were being used by large corporations than by any other part of the society. She was delighted that corporations were moving away from competition with one another. This new cooperation, she wrote, represented a "vastly different spirit from that which used to animate the business world." She was certain that, within the new cooperative spirit, corporations were developing the science of personnel management on the basis of what she had called the new psychology. This progressive personnel management was rejecting the "false psychology" that compromise must be reached between the interests of management and labor. Using the new psychology, personnel managers were recognizing that "real harmony can be obtained only by an integration of antagonistic interests," making "labor and capital into one group."

When Follett published her book, *The New State*, in 1918, she was a consultant to corporations and a lecturer to schools of business administration and departments of economics in the United States and England. She was critical of most of the major American political philosophers, such as Herbert Croly, for advocating too active a role for the national government. This, for Follett, was an effort to impose community from the top instead of allowing community to grow spontaneously. "The new state," Follett declared, "must be grown – its branches will widen as its roots spread." Follett was pleased with the nation's planned economy during World War I because, in her estimation, most of the planning was done by corporation leaders, not by government bureaucrats. The war, for her, accelerated the inexorable progressive trend toward a cooperative society built around the fusion of management and labor in the corporations, a fusion facilitated by the scientific techniques of personnel managers. Praising the experience of war, Follett wrote, "The world today is growing more spiritual, and I say this not in spite of the great war, but because of all this war has shown us of the inner forces bursting forth in fuller and fuller expression."

Placing her faith on the corporations rather than on politics as the way to reach the new state, Follett, like Herbert Hoover, remained optimistic about progress in the 1920s. She liked the way in which some corporate leaders were concerned with the whole life of their employees. They wanted their workers to find their recreational activities within the corporation. Some were concerned with the housing and life-styles of their workers. Follett had written that "all our private life is to be public life" and declared, "I am an individual not as far as I am apart from, but as far as I am a part of other men." She rejoiced, therefore, in the way in which corporations were encouraging their workers to see the corporation as encompassing all their life. "Their leisure-time problem is not how the workman can have more time for play," she argued, "it is how he can have more time for association, to take his share in the integrated thought and will and responsibility which is to make the new world."

Chapter VI

The South: Agrarian Defeat and the Negro as Scapegoat

The burst of optimism which separated the first decade of the twentieth century from the pessimism of the 1890s was largely due to the ability of so many Americans to rediscover a way to define their history as progressive. No longer was it a choice between Donnelley's black vision of an American golden age being ruthlessly corrupted and Sumner's promise of progress through corporate leadership, recruited by means of bitter competition in which the unfit would be weeded out of society. The vision of an industrial technological frontier leading mankind inexorably out of competitive complexity toward cooperative simplicity placed the ultimate triumph of democracy ahead, to a date like 1912, not behind in 1800. And it promised a universal democracy from which neither particular classes nor nations would be excluded. This was a theory of progress designed for the new urban-industrial society. Inevitably, therefore, much of rural America continued to cling to the view that the arcadian democracy of 1828 must be restored. This was especially true for the South. That region remained overwhelmingly rural in 1900, and the vast majority of its white people were Anglo-Saxon evangelical Protestants. From the end of the Civil War until 1890 the southern states were governed by upper middle-class men who were committed to creating a New South, one which shared the expanding urban-industrial revolution. Dependent upon northern capital for this hoped-for transformation, these leaders had accepted the Fourteenth and Fifteenth Amendments which had established Negro citizenship and voting rights.

Traditionally, the South and the nation had defined the Negro in terms of two stereotypes—as Sambo or as the devil. The Sambo stereotype described the Negro as innately childlike, dependent, and irresponsible, fun-loving and given to petty thievery. The devil stereotype described the Negro male as a ruthless murderer, arsonist, and rapist. In the generation before the Civil War, the southern imagination seems to have been dominated by the fear that the Negro was the devil, and consequently the region was swept constantly by rumors of slave rebellions. But no revolts came after that of Nat Turner in 1831, and during the Civil War, when so many white men were called away from home, there was little aggression by slaves against white families. This unexpected passivity by the black population, followed by the remarkable absence of black crimes of violence against whites during Reconstruction, seems to have convinced white southerners by the 1870s that the Sambo stereotype, rather than that of the devil, was the real Negro character. And this made possible southern white acceptance of the Fourteenth and Fifteenth Amendments because these southerners could visualize a docile Sambo following white leadership.

The 1880s in the South, therefore, were characterized by racial stability as the white political leaders concentrated on policies designed to encourage the transformation of the region from agriculture to industrialism. But the South, impoverished by the war and without an economic base on which to build, could not create enough industrial jobs to keep up with the expanding population. Consequently, the people, without an industrial frontier of economic opportunity, became increasingly impoverished. This poverty was deepened by the constant drop in the price of cotton on the world market.

This economic depression for the majority of the white population that lived on farms brought, by the end of the 1880s, a political rebellion of the farmers against the office-holding spokesmen for the New South. One of the most important leaders of this discontent was Tom Watson of Georgia.

Born in 1856, Watson had experienced the physical and economic destruction of his family, well-to-do planters, by the war. Fighting his way back to prosperity through the practice of law, Watson retained an identification with the poor, and when the farmers organized at the end of the 1880s to capture control of the Democratic Party from the New South chieftains, Watson became one of the spokesmen of the political revolt.

Elected to the United States House of Representatives in 1890, Watson was dismayed to find that the insurgent farmers had failed to displace the New South leadership of the Georgia Democratic Party in spite of their majority in the state legislature. He concluded that it was impossible to capture control of the Democratic Party and that the political future of Georgia's farmers and those of the other southern and western states had to be found in a new party, the People's Party, or Populists.

Starting a People's Party newspaper, Watson described the America of 1890 in terms comparable to Donnelly's. For Watson, the people were "the victims of cold-blooded, deliberate villainy, and their homes are being taken from them through the fraudulent collusion of federal lawmakers; that industrial and political servitude is coming to them as fast as time can bring it." In the South the people were being betrayed to the forces of darkness by their present leaders. "If the devil himself were to come to this town in a palace car and propose to haul the balance of the state to his infernal kingdom, and to allow Atlanta capitalists the profits on the transaction, they would cry, 'Hurrah for the devil. He's going to build up Atlanta!'"

And even as Georgia's state government was in the hands of a corrupt conspiracy, so was the national government. "We demand," Watson wrote, that the members of the United States Senate "be elected hereafter by a direct vote of the people. Why? . . . We know that the very concentration of power, the concentration of capital, the concentration of privilege which we are fighting is enthroned and intrenched in the Senate. . . . Every great corporation of this land has its agents, its attorneys there."

Again like Donnelly, Watson hoped for a hero, another Andrew Jackson, to appear, who would unite the yeomen of the South and West in victory over an eastern conspiracy. But when Watson wrote, "Today there stands waiting in the South and West as grand an army as ever brought pride to a warrior. It only needs leaders bold and true," he saw himself as that leader who would urge the people to "let the fires of this revolution burn brighter and brighter. Pile on the fuel till the forked flames shall leap in wrath around this foul structure of government wrong—shall sweep it from basement to turret, and shall sweep it from the face of the earth."

In this war between the productive people and the parasitical aristocracy, Watson saw it as one of his major duties to unite the people. This meant in Georgia and throughout the South that white farmers must cooperate with black farmers. For Watson, "The People's Party says to these two men, 'You are kept apart that you may be separately fleeced of your earnings. You are made to hate each other because upon that hatred is rested the keystone of the arch of financial despotism which enslaves you both. You are deceived and blinded that you may not see how the race antagonism perpetuates a monetary system which beggars both.'" Speaking strongly against lynch law, Watson included a Negro on the executive committee of the Georgia Populist Party. H. S. Doyle, a young Negro minister, who gave sixty-three speeches in one Populist campaign, was protected by white farmers, summoned by Watson, from threats of violence which came from the New South Democratic leadership.

In spite of fraud and intimidation by the entrenched party officials, who attacked the Populists as "nigger-lovers" even as they organized Negro voters to defeat Watson, the Populists won almost 50 per cent of the vote in Georgia in 1894, and the momentum of revolution seemed on their side as they prepared for 1896. But then the vision of victory turned into total defeat. The national Populist Party decided to back William Jennings Bryan when the forces of agricultural reform captured the presidential nomination from the Cleveland Democrats. For Watson fusion with the Democrats meant abject surrender to the New South leaders who dominated party machinery. It meant the collapse of the effort to unify the white and black producers so that they could defeat the corporation conspiracy in state and nation. It meant that the people had been defeated by the forces of darkness. It meant that Watson had failed to repeat the victories of Jefferson and Jackson who had been able to rally the farmers of the South and West to purge the conspiracy of an eastern aristocracy which planned to establish Old World complexity in the New World and destroy America's redemptive harmony with nature. The devil had captured the United States of America.

Denounced by his brother as a traitor to the Democratic Party, victim of violence in which his supporters were beaten and shot, victim of fraud in which establishment leaders had created false voting rolls and had brought South Carolina Negroes across the river to vote against him, Watson described his reaction to disaster in these words: "How near I came to loss of mind only God who made me knows—but I was as near distraction, perhaps, as any mortal could safely be. If ever a poor devil had been outlawed and vilified and persecuted and misrepresented and howled down and mobbed and threatened until he was well nigh mad, I was he."

From 1896 to 1904, Watson became a political recluse, practicing law and writing books. The books reveal, however, that he could not surrender his deep commitment to the idea of the hero as a salvation figure who in the name of the people would destroy the dragons of chaos and preserve the peaceable kingdom.

Watson poured out in rapid succession a whole series of histories which became national best sellers. The first was *The Story of France* which reached its dramatic climax in the French revolution. It was written, Watson declared, "to mark the encroachments of absolutism upon popular rights, to describe the long-continued struggle of the many to throw off the yoke of the few . . . and the systematic plunder, year by year, of the weaker classes by the stronger." His next volume was on Napoleon who, in Watson's estimation, fulfilled the goals of the Revolution because for those who believe that "monopoly of power, patronage, wealth is wrong, there the name of Napoleon will be spoken with reverence, despot though he became, for in his innermost fibre he was a man of the people, crushing to atoms feudalism, castes, divine rights, and hereditary imposture."

Watson next wrote histories of Jefferson and Jackson, the two American heroes who had struggled to preserve the liberty natural to America from being subverted by a new feudalism, that of industrialism. The factory, he wrote, was "some hideous monster, with a hundred dull red eyes, indicative of the flames within which were consuming the men, women, and children chained to the remorseless wheel of labor. . . . Everyone of those red-eyed monsters is a Moloch, into which soulless commercialism is casting human victims—the atrocious sacrifice to an insatiable god."

Watson could not believe, as Henry Ford did, that the factory was preserving the productive values of the homestead farm. For Watson there remained in 1904, as in 1890, an absolute conflict between the serenity of agriculture and the chaos of industry. And in his historical novel *Bethany: A Story of the Old South,* he expressed his anguished nostalgia for that Jeffersonian arcadia when the "old Southern homestead was a little kingdom, a complete social and industrial organism, almost wholly sufficient unto itself, asking less of the outer world than it gave. How sound, sane, healthy it appears."

When Watson looked at American history from the end of the Civil War down to the present, he saw nothing but forty years of victory for that dragon of chaos, the factory, and its evil organizers and managers, the leaders of that artificial and parasitical institution, the corporation. From the 1880s he had engaged in political organizations trying to turn back this alien invasion, until he had experienced devastating defeat in 1896. Certainly as Watson tried to understand the American situation during his years of political retirement from 1896 to 1904, there was no rational, no logical argument that he could develop by which he might escape the conclusion that the future would see the further erosion of rural America by the forces of industrialism and urbanism. If Watson then was to save the Southern homestead, if he was to be a victorious hero after the models of Jefferson and Jackson, he would have to place the homestead within the context of a fantasy history, where it would be threatened by a fantasy dragon of chaos, not the reality of industrialism, by a make-believe dragon whom Watson, as a make-believe hero, could slay. As so much of the nation, unable to find a formula for twentieth-century progress in the 1890s, had regressed to the ritual purge of an ancient scapegoat, medieval Spain in 1898, Watson regressed by 1904 to the demand that there be a ritual purge of a new scapegoat, the Negro.

When, in 1906, Watson declared that he would support for the governorship that Georgian who called for disfranchising the Negro, he had begun to contribute to the development of an anti-Negro crusade which promised that, if the Negro were removed from the life of the white people, peace and prosperity would return as a permanent normalcy. His call was answered by the election of Hoke Smith who promised to disfranchise the Negro and build a wall of separation between white and black. Smith's victory was followed by four fantastic days in Atlanta in which Negroes were systematically shot down in the streets, followed by the speech of a Georgia congressman on the floor of the United States House of Representatives suggesting the possible need for the genocide of all Negroes to solve the problems of the United States.

Watson and many southerners seemed to be reacting to problems of poverty and economic conflict related to industrialism at the beginning of the twentieth century as many Germans would react in the 1920s and 1930s. Some southerners were making the Negro a scapegoat as some Germans would make the Jew a scapegoat for social and economic problems which seemed incapable of political control. Watson became a major spokesman of those southerners who came to argue in the progressive era that there was a normalcy of peace and harmony in their region which was threatened by an alien enemy, the Negro, and that, if this chaos-causing group could not be removed or exterminated, at least it could be removed from politics and physically segregated from white society. The profane black must be kept from contaminating the sacred white. It was during these years of national progressivism, therefore, that the patterns of Jim Crow segregation were established in the South and the Negro was effectively removed from politics by the passage of laws that denied the vote to the poor and the illiterate. Technically these laws did not violate the Fifteenth Amendment because they applied to white as well as black voters. But the literacy tests were not upheld for illiterate whites and many literate Negroes were disfranchised. The Supreme Court did not choose to listen to the state conventions in the South which, when they passed these laws, proclaimed that their aim was "to disfranchise the nigger." Nor did the Court listen to southern senators and representatives coming to Washington to boast on the floor of the House and Senate that they had taken the vote from "the nigger." Furthermore, as the southern states participated in the drive of progressivism to break machine politics by creating the primary, the Court accepted the right of the state Democratic parties explicitly to bar the Negro from the primary because the Court ruled that the primary was an election within a private organization and, therefore, not covered by the Fourteenth or Fifteenth Amendments.

The Court further accepted the anti-Negro revolution in the South by arguing that it did not violate the provision of national citizenship in the Fourteenth Amendment by establishing separate

public facilities as long as they were equal. Again the Court chose
to ignore reality as funds for white and black education fell from
a ratio of about two dollars for a white child to one dollar for a
black child in 1890 to a ratio of about twelve dollars for a white
to one dollar for a black by 1917.

In the years between 1906 and 1920 Watson described himself
as "a State Socialist through and through." He wanted public
utilities owned by the government, but he wanted production kept
in the form of private property. Watson was also opposed to finance
capitalism which he saw as corrupt internationalism threatening the
culture of the agrarian South. Further he was opposed to international socialism because it threatened the private property of the
small producer and because, Watson wrote, it "would devour the
Home, and all that is purest and best in Christian civilization,—
reducing all women to the same level of sexual depravity.... [it
would not] make a white woman secure from the lusts of the Negro."
After all, Watson concluded, Marx was a Jew.

For Watson Anglo-Saxon racial democracy was the South, an
eternal and everlasting South, which would be invulnerable to the
forces of change and corruption if the forces of international finance
capitalism and international socialism were unable to find an ally,
the Negro, whom they could use to undermine the racial purity of
the region from within.

Twenty years after he had seen himself as a hero who would
unite the white and black producers of the South against an alien
aristocracy, Watson had a vision in which he saw himself as the
redeeming hero who would save the white South from the menace
of the Negro: "A new spirit has taken possession of me and I have
to obey it. [The people are] beginning to believe that I am one of
the men whom God Himself raises up and inspires.... My mission
is to tell you what you must do to be saved—to that high and holy
purpose will be devoted the remaining years of my life. I beg you
to listen."

To the threat of international capitalism and international socialism Watson now added the threat of international Roman Catholicism as a force that would use the Negro to subvert southern racial
democracy. "The Roman Catholic Hierarchy," Watson wrote, was
"the Deadliest Menace to our Liberties and our Civilization" because of "the sinister portent of Negro priests" and "How the Con-
fessional is used by Priests to Ruin Women."

The more Watson preached a religion of hatred, the more he used demagoguery to manufacture dragons of chaos who might profane the sacred purity of white Anglo-Saxon Protestant democracy, the more successful his publications, *Watson's Jeffersonian Magazine* and *Watson's Jeffersonian Weekly*, became. These journals could not be produced rapidly enough to meet demand when Watson called for the lynching of Leo Frank, the superintendent of a factory in Atlanta. When a young worker, Mary Phagen, was murdered, Frank was accused. For Watson Frank must be guilty because of his physical appearance: "Those bulging satyr eyes ... the protruding fearfully sensual lips; and also the animal jaw." He must be guilty because he was a Jew who had a "ravenous appetite for the forbidden fruit—a lustful eagerness enhanced by the racial novelty of the girl of the uncircumcized." And, wrote Watson, he would not be convicted in a court because of the "gigantic conspiracy of Big Money.... Frank belonged to the Jewish aristocracy, and it was determined by the rich Jews that no aristocrat of their race should die for the death of a working-class Gentile."

Watson's call for Frank's lynching was promptly fulfilled by a group of unmasked men who went unpunished. Watson now asked in 1915 for the recreation of the Ku Klux Klan to symbolize that racial democracy which found it necessary to seek ultimate defense outside the law through the spontaneous and violent expression of the will of the people. Founded in 1915, this new Klan spread throughout the entire nation in the 1920s and enrolled millions of Americans. The spread of the Klan was indicative of the many people outside the South, especially in the Midwest and West, who had not shared the progressive commitment to industrialism and instead turned to the use of the Negro, the Jew, and the Catholic as symbolic scapegoats for the impersonal social and economic forces of modernization. If the Negro could be disfranchised and segregated, if the immigration of the Catholic and Jew could be stopped, if prohibition of the sale of liquor could be imposed on the urban centers so that they could not corrupt rural youth, if academics could be kept from teaching the false doctrine of evolutionary change, then Anglo-Saxon democracy could be preserved in the state of a timeless New World Eden. Increasingly from 1900 to 1917 rural and small-town America mobilized to push through this counter-revolution against progressivism.

This demagoguery appealed to the latent fears of much of urban

America as well. It was easier to search for scapegoats that could be destroyed than to commit oneself to the endless task of reform of the urban environment. The wide sale of the novels of the southern writer Thomas Dixon throughout northern cities and the immense popularity among urban audiences of the movie "The Birth of a Nation," made in 1915 from his novel *The Clansman*, attests to a continuing loyalty to the idea of racial and rural demagoguery throughout the entire nation. And it attests to the particularly dramatic change of the white stereotype of the Negro as Sambo, dominant in the late nineteenth century, to that of the Negro as the devil.

Dixon, a North Carolinian who was a college friend of Woodrow Wilson and whose career changed from that of a Southern Baptist minister to that of national actor, novelist, playwright, and screen writer, attempted in his first novel, *The Leopard's Spots* (1902), explicitly to convert southerners and northerners from the view of the Negro as Sambo to that of the devil.

The philosophical framework which Dixon used for his novels was that established by the New England historians, Bancroft, Prescott, Motley, and Parkman, in the mid-nineteenth century and used to give redemptive meaning to the Spanish-American War. Dixon asked his readers to remember that these historians had shown that progress away from the corruption of medieval civilization had been limited to Anglo-Saxons, who alone had the racial strength to reject the materialistic temptations of the decadent institutions of Rome. Only the Anglo-Saxons had the racial strength to be Protestants and to commit themselves to the spiritual value of the free individual. The United States of America, Dixon reminded his readers, represented the culmination of this progress, when a democracy of free citizens had been achieved, a democracy whose citizens were necessarily white Anglo-Saxon Protestants.

Dixon agreed that the great internal contradiction to this democracy had been the institution of slavery and the slave-holding aristocracy of the South. And he announced that he and most southerners were delighted with the abolition of slavery and the destruction of the aristocracy. Describing Lincoln as the greatest American hero, Dixon also described him as a southerner and a democrat who had freed the people of the South from the curse of slavery and aristocracy to share fully in the classless American system of free and equal white citizens. Dixon quoted Lincoln's statement that "I am not nor ever have been in favor of bringing about in any way the social and political equality of the white and black races." For Lincoln slavery must end but, because the Negro's biological inferiority kept him from being an equal citizen, the Negro must be sent back to Africa.

Tragically, Dixon declared, Lincoln's assassination allowed a handful of unrepresentative Radical Republicans to seize control of the government, and to attempt to destroy Anglo-Saxon democracy in the South, and to threaten the identity of the entire Anglo-Saxon race by forcing social equality with the Negro that must culminate in racial intermarriage. As Dixon unfolded this grotesque history, he explained that northerners had initially supported the Radical Republicans because they accepted the radical argument that the Fourteenth and Fifteenth Amendments were necessary to create citizenship and voting rights for the Negro in order to destroy completely the power of the southern aristocracy which they blamed for Lincoln's assassination. Most northerners, however, accepted political citizenship for the Negro without assuming that the Negro would have social equality. For them, the Negro was Sambo, passive and docile, willing to be subservient and loyal to his white leaders. But this image of the Negro as Sambo was a ghastly mistake, Dixon wrote; the Negro had been trained, as any wild beast could be trained, to perform certain tasks on the plantation, but his true nature, the wild beast within, remained. Now with the destruction of the plantation, the Negro reverted to that bestial nature, the leopard's spots could not be changed, and with freedom the Negro lusted for supremacy over his former masters, lusted to take white women and force them to the Negro's animal level.

Dixon's method of converting his readers to see the Negro as a dangerous beast was to have them identify with the hero of his novel, Charles Gaston. Gaston's father, a colonel from the planter class, has died on the battlefield, a symbol of the death of the aristocracy. His delicate mother has collapsed with the loss of her husband and the confiscation of her property. And Charles is left to be raised by a spokesman of the people, the Baptist preacher, John Durham, who constantly reiterates to the boy that there is no place for the Negro as a citizen in a democracy because the concept of citizenship implies equality, and the acceptance of Negro equality means racial suicide for the Aryan race.

Charles, however, knows the Negro only as Sambo in the form

of his father's body servant, Nelse, who has loyally returned to serve and defend his master's son after the death of the father. Charles has a paternalistic fondness for the Negro and cannot understand the attitude of the yeoman farmer, Tom Camp, who tells him that "I always hated a nigger since I was knee-high. My daddy and my mammy hated 'em before me." Instinctively, Dixon wrote, the common man understands the inner bestial nature of the Negroes and hates and fears their presence. The efforts of Preacher Durham and Tom Camp to make Charles see the Negro as he really is fail until the young Negro orphan, Dick, whom Charles has chosen to be his own body servant, runs away and rapes and kills Tom Camp's daughter, Flora.

Almost a generation earlier, however, during the years of Radical Reconstruction, Tom Camp has seen another daughter sacrificed to the black dragon of chaos. In 1867 North Carolina has been taken over by the scalawag, Amos Hogg, a leading secessionist of the planter aristocracy. Unsympathetic to the white people when he was a parasitical slaveholder, he now continues his undemocratic ways. One of his lieutenants is the carpetbagger, Simon Legree, who has also been alienated from the productive common man before the war in his role as a northern-born slave driver serving the slavocracy. His other lieutenant is the Negro, Tim Shelby, educated in Canada to dream of equality and intermarriage. Together these three devils disarm and disfranchise the whites and arm and enfranchise the blacks whom they then turn loose to engage in widespread murder, arson, and rape.

A band of Negro soldiers kidnap Tom Camp's daughter during her wedding ceremony but fortunately she escapes rape when she is killed as the wedding party fires on the fleeing black soldiers. The death of a white maiden at the hands of the black dragon forces white men out of their defeatist attitude and spontaneously they band together as the Ku Klux Klan to save white civilization. Tim Shelby is lynched and "His thick lips had been split with a sharp knife, and from his teeth hung this placard 'The answer of the Anglo-Saxon race to Negro lips that dare pollute with words the womanhood of the South. K.K.K.' "

The white people have been able to save Anglo-Saxon democracy by driving out Scalawag and Carpetbag and Negro leaders but Aryan civilization is not yet secure. The Negro still remains within the United States, and as long as he remains, he poses a threat to the racial purity which has made Americans a chosen people. Moreover, although the threat of Negro leadership has been temporarily destroyed by the Ku Klux Klan, the Negro has kept the rights of citizenship granted by the Fourteenth and Fifteenth Amendments. It is possible, therefore, if white men become involved in political conflict with one another, that the Negro can assume the balance of power, seize political leadership, and once more threaten the sanctity of white women.

And, Dixon continued, this awful possibility has become horrible reality in the 1890s in North Carolina. What has happened in this unhappy state is indicative, however, of a national sickness. More and more Americans, especially northerners, have lost their commitment to the spiritual values of Anglo-Saxon civilization; more and more, they have succumbed to the seduction of materialism. It is this growing moral blindness which has made it possible for so many northerners to ignore the attempt of the Radical Republicans to destroy the racial and spiritual purity of their race. It is this moral blindness which has made it possible for northerners and southerners to continue to tolerate the monstrous Fourteenth and Fifteenth Amendments after the Radical Republicans have been driven from power. In North Carolina this national sickness is represented by General Worth and the Farmer's Alliance.

Basically General Worth is a good man, for "an expert in anthropology would have selected his face from among a thousand as the typical man of the Caucasian race." A Whig unionist, the General believes that all the problems of his state and region will be solved by importing factories. On the other hand, the farmers have come to believe that their salvation will also come through economic policies of government aid to agriculture and government control of the currency. This national emphasis on materialism is allowing physical degenerates of the Anglo-Saxon race, like Simon Legree with his "bloated face, beastly jaw and coarse lips, lecherous eyes twinkling like snakes and saliva trickling from the corners of his mouth... [to have] power...greater than a monarch. He controls fleets of ships, mines and mills.... He buys judges, juries, legislatures, and governers." What Legree, now operating from Wall Street, represents at a national level, Allan McLeod represents in North Carolina. Inheriting the physical degeneracy of his mother, who was a drunkard, McLeod's moral degeneracy has led him from upright membership in the Klan to the leadership of the Negro attempt to seize control of North Carolina in the 1890s. Legree and McLeod, because of their physical degeneracy, are essentially beasts like the Negro and want nothing more than to destroy the integrity of the Anglo-Saxon race by destroying the integrity of its maidens.

In 1890 Charles Gaston, well-trained by Preacher Durham to the importance of racial spirituality, is tempted by both General Worth and McLeod. Gaston has fallen in love with Sallie Worth. The General, however, refuses to give his daughter to Gaston until the young man gives up politics for a business career. And McLeod offers Charles immediate wealth and power if he will become the head of the Republican Party. In rejecting these temptations, Charles informs the General that "politics is a religion. . . . I believe that the government is the organized virtue of the community, that politics is religion in action. . . . I believe that the state is now the only organ through which the whole people can search for righteousness." And to McLeod he replies, "Man shall not live by bread alone."

Now convinced by Dick's rape of Flora that the Negro is indeed the devil and not Sambo, Charles begins to build a spiritual crusade in politics to purify the white community by removing the Negro. In this crusade the rival economic concerns of General Worth and the farmers are irrelevant and, to the extent that men from both sides are converted to the truth that they are white brothers, the antagonisms that divide them will disappear.

Blocked from leadership in the convention of the state Democratic Party by General Worth's boss control which has led to the writing of a materialistic platform, Gaston dramatically speaks from the floor to offer a substitute platform:

Whereas, it is impossible to build a state inside a state of two antagonistic races; and whereas, the future North Carolina must therefore be an Anglo-Saxon or a mulatto,

Resolved, that the hour has now come in our history to eliminate the Negro from our life. . . . The Old South fought against the stars in their courses—the resistless tide of the rising consciousness of nationalism and world mission.

The Young South greets the new era and glories in its manhood. He joins his voice in the cheers of triumph which are ushering in the all-conquering Saxon. Our old men dreamed of local supremacy. We dream of the conquest of the globe. . . . We believe that God has raised up our race, as he ordained Israel of old, in this world crisis. . . . I believe in God's call to our race to do His work in history. What other races failed to do, you wrought in this continental wilderness . . . until out of it all has grown the mightiest nation of the earth.

Is the Negro worthy to rule over you?

I am in a sense narrow and provincial. I love mine own people. . . . I hate the dishwater of modern world citizenship. A shallow cosmopolitanism is the mask of death for the individual. Race and race pride are the ordinances of life.

In Dixon's novel the delegates are filled with the excitement of a religious revival as they are converted to this crusade. General Worth is also converted and not only blesses the marriage of his daughter but has one of his political leaders leap to the platform and cry out, "And now that our eyes have seen the glory of the Lord, as we heard the messenger annointed to lead His People, I move that the convention nominate by acclamation for Governor—Charles Gaston."

Gaston now leads the delegates, "the Anglo-Saxon race . . . fused into a solid mass," armed with "omnipotent racial power," "to nullify the Fourteenth and Fifteenth Amendments to the Constitution of the Republic" by destroying Negro citizenship, to segregate the black from the white, and to prepare to send the Negro back to Africa.

In this novel Dixon was offering the entire nation salvation through the political religion of an anti-Negro crusade. The ills of the South were the ills of the nation. But, from Dixon's perspective, the salvation figure, the hero, who would restore the racial vitality and harmony of the Aryan nation must come from the South. The horror of Reconstruction had taught perceptive men in the South, like Preacher Durham, that the only real danger to the nation came from the alien African. And the iron that had entered into the souls of the John Durhams during these years of suffering saved them from being seduced by the false religion of materialistic progress. Because of its legacy of suffering and poverty, the South retained the purity to produce a leader, like Charles Gaston, who could save the North from its materialistic madness. In their greed that had made them forget their racial heritage, northerners had been importing millions of Latins and Slavs to work in their mines and factories. They overlooked the fact that these non-Anglo-Saxons, like the Negro, must ultimately attempt that intermarriage which would

compromise Anglo-Saxon blood. As Preacher Durham had told
Boston's aristocracy when he refused its offer of a highly paid pulpit,
"the ark of the covenant of American ideas rests today on the
Appalachian mountain range of the South. When your metropolitan
mobs shall knock at the doors of your life . . . from these poverty-
stricken homes . . . will come the fierce athletic sons and sweet-voiced
daughters in whom the nation will find a new birth."

Like Ignatius Donnelly and the young Tom Watson, Thomas
Dixon was arguing that America stood at Armageddon in the 1890s.
But while Donnelly and Watson saw the crisis as the corruption of
the simplicity of the Jeffersonian arcadia and its yeomen inhabitants
by complex and alien economic and social institutions, Dixon defined
the crisis as the threatened corruption of Anglo-Saxon racial purity
by alien races. For Donnelly and Watson the election of 1896 would
see a repetition of the political-religious rituals of 1800 and 1828 when
Jefferson and Jackson had preserved the American arcadia from the
threat of Hamiltonian economic complexity. For Dixon these economic concerns were irrelevant because the 1890s must see the repetition of the 1870s when a political-religious ritual headed by the
Ku Klux Klan had saved the nation from racial intermarriage with
the Negro. And when many southern farmers, like Tom Watson,
were faced with the possibility that the forces of economic darkness
had won in 1896, that the purity of the nation was lost forever, men
like Dixon were there to reassure them that this was not true, that
the truly sacred aspect of America, its Aryan blood, was still intact
and that, just as the Anglo-Saxon nation could find an external devil,
Spain, which it was guaranteed to defeat, so white America could
find in the Negro a devil whose defeat was guaranteed.

Defeat of the Negro was guaranteed in 1900, Dixon wrote,
because if the Negro had been defeated in 1870 when all the odds
were in his favor, how could the Negro win at the beginning of the
twentieth century when he no longer had the political and military
support he had enjoyed from the Radical Republicans during Reconstruction. In his second novel, *The Clansman,* Dixon was to give
dramatic emphasis to his assertion that Reconstruction was the most
important moment in American history when the national identity
as a democracy of free and equal white Anglo-Saxon Protestant
citizens had received its greatest threat of destruction through the
profaning of the Aryan people by the Negro. He reassured Americans in the first decade of the twentieth century that their identity

crisis was insignificant compared to that of 1870. He reassured them that Armageddon had come a generation earlier and that the forces of light had decisively defeated the forces of darkness. They now had only to preserve the fruits of that epic victory.

The Clansman revolves around Austin Stoneman who is the fictionalized figure of Thaddeus Stevens. Stoneman is presented as a Dr. Frankenstein, who is alienated from normal people and who in his pride and madness attempts to play the role of God in creating man, in this case making the Negro a citizen. To explain the motivation of this traitor to the Anglo-Saxon race, Dixon first presents him as a physical degenerate whose "left leg ended in a mere bunch of flesh, resembling more closely an elephant's hoof than the foot of a man." Second Stoneman has been caught up by the growing national greed for material possessions. Lusting for wealth, he had built an empire in iron mills which Lee destroyed in his invasion of Pennsylvania. And now he wants revenge on the South. But, finally and most importantly, Stoneman has been seduced by his Negro housekeeper, Lydia Brown, "a strange brown woman of sinister animal beauty and the restless eyes of a leopardess." It is she who persuades him that the Negro can be the equal of the Anglo-Saxon.

A brilliant man, Stoneman takes advantage of the political confusion caused by Lincoln's assassination and the mood of moral indifference caused by national greed to begin his experiment of creating a human being out of the Negro. Suddenly, "Washington, choked with scrofulous wealth, bowed the knee to the Almighty Dollar . . . and a new mob of onion-laden-breath, mixed with perspiring African odour, became the symbol of American democracy." With a heavy hand, Dixon painted the awful scene in which this mad scientist, in control of the national government, begins his experiment in playing God:

The Negroes placed him in an armchair facing the semicircle of Senators, and crouched down on their haunches beside him. Their kinky heads, black skin, thick lips, white teeth, and flat noses made for the moment a curious symbolic frame for the chalk-white passion of the old commoner's face.

No sculptor ever dreamed a more sinister emblem of the corruption of a race of empire-builders than this group. Its black figures, wrapped in the night of four thousand years of barbarism, squatted there the "equal" of their master, grinning at his forms of justice, the evolution of forty centuries of Aryan genius, or genus? To their brute strength the white fanatic in the madness of his hate had appealed, and for their hire he had bartered the birthright of a mighty race of freemen.

Stoneman has set in motion a conspiracy, operating secretly through the Union League, to organize the Negro politically and militarily in the South, to disfranchise and disarm the white southerners, and to confiscate their property and transfer it to the Negro. He would make a laboratory of the South to test his experiment in making the Negro capable of responsible citizenship. Ironically, a physical breakdown forces Stoneman to recuperate in South Carolina where the children of his deceased wife, Elsie and Phil, have made close friends with the Cameron family. Phil, hoping to marry Margaret Cameron, and Elsie, hoping to marry Ben Cameron, are unaware that the conspiracy of the Union League is headed by their father. Both have identified with the struggle of the white South to preserve its racial integrity. Dixon has Phil say, "I love these green hills and mountains, these rivers musical with cascade and fall, these solemn forests—but for the Black Curse, the South would be today the Garden of the world!"

An invalid, Stoneman has lost control of his conspiratorial experiment. Lydia Brown, unfaithful to him, has a Negro lover, Lynch, with whom she has seized power. Having established political and military power over the white southerners, they now turn loose all the Negroes to burn, to loot, to murder, and to rape. Here is the beast that Stoneman had hoped to humanize:

He had the short heavy-set neck of the lower order of animals. His skin was coal black, his lips so thick they curled both ways up and down with crooked blood marks across them. His nose was flat, and its enormous nostrils seemed in perpetual dilation. The sinister bead eyes ... were set wide apart and gleamed apelike under his scant brows. His enormous cheekbones and jaws seemed to protrude beyond the ears and almost hide them.

The horror of Negro freedom reaches its climax when a friend of the Camerons, Margaret Lenoir, is raped. Profaned, she dresses in white and with her mother, "hand in hand, they stepped from the cliff into the mists and on through the opal gales of death."

As in *The Leopard's Spots*, the destruction of a white virgin by the dragon forces the white men to organize to protect the innocence of their women. Spontaneously they form the Ku Klux Klan. "It was the resistless movement of a race. . . . Society was fused in the white heat of one sublime thought and beat with the pulse of the single will of the Grand Wizard of the Klan." Poetically, Phil Stoneman is rescued by the Klan from the Union League conspiracy and old Stoneman is redeemed as he confesses his sin in attempting to overcome the laws of nature.

Because the most important historians of the progressive era, like Charles Beard, accepted this myth of Reconstruction during the years 1890–1917, it became the standard interpretation in American history textbooks until after World War II. Not until the present has it been recognized that, if both the white New South leaders and the white agrarian dissidents worked politically with the Negro in the 1880s and 1890s, they did not consider the Negro as a devil figure in the 1870s. It has become clear that the dominant attitude toward the Negro was that of Sambo and that the fundamental racial calm during Reconstruction did not give rise at that time to a political-religious crusade against the Negro. This crusade came in the period .1890–1917 and was the result of severe conflict within the white community and the inability of most white southerners to share in the new, positive attitude toward industrialism. It was not until after 1890 that many southern whites were converted to the belief that the Negro was a kind of devil corrupting the American garden; it was not until this later period that a ritual lynching of Negroes became prevalent and men, women, and children gathered to witness the burning of a Negro and to celebrate the purging of this symbol of blackness from their white Eden.

When one asks why the majority of progressive historians, like Beard, were willing to accept this "big lie"—that Reconstruction had been a monstrous period of chaos and terror for the South which had resulted in the great hatred of the whites for the blacks—the basic conspiratorial view of history held by the progressives is dramatized. For Beard the end of the Civil War began the worst period in American history. It was then that the robber barons had imposed the most malignant artificial social and economic patterns; it was then that the parasitical aristocracy had most viciously corrupted politics. For Beard the progressive movement was a political-religious purge that destroyed all the artful and unnatural patterns imposed by the robber barons, who were, in his eyes, the descendants of the Radical Republicans.

Here, however, the similarity ends. Beard and the northern

progressives assumed that industrialism was predestined to disintegrate the artificial establishment. For them the great victory was in the future. For Dixon and the later Tom Watson the great victory was in the past, and it must be defended against the forces of history, industrialism, corporation capitalism, and socialism by the triumph of the will of those who remained loyal to the integrity of the Aryan race.

The emphasis on the triumph of the will was not unique to the South in the progressive period. The Spanish-American war was to a large extent defined as the triumph of the national will. The myth of the cowboy which so attracted Theodore Roosevelt as well as millions of other Americans placed great emphasis on the triumph of the will. But southern political thought put particular stress on it. Beginning with the victory of Ben Tillman in South Carolina in 1890, most southern states saw the emergence of demagogic leaders who identified themselves as representatives of the white masses. These men preached the validity of one-party politics, arguing that, if there was one people, there could be only one party and one leader to express the voice of the people. Along with one party democracy, they also preached the need for the people to remain vital through the exercise of violence. Focusing on the use of this violence against the Negro who had no place in the one-party democracy of the Anglo-Saxon race, these demagogues symbolize the degree to which Americans, suffering from poverty and unable to link themselves to a progressive future, engaged in a form of reactionary totalitarian politics at the beginning of the twentieth century.

It was during the years of progressivism, therefore, that the foundation for the recent sectional conflict between North and South was established. Most of the South remained loyal to the old, nineteenth-century identity, while much of the North was moving toward a new identity which enlarged the boundaries of the community to include the machine and the new Jewish and Catholic immigrants. But the South, in order to feel successful in preserving the older identity, had to sacrifice the Negro as a scapegoat and symbolically destroy the Negro status of second-class citizenship. It narrowed its definition of community even as the North was enlarging its definition.

Chapter VII

The Negro and Progressivism: South and North

The leaders of the Negro community during the years between 1890 and 1917 were caught up in the major trends of the white society and either participated in them or reacted against them. The overwhelming proportion of the Negro population continued to live in the South and could not escape the anti-Negro crusade which swept that region. Nor could southern Negro leadership look to the North for help in preserving voting rights and the civil rights of equal treatment in the courts, schools, and public facilities. Too much of the Anglo-Saxon racism, which had experienced an upsurge in the war against Spain, remained throughout the period to permit any popular sympathy for the Negro.

And while the counter-current of environmentalism among the social scientists and social philosophers helped to cause large numbers of businessmen and politicians in the North to modify their racial prejudice toward the new Catholic and Jewish immigrants from southern and eastern Europe, this spirit of greater tolerance was not applied to the Negro. Indeed, at the popular level in the North as in the South, hostility toward the Negro seemed to increase between 1900 and 1917. This meant that only a small group of academic and professional men and women in the North experienced a major change in attitude toward the Negro. But this change was revolutionary because these were the first white Americans who were able to understand some of the social, psychological, and economic factors in the historical environment in the United States which had impoverished the Negro community, damaged the Negro personality, and effectively kept the Negro from being able to compete on an equal plane with the white man.

While the division between the white South and North over the issue of second-class citizenship was established before 1917, it was not to become apparent until it began to affect national politics in the 1920s and 1930s. But the stark contrast between the view of many southern white writers and political leaders that the Negro was the devil and should be stripped of second-class citizenship and the view of a group of northern white intellectuals that the Negro was an equal human being and should transcend the humiliation of second-class citizenship to exercise his rights as a first-class citizen had the immediate effect of creating two antagonistic groups of Negro leaders, one based in the South and the other in the North. These groups are symbolized by Booker T. Washington and W.E.B. DuBois.

Washington had been born into slavery in Virginia at the end of the 1850s. A series of chance circumstances began his education into literacy. Then he walked hundreds of miles to enroll in Hampton Institute in Virginia. This school had been established by white New England religious philanthropists to provide a training center for Negro teachers who were to help the members of their race to achieve economic and social self-sufficiency and to escape the dependency of their slave heritage.

When white men in Alabama decided to provide a small state grant to begin a similar school in the black-belt plantation area of their state, they requested Hampton to send them a teacher and organizer. Given a vote of confidence by his white teachers as a young man of strong character, great ambition, and leadership ability, Washington arrived in Alabama to find that state funds were totally inadequate and that the school would have to be built by Negro self-help in money and labor and gifts from white northern philanthropists.

In little more than a decade, from the 1880s to the end of the 1890s, Washington directed the construction of a major campus with a large corps of teachers and students. His educational policy was designed to break down the slave heritage of the Sambo personality with its dependency upon white leadership and to teach the Negro to be personally self-reliant and self-disciplined and to learn the skills in agriculture and the trades which would allow him to become economically independent.

These values fitted those of the nineteenth-century white community which had idealized the independence of the yeoman farmer and the small-town mechanic, and, as critics of Washington have pointed out, they ignored the transformation of the nation from a rural small-town past to industrialism and urbanism. But on the other hand the South in the 1890s was 90 per cent rural and was not participating to any significant extent in the industrialization and urbanization of the nation.

Washington's educational philosophy, which represented the viewpoint of the majority of southern Negro leaders in the 1880s and 1890s, was not the cause of his emergence as the best-known and most powerful Negro leader in the South and the nation by 1900. Rather his leadership depended upon his political and psychological skills in meeting the crisis of the anti-Negro crusade. Washington leaped into national prominence with a speech given at the Atlanta Exposition of 1895. Here the white leaders of the New South were celebrating the modest economic growth that had taken place and, more importantly, were projecting a future of major industrial transformation. Washington addressed himself to the place of the Negro in the hoped-for New South of constantly expanding economic growth. First Washington declared that it had been a mistake for the Negro to have been given so much political power during Reconstruction because, he argued, political power must rest upon social and economic achievement. It followed then that the Negro would not now ask for political equality but would work to establish himself as a productive economic force in the South and would achieve good habits of social discipline and character before becoming concerned with political rights.

The strategy of Washington's speech can be understood only within the context of the growing anti-Negro crusade of the 1890s. Washington was aware that the precedent of the constitutional conventions called in Mississippi and South Carolina to disfranchise the Negro was being discussed favorably in all the southern states. He was aware that the rate of lynchings was increasing and that they were taking on the more rigidly ceremonial form of burning

Negroes in front of large public gatherings of men, women, and children. He was aware that there was momentum in the direction of completely ending the Negro's status as even a second-class citizen.

His task then in a South dominated by a white population that was increasingly using the Negro as a scapegoat for its frustrations was to save as much of the status of citizenship for the Negro as possible and to try to preserve an environment in which it would be possible for the Negro to continue to make progress away from the culture of slavery and toward some independence in social and economic decision making.

One of the major emotional techniques Washington used in this speech, and one which would continue to characterize his leadership, was to put on the mask of Sambo dependence. The southern white demagogue claimed that the Negro was not naturally Sambo but was rather a devil. Only the threat of coercion, men like Thomas Dixon argued, kept the aggressive Negro in his place. But Washington assured his audience in Atlanta in 1895, and every white audience he spoke to or wrote for until his death in 1915, that the Negroes were "the most patient, faithful, law-abiding, and unresentful people that the world had seen." Unaggressive, the Negro had not wanted political leadership in 1870. And now, in the 1890s, the Negro wanted only to be able to make a contribution to the economic well-being of a South which was two-thirds white.

To keep from handicapping the economic progress of the region and the nation, to keep from handicapping the economic progress of white America, the Negro needed education to become a more efficient and productive worker. This was the crucial point for Washington. All would not be lost if the Negro temporarily was pushed out of politics. All would not be lost if the Negro temporarily was pushed into segregated public facilities. All would be lost, however, if the Negro was barred from education and the right to hold property. And this, of course, was the recommendation of Preacher Durham to Governor Charles Gaston in Dixon's novel, *The Leopard's Spots.* The logic of the anti-Negro crusade when pushed to its extreme demanded that the Negro lose every right of citizenship, including education and the holding of property.

Washington fought this logic by emphasizing the natural docility of the Negro, his innate Sambo quality, and by insisting that the Negro would gratefully accept a restricted and qualified second-class citizenship. Then he stressed the economic benefits of this second-class citizenship for the white South, which needed a trained, docile labor force if economic growth was to take place. Desperately Washington appealed to the white southern capitalists that "in all things that are purely social we can be as separate as the five fingers, yet one as the hand in all things essential to mutual progress."

In 1889 Washington and many other southern Negro leaders applauded the speech of the great Negro leader, Frederick Douglass, which had attacked the growing sentiment among whites to disfranchise the Negro and establish Jim Crow segregation. Until 1890 these leaders could hope that an appeal to white conscience in the name of the human dignity of the Negro might be effective. "The real question," Douglass had declared, "is whether American justice, American liberty, American civilization, American law, and American Christianity can be made to include . . . all American citizens." By 1900, however, there was no major Negro leader in the South who would openly criticize disfranchisement and Jim Crow. All had joined Washington in recognizing that the white South had become a semitotalitarian society dedicated to an anti-Negro crusade. All joined Washington in the idea that only underground resistance was possible in this atmosphere of armed hostility toward the Negro.

Their hope was that "the combined forces of opposition cannot prevent us from advancing so long as we have the road to books and schools open to us. Even the snub that has been given to our political condition is as nothing compared with what it would be to shut against us the doors of schools." From underground Washington and the others fought against the spread of disfranchisement to other southern states like Alabama, Louisiana, Georgia, and Maryland. Through the use of lawyers who received payment from anonymous sources, they fought against the further spread of Jim Crow laws in public transportation. Always, however, after 1895 they worked from underground, presenting to the white man the mask of a servile nonaggressive Sambo who was loyal and grateful to white leadership for whatever favors were received.

To the disgust of the radical leaders of the anti-Negro crusade like Dixon, the latter-day Tom Watson, Governor Vardaman of Mississippi, and many others, the anti-Negro crusade did crest without the total destruction of Negro citizenship. This remaining area of citizenship provided the foundation in the 1950s for the Negro revolution that sought to restore political rights and destroy Jim Crow.

Washington had told his people in the underground that "I believe the past and present teach but one lesson ... that there is but one way out ... and that is for the Negro in every part of America to resolve from henceforth that he will throw aside every non-essential and cling only to the essential—that his pillar of fire by night and pillar of cloud by day shall be property, economy, education, and Christian character. To us just now these are the wheat, all else the chaff. The individual or race that owns the property, pays the taxes, possesses the intelligence and substantial character, is the one which is going to exercise the greatest control in government, whether he lives in the North or whether he lives in the South." By putting on the Sambo mask, southern Negro leaders kept education from being destroyed and therefore kept open the possibility of overcoming the heritage of slave culture. While it probably would not have been acceptable to the Supreme Court to have the public education system totally destroyed in the southern states, we know from the great gap which the Court permitted to develop between expenditures for white and black children during the progressive period that the situation could have become worse.

The major cause for the diverging costs for white and black public education during these years was basically the increased expenditures for the newly established public high schools for white children and higher education for whites. High schools and colleges for Negroes at the beginning of the twentieth century in the South, the schools absolutely essential for the development of black leadership, were privately financed. As private institutions, they were vulnerable, therefore, to legal destruction by the southern states. By fawning before the white man, educated Negro leaders somehow persuaded the majority of the southern white leaders that they were Sambos incapable of constructive leadership leading to significant change. Somehow the white leaders were persuaded that the autonomous Negro colleges like Tuskegee, with its campus of thousands of acres, substantial buildings, a faculty of over one hundred, a student body of more than a thousand, were not threats to the status quo.

Similarly Negroes retained that basic right of citizenship, gained under the Fourteenth Amendment, of geographic mobility. Slowly but steadily the Negro population was moving within the South toward the Southwest and into the towns and cities, and another slow migration to the North, which was to accelerate dramatically during World War I, had begun. This movement, of course, broke down traditional patterns of white domination over the Negro. In the southern cities this loss of direct white control on the plantation seemed to find a substitute in the Jim Crow laws. The official designation of the Negro part of public facilities so that they symbolized white superiority and black inferiority apparently gave the whites the psychological security of believing that the Negro was not free to roam at will as a devil but was socially confined as a passive Sambo. Therefore, the whites made no systematic effort to suppress the development of Negro leadership in the ghetto. Unlike the present situation in South Africa, there was the legal possibility for the emergence of black teachers and ministers, lawyers and doctors, businessmen and bankers.

Unable to define the Negro in any other terms than the stereotype of Sambo or the devil, most white southerners seemed to have felt by 1914 that they had defeated the devil in a repetition of the victory of Reconstruction and, like their grandfathers, had pushed the black man into the quiescence of a changeless Sambo. Destroying the Negroes' right to vote and publicly humiliating the blacks through Jim Crow segregation, the white South was able to delude itself that in their segregated schools, churches, businesses, and professions Negroes were not transcending slave culture to acquire the social and psychological skills of leadership. But by the 1950s the young black men and women trained in this underground world would begin to march out into the streets of Montgomery and every other southern city to demand first-class citizenship.

Washington also used whatever influence he had as a recognized leader of the national Negro community to try to get the Republican Presidents, Roosevelt and Taft, to block the development in the southern states of lily-white Republican parties which drove the Negro out of traditional positions of party leadership. Reflecting the center of public sentiment in the North, however, Roosevelt and Taft refused to act to try to check the political segregation of the Negro in the South. Periodically Washington tested northern opinion by appealing directly to northern audiences for support against southern white brutality. On one instance he declared:

Within the last fortnight three members of my race have been burned at the stake; one of them was a woman. No one ... was charged with any crime even remotely connected with the abuse of a white woman. ... Two of them occurred on Sunday afternoon in sight of a Christian Church. ... The custom of burning human beings has become so common as scarcely to excite interest. ... There is no shadow of excuse for departure from legal methods in the case of individuals accused of murder. ... Until we conquer [racial prejudice] I make no empty statement when I say that we shall have a cancer gnawing at the heart of this republic that shall prove to be as dangerous as an attack from an army within or without.

Each of these public criticisms was met by great hostility in the northern press, which warned Washington that he would hurt the cause of the Negro by open statements. Unable to find support from the Supreme Court, Congress, the Presidency, or northern public opinion, Washington had no choice but to return to the use of his Sambo mask to preserve an area of underground freedom for the Negro.

By 1903, however, a number of northern Negro leaders mounted an attack on Washington's leadership and by 1910 had joined their criticism with that of a group of northern white progressives to form the National Association for the Advancement of Colored People. The only high Negro official of the NAACP in 1910 was W. E. B. DuBois, the most important of Washington's critics.

DuBois was born in Great Barrington in western Massachusetts in 1868. His family had been in the area since the Revolution and was accepted with friendliness, but not full equality, by the white community. He played with the children of the old Anglo-Saxon families and shared their prejudices against the new Catholic industrial workers as a "ragged, ignorant, drunken proletariat, great for the dirty woolen mills and the poor house." DuBois was the scholarly star of the high school and the white families provided the money for him to go to Fisk College in Tennessee. No social problems had arisen in the strict sexual segregation of the adolescents in this Victorian culture, and it was only now that DuBois became fully aware that the white townsmen expected him to become a leader in a Negro community, that they were sending him to a black and not a white college.

Fisk was even more of a shock in revealing the rigid division of a southern state into two societies. As DuBois wrote:

I was tossed boldly into the "Negro problem." From a section and circumstances where the status of me and my folk could be rationalized as the result of poverty and limited essentially by schooling and hard effort, I suddenly came to a region where the world was split into white and black halves, and where the darker half was held back by race prejudice and legal bonds, as well as by deep ignorance and dire poverty.

DuBois responded to this shock by deciding that it was his personal mission to help his race—"through the leadership of men like me and my fellows, we were going to have these enslaved Israelites out of the still enduring bondage in short order." At his graduation from Fisk, however, he had no idea of how he was to accomplish this. Provided with fellowship help, he enrolled in the graduate school at Harvard University where, after some exploration in the physical sciences, he turned in the direction of social science "with a view to the ultimate application of its principles to the social and economic rise of the Negro people." His doctoral dissertation, published in 1896, was a historical study, *The Suppression of the African Slave Trade to the United States of America, 1638–1870.* He also travelled to Germany where his interests turned more toward sociological analysis under the influence of Gustav Schmoller.

When DuBois began his career as a college teacher, he was proud of his racial heritage but distressed by the black man's lack of intellectual attainment. He was critical of the Negroes' failure to stress education because, he wrote, they are "a people who have contributed nothing to modern civilization, who are largely on the lowest stages of barbarism in these closing days of the 19th century." It was to be his task, therefore, to uplift his race intellectually and to demonstrate to the whites that, given the right social and economic circumstances, Negro scholarly achievement would equal that of the Anglo-Saxons.

In the 1890s DuBois had become certain that history was progress away from ignorance toward enlightenment, a progress made possible by the accumulation of empirical knowledge upon which statesmen could build proper social policy. What he wanted to do, therefore, was to establish a sociology department in a Negro university which would have as its aims, "1. Scientifically to study the

Negro question past and present with a view to its best solution. 2. To see how far Negro students are capable of further independent study and research in the best scientific work of the day."

After a disastrous year at Wilberforce College, where he hated the evangelical atmosphere, DuBois spent a year at the University of Pennsylvania making a statistical study of the Philadelphia Negro community. In his conclusion DuBois criticized the Negroes for their low sexual morality, their high crime rate, their excessive devotion to fun and games and drinking, the inefficiency of their self-help organizations, the irresponsibility of wealthier Negroes in failing to exercise constructive leadership, and the general corruption of Negro politics.

On the other hand, he found the white community to be so hysterical about the possibility of racial intermarriage that it was incapable of recognizing and encouraging those Negro individuals who were responsible. He argued, too, that the white community, by refusing to provide jobs for blacks in or out of unions, was greatly responsible for the crime and corruption in the black ghetto.

Moving now to Atlanta University, where he would remain until 1910, DuBois began a series of statistical studies of Negro farmers and workers which, he declared, in one hundred years would provide a complete description of black society. Certain that such research would reveal the basic natural laws of social evolution, DuBois believed that "the sole aim of any society is to settle its problems in accordance with its highest ideals, and the only rational method of accomplishing this is to study those problems in the light of the best scientific research."

In 1900 DuBois was in agreement with Washington that Negro progress up from slavery was to be slow and difficult. But DuBois, like so many of his fellow white social philosophers of progressivism, coupled his philosophy of inevitable evolutionary progress with the possibility of sudden and dramatic conversion of the people from a false and artificial establishment. Such mass conversion would be the result of heroic, charismatic leadership. And at the beginning of the twentieth century DuBois began to see Washington as the head of a conspiratorial Negro establishment which was attempting to place the black masses in permanent servitude. Washington, declared DuBois in 1903, was asking Negroes to give up political power, civil rights, and liberal arts colleges; he was, for DuBois, asking Negroes to give up participation in evolutionary social progress. And Washington was carrying on his war against the Negro people through his control of most Negro newspapers throughout the entire nation, his control of most Negro ministers, his control of most Negro presidents of black colleges, his control of most Negro politicians. By 1905 DuBois had defined a progressive drama for black America which paralleled that of white America. He, like Beard or Veblen or Dewey, postulated that there was a law of progress operating in the world. He too insisted that, in addition to this natural history of progress, there was an unnatural history, artificially created by evil men. He too declared that the people suffered the existence of this conspiracy only because they did not recognize it. He too believed in the necessity of muckraking to expose this unnatural establishment. He too hoped that once the people were given the possibility of choosing between the false aristocracy and the true democracy, between a decadent status quo and vital progress, they would inevitably purge unnatural history and follow the good men who were leading them back into harmony with the natural history of evolutionary progress.

In the 1890s DuBois had seen the problem of Negro progress as solely the result of the Negroes' ignorance of the skills that would allow the black man to participate in evolutionary progress and the whites' ignorance that the Negro had the innate potential to acquire those skills. Now, however, after 1905, DuBois joined the white progressives in arguing that this ignorance was encouraged by selfish men who benefited economically from the backwardness of white and black labor. But DuBois shared with the white progressives the belief that the robber barons, white and black, who were exploiting the people were nonfunctional to the economy and society—that they were parasites and could be removed easily from a society that was basically cooperative and democratic.

His great efforts, therefore, between 1903 and 1910 were to educate white and black men to the plight of the Negro under Washington's leadership and to work for the organization of a black leadership group to overthrow Washington. He published widely in national magazines and began his own magazine, *Horizon,* to carry out his muckraking and educational concerns; in 1905 he brought together Negro leaders hostile to Washington at a meeting at Niagara Falls in Canada.

This Niagara group was not large enough or unified enough to accomplish anything significant and DuBois' magazine, *Horizon,* also failed to establish itself. In 1909 DuBois appeared to be defeated in his war against Washington when suddenly he was offered the chance to leave Atlanta and come north to edit the journal of the newly formed NAACP. Particularly vicious white atrocities in mass violence and lynching of Negroes in Springfield, Illinois, in 1908 brought to a focus the growing sympathy for and understanding of the Negroes among a small group of white intellectuals and professional people in the North which was the result of the new emphasis on environmentalism in the social sciences. Led by William English Walling, Oswald Garrison Villard, and Mary White Ovington, a conference was called which resulted in the formation of the NAACP.

In 1910 as editor of a magazine, *The Crisis,* with adequate financial support from the white community, DuBois prophesied the quick end of the establishment, black and white. "From contempt and amusement," he wrote, the Negroes "have passed to the pity and perplexity of their neighbors, while within their own souls they have arisen from apathy and timid complaint to open protest and more and more manly assertion." The liberation of the Negro, he continued, was part of the general democratic liberation of mankind, expressed by the emancipation of women, the socialization of wealth, and the coming of universal peace. DuBois had "the vision of future cooperation, not simply as in the past, between giver and beggar—the older idea of charity—but a new alliance between experienced social workers and reformers in touch on the one hand with scientific philanthropy and on the other hand with the great struggling mass of laborers of all kinds, whose conditions and needs know no color line."

At the same time that white liberals, who had the reputation for being pragmatic, were founding the *New Republic* magazine to symbolize that America had experienced a rebirth and was beginning a new era in which a cooperative, nonpartisan democracy would endure in peace forever, DuBois was setting forth his philosophy of the new era on the editorial pages of *The Crisis:* "Evolution is evolving the millennium, but one of the unescapable factors in evolution are the men who hate wickedness and oppression with perfect hatred, who will not equivocate, will not excuse and will be heard."

DuBois, like the editors of the *New Republic,* Herbert Croly, Walter Lippmann, and Walter Weyl, supported Theodore Roosevelt in 1912 and Woodrow Wilson in 1916, only to be disappointed both times by the failure of these candidates to clarify the nature of the onrushing cooperative commonwealth. But the editors of the *New Republic* and the editor of *The Crisis* were both certain that the participation of the United States in World War I would break down the final resistance of organized selfishness and that the need for cooperation in the face of a common enemy would hasten the emergence of the new era of perfect democratic brotherhood. And so DuBois proclaimed that "the walls of prejudice crumble before the onslaught of common sense and racial progress." "We make no ordinary sacrifice," he wrote of the Negro community, "but we make it gladly and willingly with our eyes lifted to the hills."

The white editors of the *New Republic* were left without a meaningful future in 1919 by the failure of their millennial vision, and they entered the 1920s totally confused and bitterly disappointed. But their confusion and bitterness were nothing compared to that of DuBois who had come to define the years of progressivism between 1905 and 1918 in terms of the most optimistic and enthusiastic white liberals. DuBois had never understood the existence of the anti-Negro crusade in the South and, living in the world of the white progressive intellectuals, he, like them, had no sense of the popular hostility to the Negro in the North. And so he greeted the failure of Armageddon and the return to normalcy with bitter self-contempt. "Fools, yes that's it. Fools. All of us fools fought a long, cruel, bloody and unnecessary war and we not only killed our boys— we killed Faith and Hope." Like the greatest of the middle-class muckrakers, Lincoln Steffens, DuBois' reaction to this loss of faith and hope would lead him ultimately toward communism.

World War I, by shutting off European immigration, marked the beginning of a very rapid exodus of southern Negroes off the land and into the slums of the northern cities. These uprooted and bewildered people reacted to the urban chaos by accepting a curiously inverted version of the Puritan myth which the progressives were attempting so desperately to modify. By 1917 two prophets, Marcus Garvey from Jamaica and Noble Drew Ali from North Carolina, had begun to preach a new religion to the Negro city poor.

The cultural identity of white America which was in crisis by 1890 had asserted that the Anglo-Saxons had rebelled against Rome to begin the Reformation because the Anglo-Saxons had never engaged in the sin of cultural creativity but had always lived simply and innocently by God's law until Rome had forced its profane and artificial patterns upon them. Outwardly corrupted, the Anglo-Saxons remained inwardly innocent because they, unlike the Latin people, had not voluntarily created false traditions and institutions in blasphemous rebellion against God. Rome had imposed its man-made civilization across the face of Europe, but it was possible for Anglo-Saxons to regain the innocence they had once enjoyed in the virgin forests of Germany before they had been desecrated by Roman ceremonies. They could do this by coming to America, to its virgin land, where they could once more live simply and without artifice, spontaneously and without cultural complexity. Symbolic of human blasphemy in the face of God's command to live in His world as He had created it was the city. The city of Rome as contrasted to the German forest demonstrated Latin artifice as contrasted to Anglo-Saxon humility.

Now, of course, in 1890, America's virgin land was replaced by the city and white Americans had to redefine their identity; they had to argue that in a state of nature man was social and gregarious and that it was, therefore, natural and not unnatural for him to live in groups. They had to argue that industrial creativity was natural and not unnatural.

But Garvey and Noble Drew Ali in 1917 refused to accept the loss of virgin land as necessary. Instead they claimed that the black man in the forests of Africa had lived simply and innocently, obedient to God's will, not disobediently creating artificial culture, not creating cities. Then, of course, the white man, Latin and Anglo-Saxon, had come and carried off many of these pious blacks and imprisoned them in the artificial environment he had created in defiance of God. The white man, Latin or Anglo-Saxon, was the child of the devil who built monuments to his pride wherever he went —cities. Wherever one met the white man in southern or northern Europe, in South or North America, one found his cities. Because the cities were the work of the devil and not of God, they were an environment of chaos, conflict, corruption, and terror.

The only salvation for the black man in America, Garvey preached, was to escape the devil and all his works and to return to Africa, rejoining the black Africans who had kept the covenant with God by refusing to be culturally creative. White Anglo-Saxon Protestant Americans in the middle of the nineteenth century had tried to distinguish between Europe as space profaned by Rome

and America as sacred space, between Europe dominated by a profane manmade history and America with a sacred God-given history.
Now these black prophets were proclaiming that white Americans
were the descendants of white Europeans who had brought profane manmade history with them and had proceeded to profane the
New World space as thoroughly as they had profaned the space of
Europe. And the evidence, they told the black urban masses, was in
their lives, trapped in the grotesque, monstrous cities which these
white hypocrites had built—hypocrites because they claimed to
be God-fearing but then built their own artificial world, the awful,
terrible towers of Babel, the city.

Clearly, Garvey and Ali declared, the black saints, biologically
superior to the white man because the black man had never surrendered to the temptation to deny God through the act of cultural
creativity, must separate themselves from the corrupting presence
of the white man, from the temptation of the white devil. While
Garvey insisted that the black Puritans must make their way back
into the African wilderness, Noble Drew Ali suggested that, when
the moment came for God to destroy the white man and his works,
the blacks could withdraw into the American desert and, when
God's purge of the white man's cities was complete and the land
was purified, the Negro could then reoccupy a restored garden of
Eden.

Both Washington and, to a greater extent, DuBois had been
interested in the growth of Pan-African movements in the Old
World. When DuBois' dream of the progressive millennium was
smashed and he turned more seriously to Pan-Africanism, he was
met by a new kind of racial prejudice. DuBois, like Washington,
had white ancestors and Garvey told DuBois that he had been corrupted by this background. Completing the inversion of nineteenth-
century white Anglo-Saxon Protestant democracy, Garvey, like Tom
Watson, attacked an eastern establishment. In the democracy of the
common man, there was no room for obvious distinction; the educated intellectual was suspect and DuBois had a Harvard Ph.D.
Where did DuBois get his aristocracy from, Garvey shouted:

> He just got it into his head that he should be an aristocrat and
> ever since that time has been keeping his very beard as an aristo-
> crat; he has been trying to be everything else but a Negro.
> Sometimes we hear he is a Frenchman and another time he is

Dutch and when it is convenient he is a Negro. Now I have no Dutch, I have no French, I have no Anglo-Saxon to imitate; I have but the ancient glories of Ethiopia to imitate.... Anyone you hear always talking about the kind of blood he has in him other than the blood you can see, he is dissatisfied with something, and ... if there is a man who is most dissatisfied with himself, it is Dr. DuBois.

Chapter VIII

Freedom from Form: Progressivism in Architecture, Art, and Music

The creative artists were particularly sensitive to the crisis in national identity and many played enthusiastic and energetic roles in the attempt to overcome the fear of decay by guiding the nation once more along the path of progress away from an artificial culture that must grow old toward unity with timeless and ever-youthful nature. Nowhere was this emphasis on the need for renaissance and reformation more dramatically expressed than in the area of architecture. Between 1890 and 1917 two great architects, Louis Sullivan and Frank Lloyd Wright, became major spokesmen for the need of a new, progressive, American architecture to replace what they saw as the decadent, European architecture which had oppressed and suffocated the American landscape throughout the entire sweep of national history. Like Charles Beard, Sullivan and Wright refused to believe that the Founding Fathers had achieved a covenant with nature which was threatened by the development of cultural complexity in the nineteenth century. Like Beard, they believed that the American Revolution which was to end European cultural influence in the New World still was to be fought. And, like Beard, they saw in the machine the new frontier force which

133

was necessary before men could experience the rebirth and renewal that must come when humanity was freed from artificial institutions and traditions to achieve organic unity with physicial nature.

For Sullivan and Wright the architecture of the authentic American Revolution was to be called specifically "organic architecture." They believed that the Founding Fathers had revealed their commitment to un-American, unnatural principles in their dedication to classical architecture. Jefferson had claimed that the new Republic was based on natural law. But for Sullivan and Wright, Jefferson had given the natural law architectural expression in an abstract, rational style borrowed from the Old World. Surely nothing could more clearly indicate the inability of these late eighteenth-century men to comprehend what was really natural. The tragic corollary of this false American Revolution was to be found in the continued borrowing of European architectural styles throughout the nineteenth century. There was no American architecture; there was no American style; there was no American identity. Unable to give themselves an authentic New World identity, Americans must borrow without guidelines. The result was the triumph of a ghastly eclecticism. The result also was the building of hideous, anarchical European cities along the east coast of the United States.

Louis Sullivan, like Ignatius Donnelly, was the son of an immigrant. Raised in the East, he too was to identify the Middle West as the real America. He too was to create a vision of Armageddon in which the virtuous Midwest must redeem an evil East before the East corrupted the midwestern garden. Born in Boston in 1856, Sullivan spent his earliest years on his grandfather's farm. In his autobiography Sullivan wrote that as a young child he developed a great love of physical nature; that his earliest memories were of an almost instinctive rejection of the message of the church that man was a sinful and divided being, in favor of the theological message, symbolized by the great trees on the farm, that there was a healthful and happy unity of all living things in the universe. Then he was taken into Boston to be educated and Sullivan described his trauma in these words:

As one might move a flourishing plant from the open to a dark cellar ... so the miasma of the big city poisoned a small boy.... Against the big city his heart swelled in impatient, impotent rebellion. Its many streets, its crooked streets, its filthy streets, lined with stupid houses, crowded together shoulder to shoulder like selfish hogs upon these trough-like lanes, irritated him, suffocated him; the crowds of people ... hurrying here and there so aimlessly ... confused and overwhelmed him, arousing ... nausea and dismay. ... In the city all was contraction, density, limitation, and a cruel concentration.

He survived his adolescence in the city by dreaming of running away: "To run where? Anywhere to liberty and freedom!" And when opportunity came, he fled west to Chicago. As he crossed the Indiana prairie, as he felt the power and openness of the prairie, and the sky, and the great blue lake, he once more experienced the joy of communion with nature.

No longer in the late nineteenth century, however, could Sullivan believe that the West had the power to keep America a nation of yeomen farmers. The city was part of America, a constantly growing part. But the virgin land of the Midwest, Sullivan believed, did make possible the creation of American and not European cities, of garden cities and not the repetition of Old World cesspools like Boston, New York, and Philadelphia.

The key to this possibility was architecture. If cities were to be healthful and natural, the architecture of their buildings must be healthful and natural. For Sullivan, if the nation was to be saved, if it was to become healthful and natural, its salvation figure would be an architect. Shamelessly Sullivan offered himself to his country as its savior. "With me," he wrote, "architecture is not an art but a religion and that religion but a part of democracy." He saw himself as a muckraker who would expose the fact that "American architecture is ... ninety parts aberration, eight parts indifference, one part poverty and one part Little Lord Fauntleroy." He saw himself as an evangelist who would call the young architects away from this profane tradition to become, themselves, spokesmen for the sacred future. "Do you intend or do you not intend ... to become architects in whose care an unfolding Democracy may entrust the interpretation of its material wants, its psychic aspirations." He saw himself as a prophet and teacher who would reveal that the kingdom of God was within every man, because each man began life as an innocent child. To lose our corruption, we need only to become as little children again—"if the mind is ... left free to act with spontaneity, individuality of expression will come to you as the flower comes to the plant—for it is nature's law." Such innocence was universal to mankind, but Americans had a special opportunity to become as little children because, while the identity of Europe was cultural complexity, the identity of America was nature itself. America, Sullivan proclaimed, was "the garden of our world." Here "tradition is without shackles, and the soul of man free to grow, to mature, to seek its own." This was "a new land, a Promised Land. Here destiny has decreed there shall be enacted the final part in the drama of man's emancipation—the redemption of his soul!"

All civilization, Sullivan wrote, could be characterized as feudal. "Glancing at our modern civilization," he continued, "we find on the surface crust essentially the same idea at work that has prevailed throughout the past." This was the dualism of the feudal idea which "holds to the concept of good and evil" in contrast to the democratic idea which is "single, integral. It holds to the good alone."

Writing that "historic feudal thought . . . found its form in a series of civilizations resting upon a denial of man by the multitudes themselves," Sullivan explained man's tragic history as the failure of men to understand themselves as part of nature. Instead they had assumed the need to create an artificial environment for themselves. They had cut themselves off from nature by constructing an artful culture. They had imagined that they must replace childish simplicity by adult complexity. And so, cut off from the life-giving power of nature, they had lived lives of fear and inhibition.

Now, however, the fruitful power of industrialism was reminding man of his organic unity with the fruitful power of nature. Sullivan wrote that, when he was young and innocent, he had instinctively sensed the difference between the artificial and inhibited creativity that had constructed a city like Boston and the artless and fruitful creativity which was expressed in a great steel bridge, simple and honest in design. His childish response to the bridge was "How great must men be, how wonderful, how powerful, that they could make such a bridge; and again he worshipped the worker."

If now Sullivan could teach Americans that all their buildings, like that bridge, should express the architectural principle that "form follows function," that every aspect of the community should express the simplicity and honesty of that rule that "form follows function," then he could lead them into that "garden of the heart wherein the simple, obvious truths, the truths that any child might consent to, are brought fresh to the faculties and are held to be good because they are true and real." He could restore "the child mind [which] can grasp an understanding of things and ideas supposed now in our pride of feudal thought to be beyond its reach."

For Sullivan industrialism was best able to restore man to his childlike understanding of his instinctive harmony with nature in the Midwest where, unlike the corrupt and complex east coast, the factory and the virgin land came together in a direct, face-to-face relationship, a marriage of productive partners. This was why Chicago, unlike Boston or New York, was a city of joy. In the old cities, men huddled together, inhibited by fear because they were separated from nature. Their buildings were fortresses or prisons. But in Chicago men had rediscovered that as natural men, they, like nature, were producers. Like the trees, they could plant themselves in the ground and reach toward the sky. This, Sullivan insisted, was why "the architects of Chicago welcomed the steel frame and did something with it." This was why "the architects of the East were appalled by it and could make no contribution to it." This was why the skyscraper was born in Chicago. It was the architecture of joy.

Sullivan designed the high buildings made possible by the use of the steel framework and he covered them with elaborate decorations of carved leaves. For Sullivan there was no contradiction between his emphasis on simplicity and honesty in architecture based on his rule that form follows function and this complex decoration. He hoped Chicago and ultimately all cities would be "garden cities," organic outgrowths, like trees, from the earth itself. In his mind his decoration was artless, not artful. It was not the decoration of civilization, imposed by the human imagination. It was natural decoration, implicit in the union of the building with its physical context.

Sullivan could escape Jefferson's fear that all cities must be sores on the body politic not only because he distinguished between artificial cities and garden cities but also because he accepted the political philosophy of Rousseau. The Founding Fathers, including Jefferson, had feared the conflict between majority and minority interests, between the group and the individual. But Sullivan, like so many of his contemporaries in the progressive movement, affirmed the position of Rousseau that in a perfect society there would be a General Will in which perfect consensus among all individuals would be expressed. Sullivan, too, was trying to shift his generation away from a commitment to a state of nature composed of atomistic individuals toward the acceptance of the state of nature based on social man who had been perfectly harmonious and cooperative before he had made the mistake of creating artificial institutions and traditions which had caused divisions and conflicts. Sullivan, therefore, saw his organic architecture as one aspect of the intellectual revolution that had rediscovered the social nature of man. The general name of this revolution, for Sullivan, was embodied in the new science of sociology which he described as "the art, the science of gregarious man.... This is the unity, science, poem, and drama of Sociology, the precursor of Democracy—its explorer, its evangel."

For Sullivan in 1890 all the impersonal forces of industrialism and social science were leading to the destruction of feudal civilization. And in 1893 at the Columbian Exposition at Chicago, the new architecture could begin the final education and liberation of the American people by illustrating in organic functionalism the true, natural, productive, and innocent nature of man. Here, at Chicago, there could be "a superb revelation of America's potency—an oration, a portrayal to arouse that which was hidden, to call it forth into the light." The new organic, democratic architecture would demonstrate how there could be created "out of the cruel feudal chaos of cross purposes, a civilization, in equilibrium, for free men conscious of their power."

But in Chicago there was an architect, Daniel Burnham, who, Sullivan wrote, "was obsessed by the feudal idea of power." And Sullivan believed that Burnham conspired to have the architecture of the exposition dominated by architects from the east coast. For Sullivan progress from complexity to simplicity was natural, but change from simplicity to complexity, the coming of decadence, must be the result of deliberate, unnatural conspiracy. Sullivan, unlike Frederick Jackson Turner in 1893, had seen Chicago as the beginning of a new frontier of hope. But the years between 1893 and 1917 were ones of disillusionment for Sullivan. He had prophesied the triumph of organic architecture, American architecture, and he witnessed the continued dominance of what he believed was feudal, European architecture. He had prophesied a new reformation and renaissance for America and instead he saw what he believed was the corruption of the Midwest by eastern conspiracy. Personally his importance declined; he was ignored; he grew old alone, alienated and impoverished. In 1917 he wrote: "As for me the bottom has dropped out, and the future is a blank."

The second great architect of the progressive era, Frank Lloyd Wright, was to find his greatest recognition and acceptance at the very end of his long career, from the 1930s to the 1950s, but for him, also, the years between 1890 and 1917 were to be ones of a prophecy which failed.

Born in Wisconsin in 1869, Wright came to Chicago to become an architect, convinced like so many young American intellectuals, from the East as well as the West, that Chicago must become the cultural capital of a nation that needed to be purged and redeemed from the corruption and complexity most dramatically symbolized by the cities of the east coast, especially New York. The psychology of muckraking, the need to detail the horrors of the corruption of a vicious feudal establishment, was as central to Wright's writings on architecture as it had been for Sullivan. Wright, too, was a young Jeremiah as he pointed out the need for a reformation which would purify the profane and restore the sacred. In Veblenian terms he wrote:

> The pernicious social fabric so excruciated by adornment was a moral, social, aesthetic excrement that was only the rubbish heap of a nation-wide waste of all natural resources.... So all this I saw around me seemed affectation, nonsense, or profane. The first feeling was hunger for reality, for sincerity. A desire for simplicity that would yield a broader, deeper sense of comfort was natural, too, to this first feeling. A growing idea of simplicity as organic ... was new as a quality of thought, able to strengthen and refresh the spirit in any circumstance.

For Wright, as for Sullivan, the cause of the ugly and evil architecture that was corrupting America came from the continuing commitment of Americans to artificial culture, a culture spun out of the human imagination, a culture which separated man from the life-giving union with nature. Current American architecture was evil and ugly because, like a Frankenstein monster, it represented an unnatural creativity by men. Men need not create new forms; indeed men should not create new forms. All forms were to be found in nature, and the architect, like all other men, should go to nature for his education; then and then only could the architect design the good, the true, and the beautiful. Again for Wright, as for Sullivan, the attempt to change the nation's attitude toward architecture was an attempt to change the religious life of the nation. A heresy must be rejected and a true faith reestablished. "The building as architecture is born out of the heart of man, permanent consort to the ground, comrade to the trees, true reflection of man in the realm of his own spirit. His building is therefore consecrated space." Therefore, Wright's liturgy continued, we must "worship at the skein of nature and go to her for inspiration: to learn why we have laid upon us an artificiality that blights and often times conceals ourselves and deforms... past recognition the fulfillment of life principles implanted in us."

In the years between 1890 and 1910 Wright's commitment to the religion of nature and the natural man led him not to the despair of a Frederick Jackson Turner but to the optimism of Charles Beard because he too had revised the theory of the state of nature to define its inhabitants as gregarious and industrious. And he too saw industrialism as helping man to escape from chaotic civilization to return to the harmony of his natural environment.

Wright added his voice to the chorus that the machine was the new messiah, "that the machine was the great forerunner of democracy," because the machine so directly challenged the artificial. The organic architecture that Wright championed was to express his variation of Sullivan's motto, "form follows function" to read "form is function." The form and function of the machine were productivity. It was clean and efficient; it was authentic; it was truth, beauty, and goodness; it was sacred in contrast to the evil of the parasitical with its nonfunctional decoration and style. Surely the machine would inhibit the imagination which had strayed away from the natural and had created, therefore, the profane chaos of manmade civilization. Surely, Wright declared, the machine would reeducate man to see that his true nature found fulfillment in productivity; surely the machine would lead man back into harmony with his inner nature and with physical nature, both of which represented the purity of the original creation. During the nineteenth century sensitive men had feared the machine because it had been misused by the parasites, the aristocratic remnants of the Dark Ages. "The machine these reformers protested because the sort of luxury which is born of greed had usurped it, and made it a terrible engine of enslavement, deluging the world with a mur-

derous ubiquity." But Wright asserted that the logic and power of
the machine was such that it would destroy these false masters and
fulfill its destiny of liberating man from the ephemeral and the
unnecessary. Therefore, Wright proclaimed, he was dedicating his
life to the idea that "the future of art lies in the machine."

Wright composed a Puritan hymn for himself that would sustain
him in his crusade to purge America of the architecture of decadent
civilization and to replace it with the organic architecture of natural
democracy.

> I'll live as I work as I am
> No work for fashion in sham
> Not to favor forsworn
> Wear mask crest or thorn
>
> My work as befitteth a man
> My work
> Work that befitteth the man

✿   ✿   ✿   ✿

> I'll act as I'll die as I am
> No slave of fashion or sham
> Of my freedom proud
> Hers shrive guard or shroud
>
> My life as betideth a man
> My life
> Aye let come what betideth the man

Wright's architectural energy and inspiration were directed,
in the first decade of the new century, toward the design of organic,
puritanical houses for the suburbs. The family, the most fundamental social unit of a naturally gregarious humanity, must be ex-
tricated from the destructive chaos of the nineteenth century, to
reachieve the harmony and order of the state of nature. The dominant theme in Wright's external design was the roof, low, wide,
overhanging, providing unity and shelter for the family. This
emphasis on a low and simple silhouette was the identifying aspect
of Wright's "prairie houses." His public buildings in these years

before 1910 also shared in this emphasis on geometric formality. Within this exterior of firm sincerity, Wright continued to emphasize family unity. Central to the home was the hearth which was drammatized to give it the sacred quality of an altar. And he provided massive regularity for the dining room furniture he designed to emphasize the liturgy of the meal which united the family in perfect oneness.

Wright, like Sullivan, could accept the city if it could be reduced from historical disharmony to natural harmony, from decadent artificiality to a vital organism. In 1902 he drew the plans for a suburban block; known as the Quadruple Block, it contained four identical houses in prairie style, set far back from the street and sharing an interior wooded court in common. When asked by a group of University of Chicago professors to design a summer colony in the Montana mountains, Wright produced a plan of rigid geometric simplicity in which the cottages were spatially related to the dining lodge where the families were to share their meals in common. A critic of Wright described this Como Orchards design in these words: "Taken as a whole, the plan seems arbitrary and rigid for a wilderness site, there is no feeling for the roughness of terrain, and the cottages to the rear of the lodge are inexplicably close together, as if land were at a premium."

Until 1909 Wright seems to have shared in that major tenet of the religious faith of progressivism which held that there was no conflict between the individual and the group in a natural situation. The nineteenth-century individual had been oppressed by a society that was artificial and historical. But now the individual was escaping from that false society to achieve harmony with an authentic community. And Wright's architecture was supposed to make this distinction between true and false community. Earlier than many of his contemporaries, however, Wright lost his faith in the coming of this democratic millennium in which the individual was to find perfect fulfillment in the general will of the majority. In 1909 Wright deserted his wife and six children. His friends and neighbors had assumed that he was a happy husband and father. But, fleeing to Europe, Wright proclaimed that he no longer could sacrifice himself to the social unit. And when he returned to the United States, he established himself in rural Wisconsin. Here he began the second and more famous phase of his architectural career, arguing that organic architecture must relate the individual to physical nature and not to other men. Ten years before the nation would try to return to the normalcy of pre-1890 individualism by electing Warren Harding to the presidency, Wright had retreated to the nineteenth-century doctrine of the self-sufficient, autonomous individual.

In the middle of the nineteenth century American painters had vigorously expressed the national faith that harmony with nature had been achieved. In dramatic landscapes and in loving scenes of rural life the painters had celebrated the timeless purity of the New World garden. These artists accepted the philosophy that the task of the artist was to reveal the objective and preexisting beauty in nature. Their style was a romantic realism, reproducing the object but in a golden glow of joyful sentiment.

In the years from the Civil War to 1900 this commitment to romantic realism continued to prevail but in a sharply altered emotional context. The painters before 1865 had expressed the spontaneous joy of a nation moving toward union with nature. But every decade after 1865, every decade of urban-industrial growth, was a threat to the national identity as a pastoral Eden. The painter could no longer in all honesty depict a nation in timeless, arcadian simplicity. Rather than describe the transformation of the nation in their paintings, however, most of the artists, like their middle-class patrons, pretended that no economic revolution which was covering the landscape with factories and cities was taking place.

Instead, with improving technique and virtuosity, the artists continued to paint the American landscape. Seemingly, however, the shrinking area of virgin land had an impact on these painters because the very physical size of their landscape paintings shrank, even as the vigor of expression gave way to a quality of contrived slickness. The artificial prettiness of these late nineteenth-century landscapes was matched by the portraits. In the midst of vast social revolution and disorder, the patrons and their painters chose to emphasize the stability of the wealthy middle-class family in the security of its Victorian parlor. Here, as in the landscape, there seemed to be an unconscious awareness of the hypocrisy, and the most popular paintings of the 1890s became those of mythical maidens, portrayed in discreet neoclassical drapery, in a primly ecstatic relationship to an idyllic landscape, as in Carrol Beckwith's painting of "Spring" or Will Low's "Autumn." Other attempts to impose the facade of gayness on the terror-stricken 1890s invoked the "Divinity of Motherhood," "Love's Token," or "Day Dreams." All these frantic attempts to paint over the reality of the new urban-industrial world reveal in another form the fear that the new reality was profane, an index of the decay of the virtuous Republic of the Founding Fathers, and a descent into the hell of an artificial civilization.

In this world of art, as in the other areas of American culture, there began to appear men who argued that the artistic establishment was not conserving a sacred tradition against the encroachments of profane chaos, but rather that the establishment itself represented false and parasitical values which were at war with a vital and progressive reality. The formula for the progressives in art, as in architecture and music, or the social sciences, was to insist that the potential of American democracy had not yet been fulfilled, that the natural had not yet liberated itself from the artificial, and that the drama of the historical situation in the 1890s was not the hopeless defense of a disintegrating Eden but rather the joyful destruction of decadent historical traditions and institutions in order to march into Eden. To make this formula work in 1900, however, it was necessary in art as in sociology to define Eden in social terms, to find the potential of a cooperative democracy in the city.

In the 1890s men like John Sloan, Everett Shinn, William Glackens, and George Luks worked as illustrators for newspapers and magazines. Here they had the opportunity to stand outside the dominant position in painting that avoided reality; instead they were encouraged to report the American scene in realistic detail. They became an important aspect of the muckraking movement, paralleling the reporters, like Lincoln Steffens, in documenting the rottenness of the official order of the day. But, like the other muckrakers, they were certain that beneath the surface corruption lay a sound and healthy reality. They shared with the other progressives the faith that a new democracy was not to be created but was to be brought into a dominant position through the purge of superficial evils which obscured the existence of the good society.

The illustrators found the inspiration to begin a revolution in American painting in the writings and teachings of Robert Henri who, for more than a decade, had been engaged in an attack on the artistic establishment symbolized by the National Academy of

Design. Henri attacked what he called this academic tradition in art for not fulfilling the American philosophy that the artist should reveal the objective and preexisting beauty in nature. Instead these academics had retreated to the precious position of art for art's sake. But "what we need," Henri insisted, "is more sense of the wonder of life and less of this business of making a picture." The young John Sloan agreed with him: "A concern with the abstract beauty of forms, the objective quality of lines, planes, and colors is not sufficient to create art. The artist must have an interest in life, curiosity, and penetrating inquiry into the livingness of things. I don't believe in art for art's sake." For Henri: "The cause of revolution in art is, that, at times, feeling drops out of the work and it must fight to get back in again." The painting must be inspired by and communicate an emotion drawn directly from life.

This emotion was the goodness, virtue, and happiness of the people in the slums. Like Jane Addams and the other social workers, the younger painters insisted that these new Americans were not a threat to an established democracy but the foundation for a new democracy because they were "undefiled by good taste, etiquette or behaviour." Mounting an attack on an artificial establishment, the young painters found the urban poor to be natural and genuine because they were not bound by convention as was the eastern aristocracy.

In 1908 seven of these young painters, Arthur B. Davies, William Glackens, Ernest Lawson, George Luks, Maurice Prendergast, Everett Shinn, and John Sloan, joined with Robert Henri to exhibit their paintings in opposition to the National Academy. Their paintings explored the streets and tenements, the wharfs, trolleys, railroads, and saloons of the city. They celebrated the work of lower-class men and women and the games of the slum children. Their academic enemies labeled them the Ash Can School, but their paintings, according to the young artists, expressed the "wonder of life," and "the marvel of existence." The city landscapes had charm and warmth; the people were vigorous and handsome.

These artists, like the other progressives, were insisting that the American parasitical aristocracy was superficial and ephemeral. Their paintings proclaimed that the day of a perfected democracy was dawning. Only a handful of painters of the progressive period joined the very small number of dissidents who were horrified at the viciousness of the ruling class and feared its strength and capacity to destroy human dignity through the inhumanity of its social and economic system. One such artist was Eugene Higgens who painted, in contrast to the healthy poor portrayed by the Ash Can School, faceless and grotesque figures because he saw in the slums "struggle and strife, horrible suffering, livid agony of soul and body, want, misery, and despair."

But in France there were young American painters who were coming to share with the new European schools of expressionists and abstractionists the loss of faith in the existence of any reality which could be painted in the form of recognizable objects. When in 1913 these new trends were exhibited at the Armory Show, Americans had a preview of the awful vision which would confront them in 1919, when so many were forced to doubt that history was indeed a progressive purge of the complex designed to bring man into harmony with the simple.

In 1900 the best-known American composer was Edward Mac-Dowell. Trained in Europe from the age of fifteen until he was twenty-seven, MacDowell returned to the United States in 1888 to write romantic music in the German tradition which he admired so greatly. His compositions were so sophisticated and skillful that he was accepted immediately as the first American to compose at an equal level of technique with Europeans. American critics became so enthusiastic that they wrote of him that "an almost unanimous vote would rank him as the greatest of American composers, while not a few ballots would indicate him as the best of living music writers."

There is a dramatic parallel between MacDowell's mastery of musical technique learned in Europe and that of his contemporaries in painting. And there is a dramatic parallel between the use of that technique in MacDowell's music, as in the paintings of the 1880s and 1890s, to provide stability for a genteel middle-class establishment. As the artists painted "pretty" pictures in their portraits and landscapes, so MacDowell composed "pretty" musical pieces. And as the artists tended to draw ever smaller and more artificial landscapes, so MacDowell's music tended to find inspiration in a fantasy world that had no relation to the conflicts that were so savagely dividing America in the 1880s and 1890s. This escapism was expressed in the very titles of his major compositions:

Op. 17. *Two Fantastic Pieces, for piano* (1884)
    1. Legend
    2. Witches' Dance

Op. 19. *Forest Idyls, for piano* (1884)
    1. Forest Stillness
    2. Play of the Nymphs
    3. Revery
    4. Dance of the Dryads

His second suite for orchestra, the *Indian Suite*, of 1897, came no closer to reality, nor did his *New England Idyls* of 1902, which concluded with *The Joy of Autumn*. His songs of 1900, "To a Wild Rose," "From Uncle Remus," "Of Br'er Rabbit," "From a German Forest," all expressed the sense of a secure and happy environment characterized by a dainty gentility.

MacDowell's music represented, then, the kind of mechanical imitation of nineteenth-century tradition which Sullivan and Wright attacked in architecture and the Ash Can School attacked in painting. It represented what so many progressives defined as an artificial and artful facade which served to blind Americans to the reality of the corruption of the parasitical establishment.

The major progressive challenger to this musical tradition was Charles Ives, who was born in Danbury, Connecticut, in 1874. While Ives was to be exposed to the musical establishment when he went to Yale, he already had been trained by his father, the town bandmaster. This training had prepared Ives to challenge the academic musical position by teaching him to consider the possibility of polytonality, polyrhythm, and atonality. George Ives, his father, was a most unusual musical innovator who taught his children to listen to several keys, and to listen to two bands as they approached each other playing different tunes. From his father Ives also learned to consider much of the academic music as too "sweet," too "easy," too "sissified," too "feminine."

At Yale, however, under the direction of academic musicians like Horatio Parker, Ives composed songs which fitted the pattern of MacDowell; they expressed peace and tranquillity and otherworldliness; they accepted German dominance with titles like "Feldeinsamkeit" and "Ich Grolle Nicht"; they accepted genteel sentimentality with words that read:

O'er the mountains toward the west
As the children go to rest,
Faintly comes a sound,
A song of nature hovers round.
'Tis the beauty of the night;
Sleep thee well till morning light.

or

Marie, I see thee fairest one
As in a garden fair, a garden fair.
Before thee flowers and blossoms play
Tossed by soft evening air.
The Pilgrim passing on his way,
Bows low before thy shrine;
Thou art, my child, like one sweet prayer,
So good, so fair, so pure, almost divine.

The evening bells are greeting thee,
With sweetest melody,
O may no storm e'er crush thy flowers,
Or break thy heart, or break thy heart, Marie.

Ives has written that in his childhood he had a spiritual experience which revealed to him the unity of the universe with God. In the 1890s at Yale he was taught that this unity was expressed best through nineteenth-century patterns of rhythm and tonality, through genteel poetry, and not through the band music, the circus tunes, and the evangelical hymns of the common people of his childhood.

But Ives began to experience a crisis around 1900 in his acceptance of traditional nineteenth-century music because he too was being convinced, like the muckrakers, that the American establishment in all its aspects was profane and not sacred. Now doubting dominant forms, he could fall back on his father's teachings and expand them to cover every aspect of American life. All forms should be rejected in the name of experimentation. All present forms should be rejected as representative of a vicious aristocracy, and the future should belong to the real Americans, the common people. Unity with God must be expressed through a new democratic folk music which was free from the artificial restraints of aristocratic music. The new music must be spontaneous and transcend established patterns; then it could help men everywhere to transcend the imperfect status quo to achieve unity with God.

As Ives began to consider his role as a composer who would be a prophet for progress, he felt the need to establish his independence from the pressures to conform to musical orthodoxy. He agreed with Thoreau that "wherever a man goes, men will pursue him with their dirty institutions." He decided then to establish himself in a business that would both contribute to public welfare and make him financially self-sufficient so that he could compose freely without the need to please patrons of music. This he accomplished to his satisfaction in an insurance company where he was so successful that he had to limit his income for fear of materialistic corruption of his basically spiritual values.

Now, free from the pressures of the musical establishment, he was able to begin to compose music which would help the people liberate themselves from their masters. Ives defined his music as an expression of theology and political thought. His unfinished *Universe Symphony* was to include these three movements:

1. Formation of the countries and the mountains
2. Evolution in nature and humanity
3. The rise of all to the spiritual

The rise of all to the spiritual out of the profane was how Ives defined the meaning of the years of progress from 1900 to 1917.

These were years, he wrote, of dramatic conflict between the forces of darkness and the forces of light but the victory was preordained:

> The Hog-mind and its handmaidens in disorder . . . cowardice and suspicion; all a part of the minority (the non-people) . . . will give way more and more to the great primal truths; that there is more good than evil; that God is on the side of the majority (the people), that he has made men greater than man, that he has made the universal mind and the over-soul greater and a part of the individual mind and soul, that he has made the Divine a part of all.

Like Charles Cooley, Ives turned back to Emerson to find the philosophical justification for transcendence of the establishment, and Ives agreed with Emerson that the greatest prophet of transcendence yet to appear was Beethoven. For Ives: "There is an 'oracle' at the beginning of the Fifth Symphony; in those four notes lies one of Beethoven's greatest messages. We would ... strive to bring it toward the spiritual message of Emerson's revelations ... the soul of humanity knocking at the door of divine mysteries, radiant in the faith that it will be opened—and the human become divine."

Ives then would embody the philosophy of Emerson and Beethoven and compose music that would help the human become the divine. Such music, he wrote, must be composed, "fervently, transcendentally, inevitably, furiously," and then it would have "sincerity, strength, nobility, and beauty and will be American."

For Ives, Americans, real Americans, the people and not the non-people, the aristocracy, were closer to God than people anywhere else in the world. But this was only because Americans were freer from corrupting institutions and traditions. Americans then had the responsibility of helping the rest of the people in the world to move away from their burden of historical corruption. And Ives had the greatest responsibility of any American because it was through music alone that men could be united in a natural and not an artificial community. Spoken and written languages were themselves historical institutions and traditions and served to divide, not unite, men. But music, Ives declared, "is beyond any analogy to word language and ... the time is coming ... when it will develop possibilities inconceivable now,—a language so transcendent, that its heights and depths will be common to all mankind."

Furiously Ives composed in isolation from a corrupt world in order to save that world. He refused to listen to other music, so that he would be free to find the key to that sacred music which would lift mankind into a heaven on earth. As he experimented with new patterns of polytonality, polyrhythm, and atonality, trying to find the formless music which would unite all of humanity, he became more and more frustrated with traditional instruments and traditional musicians. "The Instrument!" he cried out, "There is the perennial difficulty. There is music's limitations. Is it the composer's fault that man has only ten fingers?" And his impatience exploded against the men who must perform his compositions. "I began to feel that if I wanted to write music that was worth while (that is, to me), I must keep away from musicians."

Writing music with simultaneous rhythms, concurrent melodies, complex patterns of syncopation that orchestras rejected as unplayable, Ives continued to compose at a furious rate because the world he needed to save had become so corrupt, because the people he needed to save were so crushed by suffering. In 1912, he wrote these words to a song:

> Crouched on the pavement, close by Belgrave Square
> A tramp I saw, ill, moody, and tongue-tied
> A babe was in her arms, and at her side
> A girl; their clothes were rags, their feet were bare.
> Some laboring men, whose work lay somewhere there,
> Passed opposite; She touched her girl, who hied
> Across and begged, and came back satisfied.
> The rich she had let pass with frozen stare,
> Thought I: "Above her state this spirit towers;
> She will not ask of aliens, but of friend,
> Of sharers in a common human fate.
> She turns from the cold succor, which attends
> The unknown little from the unknowing great,
> And points to a better Time than ours."

Like so many of his progressive contemporaries, Ives began to see the millennium rising out of this darkness around 1914. He sensed a spiritual awakening among the people. He saw the rejection of the old gospel of self-sufficiency and selfishness in favor of the new social gospel of community salvation and brotherly love. And in 1914 he composed his most triumphant song, "General William Booth Enters into Heaven." Against the complacent sterility of the aristocracy, he contrasted this leader of the common man who, preaching a gospel of love for the people, had transcended churchly institutions and churchly dogma. Booth was a leader who had transcended conformity to respectable norms that ignored the needs of the people. This was the fruitful leader who was leading his motley, rag-tag, democratic army "washed in the blood of the lamb" into heaven. For Ives in 1914:

> The Masses are yearning, are yearning, are yearning.
> Whence comes the hope of the world.
> The masses are dreaming, dreaming,
> The masses are dreaming,
> When comes the vision of God!
> God's in His Heaven,
> All will be well with the world.

These lines from his song, "Majority," express his faith that a constitutional amendment giving the people the right to vote on all important decisions, to participate directly as a general will, would allow them to vote themselves into a heaven on earth.

Then the war came for Ives, as it had for so many progressives, to destroy his hope. "My things," he was to write, "were done mostly in the twenty years or so between 1896 and 1916. In 1917, the war came on and I did practically nothing in music. I did not seem to feel like it." He did compose another song, however, "A Farewell to Land," in which the voice and the piano are to start at the top of the voice's range and descend steadily to the lower limits of the voice.

> Adieu, Adieu! My native shore
> Fades o'er the waters blue;
> The night winds sigh, the breakers roar
> And shrieks the wild sea-mew.
> You sun that sets upon the sea,
> We follow in his flight;
> Farewell while to him and thee,
> My native Land, good-night!

Ives, like the novelist Winston Churchill, was to live another twenty years; old before his time, an aged member of the lost generation, he too would have no messages, no songs of hope to write, to compose, to communicate.

Chapter IX

The Novelists:
Naturalism versus Progressivism

The writings of Mark Twain from the end of the Civil War to the Spanish-American War dramatize the reasons why the dominant self-image of the intellectuals of the progressive era was that of spokesmen for a new reformation that would purge a medieval establishment. Twain was well read in the American and English historians who defined history since the Reformation and Renaissance as the progressive liberation of the individual from slavery to the institutions and traditions of the Dark Ages. And in his *Innocents Abroad,* written immediately after the Civil War had apparently destroyed the last vestiges of feudalism in the New World, he celebrated America's childlike virtue in contrast to the childish superstitions which still kept Europeans from rational and enlightened behavior.

But when Twain collaborated with Charles Warner to write *The Gilded Age,* he had discovered that Americans after the Civil War had neither innocence nor virtue. Now he had to describe the corruption and materialism of the Grant administration and to admit that the people most motivated by greed came from the West. Taught by convention that corruption was greatest in the East where artificial culture was established and that virtue was greatest in the

West where nature restored man's lost innocence, Twain was forced to consider the possibility that physical nature had failed to fulfill its promise to redeem mankind. In *Tom Sawyer* he described two worlds, the materialistic and greedy world of the adults in the town of St. Petersburg on the Mississippi, and the fantasy world of the children who escape to nature: "Cardiff Hill, beyond the village and above it, was green with vegetation, and it lay just far enough away to seem a Delectable Land, dreamy, reposeful, and inviting." But when Tom seeks refuge from the adult world in the heart of nature, in the cave, he finds terror and death and gold. He is initiated into the adult world; he is trapped into violence, materialism, and greed.

When Twain turned from fiction to a book of travel description, *Life on the Mississippi,* he continued to write about nature as a god that had failed. At first he described the river as the very essence of natural and redemptive innocence, the very antithesis of human artificiality, which had given birth to an American Adam, the river pilot. Twain affirmed that he "loved the profession far better than any I have followed since and I took measureless pride in it. The reason is plain: a pilot, in those days, was the only unfettered and entirely independent human being that lived on the earth. ... In truth, every man and woman and child has a master and worries and frets in servitude; but in the day I write of, the Mississippi pilot had none." But then, Twain continued, engineers came to remove the snags, to dredge and mark the channels. And captains, who worked from artificial charts, replaced the pilots who had been in instinctive and organic harmony with the river.

By the end of the 1870s Twain was certain that history as progress from medieval darkness to liberty for the individual had reached its climax in the early nineteenth century and that now mankind was slipping back into the hell of medieval civilization because nature was not able to preserve man in an Edenlike state of innocence. His first reaction to this horrible vision was to retreat back into the past when the forces of progress had been able to defeat the forces of medieval reaction as in his children's fantasy, *The Prince and the Pauper.*

Here, in sixteenth-century England, Twain created two identical boys, one Prince Edward, the son of Henry VIII, the other Tom Canty, the son of a slum-dweller who is a drunkard, a thief, and a murderer—the qualities of the feudal king himself. Each boy wants to escape the wicked world in which he finds himself and each dreams that the other's world is innocent. Changing places, they discover the totality of evil in Henry's England and learn that they must work to reform society from top to bottom.

But in celebrating the victory of innocent children over corrupt adults, in assuming that evil was imposed on a basically good human nature by a wicked society, and that it was possible for mankind to reestablish its fundamental virtue by stepping out of society into harmony with nature, Twain was aware in 1880 that he was engaged in fantasy. He had lost faith in the essential goodness of human nature and he had lost faith in physical nature. The bleakness of this view of reality is described in his next book, *Huckleberry Finn*, which begins with a scathing criticism of the kind of romanticism found in *The Prince and the Pauper*.

Huck Finn cannot believe in Tom Sawyer's make-believe world of childish romance where good children always defeat wicked adults. Appalled by the hypocrisy of the town aristocracy and the evil of his drunken, murderous father, Huck, like Tom Canty, runs away. But he runs to Jackson's Island in the Mississippi River where he hopes to find refuge. He is driven off the island, however, and with the runaway slave, Jim, he takes to the river itself as the final symbol of natural harmony. But the river turns out to be treacherous as it brings death and violence and as it carries Huck and Jim farther and farther south, deeper and deeper into the heart of slavery.

Writing at the end of the 1880s, Twain was certain that physical nature had failed as an alternative to civilization. If men were to escape from the corruption of institutions and traditions, then there had to be another frontier force. And Twain in his next novel, *A Connecticut Yankee in King Arthur's Court*, anticipated the hope of the progressive intellectuals that industrialism would provide that frontier force which could destroy civilization and liberate individuals to live by their inner natures. But Twain was to reject this possibility and argue that industrialism could not save mankind because evil was within the individual himself.

Once more Twain returned to the clash between modern progress and medieval blackness when he transported the Yankee from nineteenth-century America back into the Dark Ages. The Yankee has every modern technological skill and practicality with which to overthrow "that artful power, the Roman Catholic Church. In two centuries, it had converted a nation of men into a nation of worms! The Church had brought Englishmen to a completely subservient and passive level of patience, resignation, an uncomplaining acceptance of whatever fate befalls them in this life."

But at the end of the novel, after the Yankee has built schools and factories to make the people free; rational, and prosperous, they turn against him and fight for the Church to destroy his new world of business enterprise and technological efficiency.

Unable to believe that either nature or technology had the power to destroy the medievalism written in the human heart, Twain turned in 1890 to a medieval saint, Joan of Arc, in the hope that her miraculous career could provide insight into possible ways of transcending the evil of civilization. Grimly Twain wrote that this "is to be a serious book. . . . It means more to me than anything I have ever undertaken." Joan, he continued, was unique and her personality "is one to be reverently studied, loved and marveled at, but not to be wholly understood and accounted for by even the most searching analysis. . . . All the rules fail in this girl's case. In the world's history, she stands alone—quite alone. . . . She rose above the limitations and infirmities of our human nature." But her martyrdom had been in vain, she had not redeemed mankind from those limitations and infirmities by her death, and mankind remained in darkness. There was no hope.

At the beginning of the 1890s Twain wrote that he was living "in the noonday glory of the Great Civilization, a witness of its gracious and beautiful youth, witness of its middle time of gaunt power, sordid splendor and mean ambitions, and witness also of its declining vigor and the first stages of its hopeless retreat before the resistless forces which itself had created and which were to destroy it . . . wonderful in scientific marvels . . . in material inflation which it calls Progress. . . . It is a civilization, which has destroyed the simplicity and repose of life; replaced its contentment, its poetry . . . with money-fever."

His final vision of the American future was a holocaust created by an engineer-dictator who destroyed everything with the finest product of American science and technology—the ultimate weapon.

Twain's realism, his exploration of the gap between the ideal of American natural perfection in 1865 and the growing cultural complexity of the 1870s and 1880s, was paralleled by the other two great American novelists of his generation, William Dean Howells and Henry James. Both assumed in the 1860s that the United States was a nation of free, innocent, and virtuous individuals, a chosen people who had escaped the corruption and conflict of Europe. Both wrote novels that described the attempt of American individuals to live by this myth. But Howells and James, unlike Twain, had decided by 1890 that the ideal of the innocent and self-reliant American individual, the American Adam, was not only unworkable but even evil. Howells, in his great novel of 1890, *The Hazard of New Fortunes*, described the alienation of the American farmer who had become rich. Dryfoos is alienated because he cannot create social attachments to his wife and children, to his neighbors and workers. Trapped by the doctrine of self-sufficiency, he is isolated from humanity and doomed to loneliness. Howells' alternative, what he had come to describe as the destructiveness of competitive individualism, was expressed in the 1890s by his Altrurian romance as utopian socialism.

Henry James also came to describe the concept of the free individual as one that led to the impoverishment of the individual through alienation from other human beings and from that treasure of collective human effort, artistic cultural creativity. His novels, like *The American*, *Portrait of a Lady*, and *The Ambassadors*, stressed the need of Americans for the humanity and the art of Europe. But until his last great novel, *The Golden Bowl*, he wrote about American individuals who refused to recognize these needs and who, because they did not surrender their concept of self-sufficiency, could not develop meaningful relations to other human beings or to culture. Then, in *The Golden Bowl*, he created a heroine, Maggie Verver, who does discover her need to surrender her autonomy to the social institution of marriage. Maggie, for James, discovers that love requires sacrifice and violation of one's independence to bring about a greater fulfillment in union with someone else.

But the next generation of novelists, Stephen Crane, Theodore Dreiser, and Frank Norris, broke dramatically from the discovery by these realists of the significance of the cultural context for human activity. Instead, beginning to write in the 1890s, they are known as naturalists because they reaffirmed that the crucial environment for man was physical nature and not culture.

Frank Norris, especially, reached out to the Darwinian theory of evolutionary nature as an alternative to the Jeffersonian concept of nature as a peaceable kingdom. In this way, he, like William Graham

Sumner, could deny that the disharmony which characterized the 1880s and 1890s was the result of growing cultural complexity. He too, with Sumner, could argue that disharmony was the definition of nature itself and must be accepted because man had no choice but to live by the laws of nature. And as Sumner tried to escape Donnelly's vision of doom, so Norris tried to escape the vision of Twain.

In Frank Norris' novel, *The Octopus*, published in 1901, one can find the clearest expression of Social Darwinism as the philosophic basis for literary naturalism. Here Norris accepted explicitly the theory of the classical economists that the disharmony of the nineteenth century was radically different from that of the past. Cultural disharmony had been corrupting; men had wandered in a wilderness of meaningless institutions and traditions, but modern man in accepting laissez-faire had escaped from the evil of manmade law and he lived now in the redemptive disharmony of the great natural law of evolution. Norris accepted the theory of evolution operating according to the mechanism of competition, of survival of the fittest. In a competitive capitalist society, evolution would force men to progress upwards, always weeding out the unfit, until finally there was a saving remnant of cleansed and purified people deserving of citizenship in the heavenly city of earth.

The central theme of *The Octopus* is the education of a young man, Presley. Presley is to be taught the falsity of the Jeffersonian view of nature and the truth of the Darwinian. He is to be taught the falsity of the Populist view that artificial economic institutions are destroying the peaceable kingdom of the yeoman farmer.

The novel begins as Presley, a poet, arrives in California to write the great American poem. He believes that he can find inspiration for this epic in the West because there, "a new race, a new people— hardy—brave, and passionate—were building an empire; where the tumultuous life ran like fire from dawn to dark, and from dark to dawn again, primitive, brutal, honest and without fear."

Norris described Presley as holding almost a parody of Frederick Jackson Turner's frontier thesis. Presley has fled the cities and the factories of the East, hoping to find on the Pacific coast an oasis of virgin land. Presley wants the inspiration of Jefferson's Republic with its promise of timeless harmony; he wants to recapture its faith in a nature serene in its completeness, to find inspiration for his poem in a dream Norris claims never was and never can be. Presley is presented as a naive romantic who is persuaded that his fantasy expresses the reality of nature.

But Presley, and every American, is to be taught by Norris the truth about nature. Presley has taken up residence on a wheat ranch in a vast, fertile valley of California to achieve organic harmony with the land and the farmers. But he cannot write. The farmers are not living in harmony; even here on the last frontier eastern complexity has disturbed the artless marriage of man and land. Into this last stronghold of the American state of nature, there has crept the octopus, the railroad.

All is lost for Presley and America unless this small band of farmers, the last American free men, begin a second American revolution which will destroy the octopus and lift the tyranny of human institutions from the land. The railroad, for Presley, is "the symbol of a vast power, huge, terrible, flinging the echo of its thunder over all the reaches of the valley." Smashing through a flock of sheep, smashing through American agrarian innocence, "leaving blood and destruction in its path," this is "the leviathan, with tentacles of steel clutching into the soil, the soulless Force, the iron-hearted Power, the Monster, the Colossus, the Octopus."

Presley has achieved a vision of doom for the American Eden which parallels that of Ignatius Donnelly and Mark Twain. But, like Donnelly, he still remains true to his Jeffersonian-Jacksonian principles, to a belief that there can be progress away from complexity to simplicity. After all, human institutions are artificial; they have no intrinsic strength. Farmers, men of the soil, are so strengthened by nature that even this small band of embattled men may begin to turn the tide and destroy the vast urban-industrial complex which has spread from Europe across the East and ever farther west.

For Presley, like Ignatius Donnelly, the railroad represents a financial conspiracy by evil men. The farmers have only to fight a parasitical alien like the railroad representative, S. Behrman, "a large, fat man, with a great stomach; his chest and the upper part of his thick neck ran together to form a great tremulous jowl, shaven and blue-grey in colour; a roll of fat, sprinkled with sparse hair, moist in perspiration, protruded over the back of his collar."

In contrast to this villain, as wicked as any in Donnelly's *Caesar's Column* or *The Golden Bottle*, Presley finds a clear-eyed hero, ap-

parently as virtuous as any described by Donnelly. Magnus Derrick
seems like one of the patriot leaders who inspired their neighbors in
that spring of 1775 to take a stand against British tyranny.

> Here in this corner of a great nation, here on the edge of the
> continent, here in this valley of the West, far from the great
> centres, isolated, remote, lost, the great iron hand crushes life
> from us, crushes liberty.... Yet it is Lexington—God help us. God
> enlighten us. God rouse us from our lethargy—it is Lexington;
> farmers with guns in their hands fighting for liberty.... is it not
> symbolical of the great and terrible conflict that is going on
> everywhere in these United States?

Presley prepares now to write his epic poem to glorify the victory
of the yeomen against the forces of feudal darkness. How can they
lose, when they are led by a great hero, a latter-day Jackson, Magnus
Derrick, who represents the Jeffersonian republic. Here "was the
last protest of the Old School, rising up there in denunciation of the
new order of things, the statesman opposed to the politician; honesty,
rectitude. Uncompromising integrity prevailing for the last time
against the devious maneuvering... the rotten expediency of a corrupted institution."

Then before the poet's horrified eyes the farmers are shot down
behind their barricades, their lands are taken, their widows and
orphans driven into poverty, even prostitution. Apparently the evil
Behrman has triumphed. And why not? Why should Presley expect
this miracle when the Octopus has won every battle beginning in
the East, continuing across the Midwest, and now culminating in
California. There is no more frontier. There is no more yeomanry.
Donnelly's prophecy of a twentieth-century America dwelling in
hellish corruption is to be fulfilled.

But suddenly Presley discovers that his description of the drama
is false because it is based on the premise that there has been a
yeomanry living in innocent harmony with nature. He discovers that
the farmers and their leader, Derrick, are as corrupt as S. Behrman.
They too lust for money and power. He remembers the cry of
Magnus Derrick, "For one moment to be able to strike back, to crush
his enemy, to defeat the railroad, hold the corporation in the grip
of his fist, put down S. Behrman.... to be once more powerful, to
command, to dominate." Here is no desire for harmony with nature,

no desire for innocence. How is Derrick different from Behrman? Is it not true that

> for all his public spirit, for all his championship of justice and truth, his respect for law, Magnus remained the gambler, willing to play for colossal stakes. . . . It was in this frame of mind that Magnus and the multitude of other ranchers . . . farmed their ranches. They had no love for their land. They were not attached to the soil. . . . To get all there was out of the land, to squeeze it dry, to exhaust it, seemed their policy. When, at last, the land was worn out, would refuse to yield, they would invest their money in something else.

Presley is no longer able to read American history as a dramatic conflict between virtuous yeomen and corrupt institutions. The farmers, because they too are corrupt, have been defeated by nature, not by the railroad. Norris now wants to reassure his readers that if nature is violent, it is nonetheless benevolent and redemptive. He wants them to have faith that a living, dynamic nature is making evolutionary progress toward an ultimate good and that this process, while it may appear superficially dreadful and cruel, is necessary to man's ultimate salvation.

This is the authentic nature that Presley discovers when he abandons the Jeffersonian concept that is sterile in its deathlike and rigid permanence. He has begun to find a new theme for his poem about the West, a West which symbolizes a vibrant, vital nature.

> Deep down there in the recesses of the soil, the great heart throbbed once more. Thrilling with passion, vibrating with desire, offering itself to the career of the plough, insistent, eager, imperious. Dimly one felt the deep-seated tremble of the earth, the uneasy agitation of its members, the hidden tumult of its womb, demanding to be made fruitful, to reproduce, to disengage the eternal renascent germ of Life that stirred and struggled in its loins.

The West is not people, fallible and corrupt; it is nature, strong and fertile. It is only in the seasons of the earth itself that there is drama. All human history is meaningless. Presley is now prepared to believe Shelgrim, president of the railroad, when he tells him that there is no octopus, that no human is responsible for the suffering of the farmers; the railroad is only a necessary adjunct to nature, necessary to distribute the fruits of her loins.

It rang with a clear reverberation of truth.... There was no malevolence in nature. Men ... were shot down in the very noon of life, hearts were broken, little children started in life lamentably handicapped; young girls were brought to a life of shame; old women died ... for lack of food. In that little isolated group of human insects, misery, death, and anguish spun like a wheel of fire. But the wheat remained. Untouched, unassailable, undefiled, that mighty world force ... wrapped in nirvanic calm ... moved onward in its appointed grooves.... Falseness dies; injustice and oppression ... fade and vanish away; greed, cruelty, selfishness, and inhumanity, are short-lived; the individual suffers but the race goes on.... The larger view always and through all shams, all wickednesses, discovers the truth that will, in the end, prevail, and all things, surely, inevitably, work together for the good.

And S. Behrman is suffocated by the wheat he has stolen from the farmers.

If Norris was right, Turner's fears that physical nature was being eclipsed by industrialism were mistaken. For Norris industrialism was a mechanism that served nature. And if Norris was right, Donnelly and Twain's fears that a complex civilization was destroying nature were equally mistaken. Nature could never by subdued by civilization. It would remain dominant and triumphant forever because it was not static but dynamic, not docile but conquering. If Norris was right, Americans should surrender all their fears of decadence and they should stop all their efforts at political, or economic, or social reform. Human action was irrelevant to the quality of life.

Stephen Crane, who died after only a decade of marvelous literary creativity, violently rejected Norris' worship of evolutionary nature. Instead, his writings in the 1890s explored the loneliness of a universe in which the ideal of redemptive nature had disappeared. Theodore Dreiser also was unable to share the boundless hope of Norris in the redemptive power of physical nature. Instead, Dreiser's novels between 1900 and World War I described the tragedy of individuals caught in the dualistic situation of being part both of artificial culture and physical nature. Like Norris, Dreiser promised that mankind would finally be absorbed into the ultimate evolutionary triumph of nature and all tragedy would be transcended. But in the meantime, in the lifetime of men and women at the beginning of the twentieth century, such transcendence was impossible and individuals suffered as they were forced to compromise with institutions and conventions even as their souls sought the absolute freedom of organic harmony with nature.

But most Americans of 1900 were rejecting Social Darwinism whether it was preached by academic economists like Sumner, or novelists like Norris and Dreiser. They did not reject the idea that men should live by natural law; rather they rejected the idea that natural law meant tooth and claw competition. More and more Americans, whether they were academic theoreticians or practical businessmen, were shifting to the belief that man was by nature cooperative. More and more Americans were defining cutthroat competition as a false theory which did not reflect reality. More and more Americans were willing to believe, with Veblen, that industrialism was facilitating a return to the cooperative nature of man and liberating the people from the unnatural doctrine of competition.

In the history of the novel, no talented writer appeared to give outstanding artistic expression to the views of a Beard or a Veblen. But one novelist, Winston Churchill, did capture in his books the conversion of much of middle-class America to the hope that the cooperative commonwealth, a middle-class millennium, was about to emerge in the opening decades of the twentieth century.

Winston Churchill wrote nine major novels. Five were the best sellers for the years in which they were published. Two were the second best sellers, one was third, and only one failed to evoke great response from America's middle-class readers. Churchill then is a cultural phenomenon of great importance even if he fails to achieve artistic greatness. What we find in his novels is a direct expression of the progressive argument that it was to be 1914, rather than 1828, when history was to end. It was then that men were to be redeemed and made innocent. It was then that the American garden was to be achieved.

Churchill had begun to explore the problems of the twentieth century from a perspective much like that of the Mugwumps and the old aristocracy of the late nineteenth century. In his first political novels, for example, *Coniston* and *Mr. Crewe's Career,* Churchill had described the corruption of nineteenth-century America by the doctrine of individual selfishness. He correlated the decline of national morality with the triumph of political democracy and laissez-faire capitalism. The villains of his pages, like the politician, Jethro Bass, are self-made men who suffer from the delusion that they have no responsibility to the community. These self-made men are corrupted by a culture which defines the self-sufficient individual as the only reality. And Churchill also contrasts these unhappy, these ceaselessly driven men with the surviving colonial aristocrats who had a sense of social responsibility and who could achieve personal equilibrium.

But Churchill was not content with the qualified virtue of those vestiges of aristocracy which continued to exist within the wider sea of middle-class corruption. He was straining to find a way to restore innocence to the land. Jethro Bass, for example, is lifted out of corruption by the innocent love of a young girl who is like a daughter to him. And in his next novel, *A Modern Chronicle,* Churchill wrote of the beauty of love that could bring the individual to transcend selfishness. As late as 1910, however, he argued that such acts of love might redeem individuals but not society.

But in 1913, when Churchill published *The Inside of the Cup,* it was obvious that he had become a convert to progressive millennialism. He was prepared to argue the intellectual possibility of the transcendence of corrupt culture by the hidden personality within each individual—a personality that was as perfect as Adam before the fall. Churchill had rejected all of his earlier doubts about the innate goodness of the individual. He accepted the progressive faith that all evil was from the environment. In making the Reverend John Hodder, an Episcopal minister, the central figure of his novel, Churchill was able to reject dramatically his own personal commitment to America's nineteenth-century aristocracy. The theology of the Reverend Hodder inevitably focuses on the innate sinfulness of man. And the close cultural relationship of his church to the existing aristocratic groups in America make it natural for him to believe in the importance of social structure to restrain the evil in men.

Churchill, who had previously defined himself as an aristocrat, an Episcopalian, and a patrician reformer, now has his hero experience a conversion to the religious faith of the social gospel. The optimism of the social gospel expressed in theological terms the

general faith of progressivism that evil was forced on the individual
by the institutions and traditions of society. It expressed the belief
that every individual was inherently good and that if each individual
were to refuse to act according to social standards, if each individual
were to act according to his instincts, the millennium would occur.
Hodder is suddenly brought to see that while he has not trusted individuals, "God trusted individuals. . . . What did that mean? Individual responsibility! He repeated it. Was the world on that
principle then? It was as though a searchlight were flung ahead of
him and he saw, dimly, a new order—a new order in government
and religion."

This new order is possible for Hodder because he now realizes
why God trusts individuals in spite of the record of history which
seems to demonstrate the evil of every man. Inspired by God,
Hodder sees beneath the surface to discover

> that we have a conscious, or lower, human self, and a sub-
> conscious, or better self. This subconscious self stretches down,
> as it were, into the depths of the universe and taps the source of
> spiritual power. And it is through the subconscious self that every
> man is potentially divine. Potentially, because the conscious self
> has to reach out by an effort of the will to effect this union with
> the spiritual in the subconscious. Apparently from without, as a
> gift, and therefore in theological language, it is called grace. This
> is what is meant by being "born again," the incarnation of the
> spirit in the conscious, or human. The two selves are no longer
> divided, and the higher self assumes control.

The Inside of the Cup is symbolically an autobiographical novel.
In it Churchill revealed the arguments that converted him to the
coming millennium. In his next novel, *A Far Country*, he began to
elaborate on his vision. Writing for a mass middle-class audience,
Churchill rejected the stereotype of the socialist created by middle-
class newspapers in the 1880s and 1890s. This stereotype had presented the socialist as an anti-Christ whose materialism was in
conflict with the spirituality of the middle class. Now, however,
Churchill reversed this stereotype. He created a sympathetic socialist, Hermann Krebs, who, preaching a gospel of love, converts
the middle-class hero of this book, Hugh Paret, to the inevitability
of the millennium because "the birthright of the spirit of man was
freedom, freedom to experiment, to determine, to create—to create

himself, to create society in the image of God." Krebs, as presented by Churchill, does not teach revolution by violence. Neither is he, however, an ethereal saint who has no contact with the realities of everyday existence. Instead Churchill describes him as having the earthly drive and the practical knowledge of a successful business leader.

But while, for Churchill, Americans must relearn the possibility of their dream from someone like Hermann Krebs and they must see it in terms of socialistic cooperation rather than laissez-faire capitalism, still the ultimate goal was the same as the Jeffersonian arcadia. The American Adam in an industrialized garden was still to enjoy "freedom from institutional restraint." In an article of 1916, "A Plea for the American Tradition," Churchill pointed out that the American socialist utopia was still an escape from Old World history because, unlike European socialist states, ours would have no institutionalized framework but would depend only on voluntary association and voluntary cooperation.

When one reads the intellectual biographies of the great philosophers of progressivism like Charles Beard, one becomes aware of the way in which the experience of World War I smashed their millennial dreams. The great prophets of the industrial utopia had their faith destroyed before their very eyes while they were still young men. Their apocalyptic dream suffered an apocalyptic death. They had marched to Armageddon, certain of victory, and the forces of darkness had risen up to annihilate the hosts of the virtuous. For those who had completely dedicated their hearts and their minds to the coming earthly kingdom, 1919 was almost beyond endurance. Winston Churchill was one of these.

As Churchill had observed the holocaust of war in Europe after 1914, he had gradually come to lose his faith in the essential goodness of man. By 1917, when Charles Beard was predicting a world made safe for democracy, this most popular novelist of progressivism had developed grave doubts about the possibility of democracy in the United States. His millennial vision had depended upon the triumph of the innocent individual over corrupt society. In 1917 Churchill published his last novel, *The Dwelling Place of Light.* He was never to write another because his faith in innocence symbolically perished in this book.

Janet Bumpus, the last of an old respected New England family, is symbolic of innocence. Thrown on her own by the economic decline of the family, she is forced to work in the Chippering Mills. Her life is momentarily made easier by the mill manager, Claude Ditmar, who makes her his secretary. Ditmar is symbolic of a capitalism that Churchill no longer believed to be in a process of redemption. He is thoroughly selfish and ruthless. His only concerns are profits and power. He dominates the mill and he wants to dominate Janet. Ultimately he does seduce her. Her innocence destroyed, pregnant, and alone, Janet flees from this man, this class, this system which exploits her body and which refuses to give her love. Her flight takes her toward the labor leader, Leonard Rolfe, hoping that this spokesman for the workers does represent a philosophy of love rather than exploitation. But once again she finds herself face to face with a man concerned only with materialism and power. Implicitly she is also face to face with another class and system which would treat her as a material commodity and refuse to give her love.

Now her only chance to survive, the only chance for innocence to continue to have a meaningful existence, rests with Brooks Insall, the symbolic representative of aristocratic tradition. But while that tradition survives in the twentieth century, it is basically impotent. Insall defines himself in this manner: "I? I'm a spectator—an innocent bystander." Powerless to reform America, Insall and the aristocratic tradition can provide no refuge for Janet and innocence.

By 1919, for Churchill, there was no chosen people in the New World which could isolate itself from the sinful brotherhood of mankind. The sinfulness of selfishness was the American way of life, of the rich and of the poor. Here there was no innocence to preserve, except that of the solitary individual who somehow retained personal virtue in the midst of social corruption. Broken in spirit and mind, Churchill withdrew from this world of chaos and war to survive behind the neutrality of a personal, separate peace. Stripped of his faith in progress, he had become a middle-aged prophet for the young novelists of the 1920s who, also stripped of their faith in progress, became a lost generation committed to a personal, separate peace.

Chapter X

Theodore Roosevelt and
the American Paradox

The large corporation had emerged as the dominant institution in American economic life at the beginning of the twentieth century. And its growth was accompanied by the increase in size of both the state and national governments which created administrative agencies to regulate the corporation. Both the spokesmen for big business and the American socialists argued that this trend to corporate giantism was natural and inevitable. For every business spokesman who wrote that "trusts are here and here to stay as the result of the inevitable laws of industrial development" and "the modern trust is the natural outcome or evolution of societary conditions and ethical standards which are recognized and established among men today as being necessary elements in the development of civilization," there was a socialist who added: "One cannot but acknowledge the natural development of the successive steps of monopoly. No better way could be invented by which the natural resources may be made available for the world's need. The lesson of trust, how to secure the greatest satisfaction for the least expenditure of human energy, is too good to be lost."

There is evidence that many leaders of the large corporations had concluded by the 1890s that the logic of the corporation, which must sustain a huge investment in buildings and inventory, in administrative bureauracy and work force, argued against vigorous price competition. Present stability and a planned and predictable future were necessary for the health of the corporation. It followed then that many corporate leaders began to encourage the national government to create regulatory agencies which would provide rules to rationalize and restrain competition. It was necessary for the stability of corporations that operated nationally to have this regulation by the national government rather than by the state governments, which might only encourage the kind of anarchic competition from which the business leaders were trying to escape.

There can be no doubt that the rapid growth of corporate and governmental bureaucracies encouraged a trend within the American cultural imagination toward administrative efficiency and scientific management. The expert in administration and science gained new prestige and power during these years between 1890 and 1917. But, on the other hand, there can be no doubt that the majority of Americans were not persuaded that their future lay within a corporate society or that the American version of the middle-class theory of history as the liberation of the individual from the medieval corporate society to be a self-sufficient, self-reliant atom of self-interest was dead.

As evidence for the continued vitality of the myth of the self-made man, it was during the years of the progressive movement that a new form of popular entertainment, vaudeville, became dominant. Directed toward the concentrated populations in the cities, it supplanted the circus and the minstrel show which had entertained small-town and rural America. The symbolic impact of vaudeville was to reinforce the traditional myth of success. When the urban lower- and lower middle-class people went to see a vaudeville show, they entered a palace of massive scale, with a most conspicuous and elegant facade decorated by rococo filigree and polished marble. Every patron was reminded that in America every man was a king and that every man could hope to become fabulously wealthy. And on stage they witnessed the competition of the artistic market place in which anonymous men and women could fight their way up to the national notoriety of star billing that would also provide great financial rewards.

If the fantasy life of the mass of Americans was alienated from the growing reality of the corporate structures which, ironically,

controlled the vaudeville circuits by national booking agencies which
determined when and where the performers would act, it was apparent also that much of the middle class was alienated from that
reality. In 1902 Owen Wister, a Harvard-educated, upper middle-
class aristocrat from the East, published his novel *The Virginian*.
It went through seventeen reprintings that year and has become one
of the ten best-selling novels in American publishing history. It was
the novel which has provided the cowboy archetype for most subsequent cowboy stories and movies.

Until *The Virginian* the figure of the cowboy had suffered in
contrast with the traditional mythological hero of the nineteenth
century, the yeoman farmer. Peaceful and settled, the farmer was
presented in literature from 1870 to 1900 as a figure of superior
virtue to the rootless and lawless cowboy. The realistic descriptions
of the heavy burden of farm work on both men and women, the
loneliness of farm life, the dependence on cruelly capricious weather,
and the endless financial problems of the farmer by writers like
Hamlin Garland, however, seriously undermined the yeoman myth
in the 1890s. And, of course, the farm was being replaced by the city
as the dwelling place for most of the population. If Americans were
going to continue to keep their identity as a natural and virtuous,
and not a civilized and decadent nation, a new mythical link with
nature was necessary. And Wister, by changing the rootlessness and
lawlessness of the cowboy from vices into virtues, made it possible
for the cowboy figure to provide that link in the twentieth century.

The hero of *The Virginian* is nameless. A child of the best stock
of the East, he had fled its complexity, decadence, and materialism
while only a youth to find freedom in the West. A self-made orphan
hero, he has found freedom from civilization by achieving harmony
with nature. "Often when I have camped here, it has made me want
to become the ground, become the water, become the trees, mix
with the whole thing. Not know myself from it. Never unmix again."

Wister's readers sensed that the Virginian was the archetypical
American; that he represented all the people who had left Europe
and families and history behind. They sensed that the West he came
to was no specific West but the entire United States. They knew
that the Virginian, like all Americans, was a natural aristocrat,
nature's nobleman, because only the best men survived when one
stepped out of civilization into nature. As the Virginian says, "Now
back East you can be middling and get along. But if you go to try

a thing on in this Western country, you've got to do it well. You've got to deal cards well; you've got to steal well; and if you claim to be quick with your gun, you must be quick."

Of course, for the American middle-class reader, the West, or America, was not to be pure nature, pure barbarism, pure savagery. It was to be a civilization married to nature; a civilization free to act boldly and decisively to keep itself pure; a civilization able to transcend its own rules when it was necessary to fight for survival. And so into the symbolic West comes Molly Stark Wood, eastern bred and refined, a perfect lady and the representative of civilization. She is incomplete, however, until she is married to the Virginian and learns to subordinate her manners to his natural actions, to subordinate her refinement to his virility, to subordinate her propriety to his decisiveness.

At first she is appalled by the Virginian's crudeness and directness. Instantly he decides that she must marry him and demands her hand without the elaborate indirection of civilized courtship. "You're goin' to love me before we get through," he tells her; "I wish you'd come a-ridin', Ma'am." Inevitably the Virginian wills her surrender as he wills the surrender of all who oppose him. He is the totally free man, free to dominate everyone because he gains his boundless strength from nature and expresses natural law. Responsible only to natural law, he is free to judge whether man-made law is to be obeyed or broken. He is aware of the way in which evil men often manipulate the laws of civilization for their own wicked ends.

Faced with the presence of evil men and evil conditions, the Virginian challenges evil directly on the field of battle in the classic confrontation of virtue and vice. Unaided, alone, the man of nature wills his victory over the enemy at a personal Armageddon and kills the symbol of the serpent which has slithered into the American garden. Miss Molly must accept the holy nature of the crusade, she must accept the fact that the end justifies the means, even though it shatters her sense of propriety and law when the Virginian leaves her side on their wedding day to seek the final solution of a duel to the death outside the courts of law. She must capitulate completely to this man of nature and put complete trust in his ability to distinguish between good natural law and bad social law.

These are the frightening implications of this fantasy that became so popular for the American middle-class public which demanded endless repetitions of this cowboy story by other novelists and by the infant movie industry between 1902 and 1917. Clearly there was tremendous demand for a salvation figure who could cut the Gordian knot of complexity and corruption and restore the community to absolute purity and stability. Here was a fantasy life that completely contradicted the apparent logic of the corporation on rationality and pragmatic compromise.

Owen Wister dedicated *The Virginian* to his friend and Harvard classmate, Theodore Roosevelt, because, Wister wrote, Roosevelt "had been the pioneer in taking the cowboy seriously, and I loved what he said about that bold horseman of the plains." And during his presidency, from 1901 to 1909, Roosevelt was to be constantly associated with the cowboy in the public's mind. It was almost inevitable then that when Roosevelt died in 1919, the great cartoonist of the progressive period, J. N. Darling, drew him "in cowboy dress, on his horse headed for the Great Divide; but he is turning back for a last look at us, smiling, waving his hat. On his horse: the figure from other days; the apparition; the Crusader, bidding us farewell."

Both in his own self-image and in the image popular with the American people, Roosevelt symbolizes how much of nineteenth-century romanticism survived through the years 1890 to 1917.

Theodore Roosevelt was one of the many eastern upper middle-class aristocrats who feared that the United States was becoming decadent at the end of the nineteenth century because the people had surrendered their spirituality to materialism. Certainly Roosevelt agreed with the sentiments that Wister expressed through his cowboy hero. Briefly, the Virginian has returned home after his flight to the West. "When I went back," the Virginian states, "I was twenty. They was talking about the same old things. Men of twenty-five or thirty—yet just sittin' and talkin' about the same old things . . . when I found this whole world was hawgs and turkeys to them . . . I put on my hat one mawnin' and told 'em maybe when I was fifty I'd look in on 'em again to see if they'd got any new subjects. But they'll never. My brothers don't seem to want chances."

But both Wister and Roosevelt felt the need to try to force Americans to change and to take chances. While Wister tried to inspire the people with his writings, Roosevelt tried to save the people through his public career.

In 1880 Roosevelt found his America to be characterized by the alienation of labor, by the decay of small towns and farm life, by social fragmentation in the cities, and above all by increasing materialism, a growing concern for security and comfort. He decided to dedicate his life to attempting to halt the course of his nation to destruction. And he called upon his readings in the mid-nineteenth-century historians, Bancroft, Prescott, Motley, and Parkman, for the course of action he would follow.

He was persuaded that the Europeans who came to America had escaped a sick society and formed a healthy one because the challenge of overcoming the wilderness had blended them into a dedicated, spiritual unity. This military unity had been reinforced by the challenges of both the American Revolution and the Civil War which had further welded the people into a single whole, committed to the welfare of the nation rather than concerned with selfish interest.

From the romantic historians he learned that at every moment of crisis a hero emerged who encouraged the people to reach their full idealistic potential. Normally the people were divided between higher and lower motives. It was the function of the democratic hero to inspire the people to transcend their baseness and live completely by their ideals.

In order to fulfill this inspirational function, the hero must prepare himself by purging his own weaknesses and developing his own strength. Roosevelt had gone to a ranch in the Dakota territories explicitly to strengthen his body and to derive spiritual vitality from the frontier. He was the Virginian, and it was his responsibility to marry the American East and teach it that it needed to keep in constant communication with nature if it was not to become lost within the artificialities of civilization. Roosevelt was horrified by "the preposterous ignorance of all our people in the matter of the relative superiority of at least certain forms of barbarism over the hyper-civilized man of the great industrial centers, and especially of the cities."

From the romantic historians, however, Roosevelt had learned that the hero could not inspire the people until they realized that they were in a severe crisis and had to make a choice between good and evil. While Roosevelt had strengthened his body and soul for the moment when the people would need his heroic leadership, the people clearly were not yet ready. They did not yet see the disintegration of their community. For the moment, at the end of the 1880s, all Roosevelt could do was to try to enlighten the public through his writings and to hasten the moment when the people would see that they must choose between a completely decadent materialism or a return to spiritual frontier conditions.

And so he wrote volume after volume about the American past, to instruct his fellow citizens in the redemptive qualities of frontier togetherness because "it is . . . of the utmost benefit to have men thrown together under circumstances which force them to realize their community of interest." The challenge of frontier conditions had kept Americans spiritual. Again and again in articles and speeches he proclaimed: "We cannot afford to let the old pioneer virtues lapse. . . . We must insist upon the strong, virile virtues."

In the 1890s Roosevelt began to believe that only a war could recreate the kind of frontier challenge that would force the people back to spirituality. Every war, he declared, "without any exception whatever, has left us better off, taking both moral and material considerations into account, than we should have been if we had not waged it." After all, Roosevelt continued, "the qualities needed to make a good soldier, in their final analysis, are the qualities needed to make a good citizen. . . . The democratic ideal must be that of subordinating chaos to order, of subordinating the individual to the community, of subordinating individual selfishness to collective self sacrifice for a lofty ideal."

Roosevelt was delighted, therefore, when war came with Spain and he gathered his Rough Riders to perform heroic charges in Cuba. But, at the war's conclusion, he decided that it had been too small and too brief to purge the people of selfishness and materialism. He came to the presidency, then, feeling that the times were not yet ready for heroic leadership. But, at the same time, he felt that he had a duty to maintain the minimum amount of national unity that McKinley had achieved by declaring war on Spain.

In Roosevelt's view of American politics, the Republican Party had been born to meet the challenge of national disunity. In its origins, therefore, it was pure and holy. To a considerable extent it had maintained that purpose. And Roosevelt felt he must work within its institutional framework to sustain that tradition as long as possible.

Historians have often described Theodore Roosevelt as a politician who transcended the romantic anti-institutionalism of nineteenth-century America to lead the way toward the realism of the twentieth century which accepted the inevitability of institutional structure and of the need of the individual to compromise with institutions. Certainly Roosevelt did compromise with Republican politics in New York State and City during the 1880s and 1890s. Certainly, too, as President and head of the national Republican Party, he demonstrated a keen sense of what reforms he could and could not win from Congress. His leadership was that of the art of the possible. And he encouraged the growth of administrative agencies, staffed by bureaucratic experts, to rationalize the new corporate America.

But it is important to realize that until 1910 Roosevelt defined the Republican Party as the necessary vehicle for national unity. It alone served to restrain the quickening process of social chaos and selfish materialism. He had no comparable sympathy for the institutional existence of the Democratic Party. He had no commitment to a two-party system. And when he came to believe that the Republican Party had lost its viability between 1910 and 1912, he had no hesitation in deserting it and calling for partyless democracy that would see the spontaneous expression of the will of the people.

As President, Roosevelt accepted the existence of industrialism and the inevitable growth of the corporation. He stated that "I am in no sense hostile to corporations. This is an age of combination." Roosevelt also recognized the necessary existence of labor unions as part of an industrial age. But he wanted these organizations to subordinate their special interests to national interest. Philosophically, therefore, he was opposed to free competition that expressed only self-interest, or to collective bargaining that expressed only self-interest. It is not surprising, then, that the platform of his Progressive Party in 1912 should include a plank for national regulation of interstate corporations because then "the businessman will have certain knowledge of the law, and will be able to conduct his business easily in conformity therewith; the investor will find security for his capital; dividends will be rendered more certain[;] ... under such a system of constructive regulation, legitimate business, freed from confusion, uncertainty and fruitless litigation, will develop normally."

Until 1910 Roosevelt's ideal remained that of perfect organic harmony for the nation, but his political leadership was that of artfully balancing conflicting and competing interests and groups to keep the existing imperfect unity from further disintegrating. Then, however, he believed that Taft had allowed this fragile unity to break down. As he approached 1912 Roosevelt, therefore, could say that the Republican Party had lost its spiritual role as the custodian of national unity and become as artificial and divisive as the Democratic Party. Now total chaos faced the nation and the time had come for him to play the heroic role of a Washington or Lincoln and unite the people in a moment of major crisis. Now he could directly appeal to the spiritual side of the people and ask them to declare war against evil.

In 1912, as he provided leadership for a new party, Roosevelt had fallen back on the traditional nineteenth-century American political ideology of a classless people whose will must be expressed directly rather than thwarted and corrupted by the artificial institutions of political parties. Roosevelt proclaimed himself the representative hero of the American democracy, the hero of

> the plain, everyday citizen. . . . The men of whom I am always thinking, and whose emotions and convictions I understand and represent, are men like those whom I meet at railway employees conventions, or out on ranches, or down at the lodge, where I come into contact with the bagman, the oyster-sloop captain, the express agent, the brakeman, the farmer, the small storekeeper, the man who is my cousin's gardener, my own chauffeur, and others like them. They are men beside whom I have fought the battle, beside whom I struggle in politics, with whose business and domestic ideals I sympathize.

He was opposed now, Roosevelt wrote, to the materialistic business establishment:

> According to their own lights, these men are often very respectable, very worthy, but they live on a plane of low ideals. In the atmosphere they create, imposters flourish, and leadership comes to be thought of only as success in making money . . . and all that is highest and purest in human nature is laughed at, and honesty is bought and sold in the market place.
>
> . . .
>
> Opposed undyingly to these men are the men of faith and vision, the men in whom love of righteousness burns like a flaming fire, who spurn lives of soft and selfish ease, of slothful self-indulgence, who scorn to think only of pleasure for themselves, who feel for and believe in their fellows, whose high fealty is

reserved for all that is good, that is just, that is honorable. By their very nature, these men are bound to battle for the truth and the right.

. . .

We fight, fearless of the future, unheeding of our individual fates; with unflinching hearts and undimmed eyes; we stand at Armageddon, and we battle for the Lord.

Roosevelt was not daunted by defeat. He had acted as a hero. He had lost, but were the people defeated? Had the Progressive Party served as a vehicle to begin to mobilize the people for the crusade that would purge materialism and decadence and restore the virile, barbarian virtues of the frontier past? Roosevelt believed that it had. And when World War I began, this hope was reinforced by the possibility that American participation in a great war would result in perfect spiritual unity.

Momentarily Roosevelt was discouraged by the actions of President Wilson whom Roosevelt defined as an antihero. Instead of calling on the people to develop their spiritual and martial virtues, Wilson asked them to strengthen their materialistic and decadent vices; he asked them to follow "a flabby cosmopolitanism" and "a flabby pacifism." He asked them to engage in "national emasculation." But at last the United States went to war and Roosevelt proclaimed that our entry marked "the moral salvation of our people. ...It has lifted us out of the stew of sordid materialism. It has brought us face to face with eternal verities which were manfully faced by our fathers.... It has taught us again to realize the worth of the great basic virtues."

Roosevelt defined the role of the hero as that of transcending the multiplicity of competing and conflicting institutions to achieve a vision of organic unity. Then the hero was to persuade the people to follow him away from chaos to order, away from materialism to spirituality. This victory of the hero and the people was essentially the triumph of his and their will.

The irony or paradox of Roosevelt's popular reputation when he was President was that he was not seen as a conservative attempting to check the disintegration of the community through the use of the institution of the Republican Party. Rather, from the very beginning of his presidency, he was interpreted in the press as a representative hero of the common people who would cut through the complexities of the institutional establishment to reestablish freedom for the average individual to pursue his own self-interest and to create his own career. Roosevelt was seen as a cowboy hero who would destroy all bullies and inspire the common people to imitate the cowboy's self-reliance and self-sufficiency.

Many of the newspapers, therefore, described Roosevelt as a second Andrew Jackson who, like Old Hickory, was saving the American masses from oppression by artificial and evil special interests. In describing Roosevelt in these terms, the newspapers also repeated the similarity between Roosevelt's preparation for political warfare and for actual warfare against an artificial and evil enemy. Like Jackson's victory at New Orleans, Roosevelt's in Cuba was described as the triumph of the simple man of nature willing the defeat of a complex, institutionalized army.

Roosevelt was a hundred feet in the lead. Up, up they went in the face of death, men dropping from the ranks at every step. The Rough-Riders acted like veterans. It was an inspiring sight and an awful one.... At last the top of the hill was reached. The Spaniards in the trenches could still have annihilated the Americans, but the Yankees' daring amazed them. They wavered for an instant, and then turned and ran.

> If the wounded sobbed, it was not from pain,
> But that they could fight no more,
> Then vollying low at the hidden foe,
> They rushed him—two to ten;
> They were trained in the rule of an iron school,
> And they were their colonel's men.

"Young Roosevelt," the newspaper reporters recounted, "was born with an iron, indomitable will, that never recoiled before any obstacle. His career is another illustration of the truth that that which a man wills to become, that he is sure to become."

And the famous muckraking reporter, Jacob Riis, added:

It was one of the things that early attracted me to Theodore Roosevelt, long before he became famous, that he was a believer in the gospel of will. Nothing is more certain, humanly speaking, than this, that what a man wills himself to be, that he will be. Is he willing to put in all on getting rich, rich he will get; will he have power, knowledge, strength—they are all within his grasp.

Ambitious Americans who feared that the corporations were closing the door to upward mobility for the individual were reassured then by the newspapers which stated that "the story of Roosevelt will always be an inspiration to struggling, limited youth: for he is the very pattern, in a new sense, of a self-made man." Because he was a self-made man in the White House, he was reported to be a fighter against privilege.

Mr. Roosevelt offends the vanity of sundry railway magnates by compelling them to enter the White House during the same hours and through the same doors as do Messrs. Smith and Jones and Brown and Robinson and others of the common herd. In this hour, as in the time of General Jackson, that president who really practices democracy makes himself to certain eyes a peril and a threat.... The devouring dragon of the Jacksonian Age was the iniquitous Biddle bank. General Jackson destroyed it, as Mr. Roosevelt destroyed the Northern merger and curbed the villainy of Coal. And, for so coming to the public rescue, those Tories loathed General Jackson as the Tories of today loathe Mr. Roosevelt.

Again and again Roosevelt was identified in terms comparable to those of the new stars of vaudeville, as a common man whose success proved the possibility of success for all common men, if only they imitated the vitality and enthusiasm of the vaudeville entertainers or the President.

Roosevelt, more than any man I ever knew, is "energizing" to the full extent of his capacities. His command of his capacities is even more remarkable than the capacities themselves.

In no one of his varied faculties, except in this faculty of "energizing" is Roosevelt a remarkable man.... In talking with many people who have met Roosevelt for the first time I have been impressed by their comments upon his "familiarity," his "commonness." He is "just like one of us."

The marvelous thing in his career is the way in which he has used his commonplace qualities—in every possible direction. His versatility amazes one; his energy is appalling; and yet it is only commonness energized to the Nth degree.

While Roosevelt and a large group of the intellectuals of the progressive period longed for a strong man of iron will to overcome the fragmentation of society and to reestablish organic community, many other Americans longed for a strong man of iron will to break through an increasingly rigid corporate and bureaucratic establishment and reopen traditional frontiers of individual opportunity. And many saw Theodore Roosevelt as just such a liberating hero.

Chapter XI

Woodrow Wilson and World War I: Armageddon for Progressivism

The major patterns of the intellectual history of the years 1890 to 1917 emerged as a result of the impact of advancing industrialization on America's established identity as a nation in harmony with physical nature. Americans in 1890 believed that they were a chosen people because their ancestors had escaped from the cultural complexity of Europe, a complexity characterized by conflict, to the natural simplicity of the New World where timeless peace was possible. They believed, therefore, that as long as they did not create new patterns of cultural complexity, conflict would not be part of the national scene.

Then, in the 1890s, Americans were forced to acknowledge that the frontier of virgin land was being replaced by industrialism. If they defined industrialism as cultural complexity, then their dream of the United States as a restored Eden was ended. But the dream could be saved if it was possible to define industrialism as itself a frontier force that destroyed cultural complexity and led to natural harmony.

Between 1890 and 1917 many middle-class intellectuals and businessmen did come to define industrialism in this way and escaped the pessimism of the 1890s to participate in an increasing optimism that a new and more democratic order was about to appear; that out of the conflict of the 1880s and 1890s a new peaceable kingdom was to appear; that 1912, rather than 1789, might bring perfect order out of chaos.

This dramatic new description of industrialism as a frontier force necessarily brought a radically new perspective on the relation of the United States to the rest of the world. Up to the 1890s the national identity as a chosen nation in harmony with physical nature logically pointed to a policy of isolation. The only way for Europeans to escape cultural complexity was to leave the Old World to come to the New. Their salvation, their chance to be born again by stepping out of history, depended upon the openness of the American frontier, the vast expanse of the physical frontier.

This attitude had been given official statement in the Monroe Doctrine of the 1820s which assumed that the western hemisphere was characterized by freedom and the eastern hemisphere by tyranny. It assumed that tyranny would endure forever in an Old World that was beyond redemption by the New. It also assumed that freedom would endure forever in the New World unless European evil could establish itself here by conspiracy. And, of course, the melodramatic definition of the Spanish-American War was built on these philosophic premises of the Monroe Doctrine. Then the last symbol of medieval presence in the New World had been purged.

But now, if the individual was to find the opportunity to be born again within the industrial frontier, the logic of American isolation was ended. Industrialism was an international economic force. It followed, therefore, that it could work as an international frontier force. Everywhere throughout the world men could be saved from the established institutions and traditions which caused chaos and conflict. Everywhere men could be lifted out of the artificial into harmony with the natural. No permanent distinction between Old and New Worlds was possible.

This outlook which was so important in Beard's historical writings, in Veblen's economic theory, in Dewey's philosophical position, could be interrelated with the ideas of men like Strong and Mahan and the business leaders of the 1890s who were arguing the need for American overseas expansion to find markets for the nation's surplus industrial productivity.

With growing momentum, then, the United States between 1890

and 1917 was turning away from isolation toward theories of internationalism, peaceful and warlike, altruistic and imperialistic. But in relating themselves to the outside world, most Americans did so in terms of their tradition of exceptionalism. The new industrial and international identity was related to the belief that the United States indeed had been purer and more virtuous than any other nation in the nineteenth century because of its frontier heritage. Increasingly, many Americans defined their country as carrying the responsibility of helping the rest of the world make the transition from darkness into light. Increasingly, many Americans seemed to take Theodore Roosevelt's concept of the hero as the salvation figure for his community and apply it to the United States which would act as a redemptive hero for the entire community of nations. Just as Americans demanded that if they surrendered their traditional individualism to enter into domestic community, that community must be perfectly pure, so Americans were demanding that if they surrendered their traditional nationalism to enter into international community, that community must be perfectly pure.

In 1912 and 1914 Theodore Roosevelt had condemned Woodrow Wilson, a college professor and college president, as a symbol of growing American decadence, of the loss of the patriotic virtue of vital and heroic aggressiveness in the name of national honor. It is ironic, therefore, that it was to be Woodrow Wilson who led the United States into World War I within an ideological context which could have been taken from the cowboy saga written by Roosevelt's friend Owen Wister.

Wister's Virginian had defined his escape from the East to the West as an escape from materialism to idealism. And Wilson defined the flight of Europeans from the Old World to the New in just such terms. "Sometimes people call me an idealist," Wilson wrote. "Well, that is why I know I am an American. America is the only idealistic nation in the world."

Wilson had described the progressive movement as a religious purge in which the nation had been cleansed of a wicked conspiracy by selfish men to destroy the heritage of national virtue established by the Founding Fathers:

The Nation has been deeply stirred, stirred by a solemn passion, stirred by the knowledge of wrong, of ideals lost, of government too often debauched and made an instrument of evil. The feelings with which we face this new age of right and opportunity sweep across our heartstrings like some air out of God's own presence, where justice and mercy are reconciled and the judge and the brother are one.

Wilson believed that the fundamental American social structure was that of a middle class of free individuals without an aristocracy or peasantry or proletariat in a European sense. Because of the selfishness of a few businessmen and the corruption of a few politicians, America had been threatened by the growth of a plutocracy which also brought the threat of a proletariat.

"I should be ashamed of myself," Wilson declared, "if I excited class feeling of any kind. . . . The government of our country cannot be lodged in any special class." The reform policies of his administration, he continued, would destroy these un-American classes, the plutocracy and the proletariat, through "regulated competition of a sort that will put the weak upon an equality with the strong." America, he affirmed, insists "upon recovering in practice those ideals which she has always professed, upon securing a government devoted to the general interest and not to special interest." Wilson saw himself and his fellow progressives as gardeners who were removing the "rank weeds" of plutocratic monopoly power "which were to choke out all wholesome life in the fair garden of affairs." Like the cowboy hero, the progressive was destroying evil that was alien to the community. For cowboy and progressive, reform was a showdown, a quick battle to the death between fundamental good and ephemeral evil.

By 1914, therefore, Wilson was certain that the reform legislation passed under his administration had resolved the national crisis by cleansing the American garden, and he was ready to turn his full attention to the unexpected war in Europe. Here his first reaction to the international tragedy was that "Europe is still governed by the same reactionary forces which controlled this country." But he was also certain in 1914 that the war marked a revolutionary moment in history when those forces could be purged in the Old World as in the New. And so he declared to Europe: "I say to you that the old order is dead. It is my part . . . to aid in composing those differences . . . that the new order, which shall have its foundation on human liberty and human rights, shall prevail."

Contrary to Roosevelt's estimate that he was a timid and effeminate academic, Wilson, who had been raised in the South, the son of a Presbyterian minister, had all the confidence of a Calvinist that he had been elected by God to fulfill the divine will in this world. Early in life he had confided that "I should be complete if I could inspire a great movement of opinion." His self-image was very much that of Roosevelt's hero, who in a moment of crisis could demonstrate "the power of leadership . . . of the man of literary ability in the field of diplomacy." Between 1914 and 1917 Wilson was filled with concern for how he could use American idealism to redeem Europe and add the Old World to the New as an example of the fulfillment of God's heavenly kingdom on earth.

This concept of America as a redeemer nation which could purify the entire world was widespread among Wilson's fellow college presidents, like David Starr Jordan of Stanford, who, in his book *America's Conquest of Europe*, published in 1913, proclaimed that "America stands, has always stood, for two ideals from which she cannot escape, for they are fundamental in her origin and in her growth. These are internationalism and democracy, and these ideals, being invincible, must conquer America and, through her, conquer Europe. . . . The conquest of the world by the ideals of internationalism and democracy marks the coming of universal peace."

And Wilson's first secretary of state, William Jennings Bryan, reinforced his President's messianic dream by declaring:

Behold a republic increasing in population, in wealth, in strength and in influence, solving the problems of civilization and hastening the coming of a universal brotherhood—a republic which shakes thrones and dissolves aristocracies by its silent example and gives light and inspiration to those who sit in darkness. Behold a republic gradually but surely becoming the supreme moral factor in the world's progress and the accepted arbiter of the world's disputes—a republic whose history, like the path of the just, "is as the shining light that shineth more and more unto the perfect day."

Together, Wilson and Bryan had continued Theodore Roosevelt's policy of frequent military intervention in the political life of Caribbean and Central American nations. But they disclaimed Roosevelt's motives of strategy and power and instead insisted that it was only natural that a purified United States should begin its mission of world salvation in the western hemisphere. As Wilson simply stated,

"I am going to teach the South American republics to elect good men." Or when Wilson refused to recognize the legitimacy of a new revolutionary government in Mexico, he explained that he could approve and recognize no leaders but "those who act in the interest of peace and honor, who protect private rights, and respect the restraints of constitutional provisions."

Therefore, when Wilson asked Americans in 1914 to "act and speak in the true spirit of neutrality, which is the spirit of impartiality and fairness and friendliness to all concerned," he was not speaking out of cowardice as Theodore Roosevelt claimed, out of unwillingness to use military strength to solve international problems. In his use of the armed forces to accomplish the moral education of Latin Americans, Wilson had proved his commitment to the philosophy of virtue through violence which he had declared in 1911: "There are times in the history of nations when they must take up the instruments of bloodshed in order to vindicate spiritual conceptions, and when men take up arms to set other men free, there is something sacred and holy in the warfare. I will not cry 'peace' so long as there is sin and wrong in the world."

Rather Wilson was entirely sincere when he declared that this was "a war with which we have nothing to do, whose causes cannot touch us." For him there was in the fall of 1914 no clearcut moral distinction between Germany and Austria-Hungary on one side and England and France and their allies on the other. Again, like Wister's Virginian, Wilson was reluctant to commit himself until the identity of the villain and his victim became very clear. And throughout 1915 and 1916 Wilson was not able to make such a distinction. Certainly he believed that the leaders of Germany were wicked men, but he also questioned the motives of the English and French leaders.

Defining both sides as typical of the European tradition of moral corruption, Wilson advised his fellow citizens to hold themselves aloof until the wicked belligerents had so destroyed themselves, or at least so exhausted themselves, that the United States could go to Europe and create "an association of nations, all bound together for the protection of the integrity of each," as association based on the "recognition of equal rights between small nations and great." Therefore, he urged: "Let us think of America before we think of Europe, in order that America may be fit to be Europe's friend when the day of tested friendship comes." "We," he continued, "are the mediating nation of the world.... We are compounded of the nations of the world.... We are, therefore, able to understand all nations." Finally, Wilson exhorted the people to still further acceptance of the burden of New World moral superiority: "I am interested in neutrality because there is something so much greater to do than fight; there is a distinction waiting for this Nation that no nation has ever got. That is the distinction of absolute self-control and self-mastery."

But while Wilson waited for the moment when it would be possible for his purified American to ride out of the West to save the East, diplomatic relations with Germany began to move toward a crisis.

In declaring the neutrality of this nation, Wilson had asked that the belligerents abide by the 1909 Declaration of London which specified the rights and duties of neutrals. Immediately, however, England proclaimed a blockade of Germany which violated the London agreements. The next step was for Germany to declare a submarine blockade of England which also violated the agreements. But while Wilson was unwilling to force a crisis with England over these violations, he was willing to do so with Germany. For Wilson there must be no decrease in American foreign trade because national prosperity depended upon its continuation.

A fellow graduate student with Frederick Jackson Turner at Johns Hopkins University, Woodrow Wilson was committed to the idea that the closing of the frontier in 1890 marked the end of growth within the nation. "The days of glad expansion," he had written, "are gone, our life grows tense and difficult." Like Turner, Wilson believed that the national economy must now reach overseas for foreign markets if national prosperity and social health were to be maintained. "Our industries have expanded to such a point that they will burst their jackets if they cannot find a free outlet to the markets of the world.... Our domestic markets no longer suffice. We need foreign markets."

Wilson not only agreed with Theodore Roosevelt on the need for overseas expansion; he also agreed with Roosevelt's philosophical attitude about the role of the individual and national will in a competitive world. In describing the history of the Constitution, Wilson had written: "What we have been witnessing for the past hundred years is the transformation of a Newtonian constitution into a Darwinian constitution. The place where the strongest will is present will be the seat of sovereignty."

In the expansion of overseas trade, the corollary of this triumph of the will, for Wilson, was the following advice: "Since trade ignores national boundaries and the manufacturer insists on having the world as a market, the flag of his nation must follow him, and the doors of the nations which are closed must be battered down."

Against German submarine warfare, therefore, Wilson struck the pose of Wister's cowboy hero. The Virginian had defined himself as a man of perfect freedom. The Virginian was free to go where he pleased, when he pleased. It was a point of honor to allow no man to limit his freedom. To challenge this right of perfect freedom, to challenge the Virginian's honor, was to call for the code of the showdown, of the duel to the death. And this was the way that Wilson phrased his diplomatic notes to Germany. When the liner Lusitania was sunk in 1915 with the loss of American lives, Wilson informed the public that "there is such a thing as a nation being so right that it does not need to convince others by force that it is right." And he warned Germany that the United States would not tolerate danger to American citizens just because they were travelling in war zones. To insist on the right of Americans to travel safely anywhere in the world, however, said Wilson, was to insist on the right of all people to travel safely: "The sinking of passenger ships involves principles of humanity which throw into the background any special circumstances of detail that may be thought to affect the cases.... The government of the United States is contending for something much greater than mere rights of property or privileges of commerce. It is a contending for nothing less high and sacred than the rights of humanity."

But once more it was clear that for Wilson only the United States was capable of defending the rights of humanity. Therefore, the issue of universal rights became personalized into American rights, and international law became personalized into American honor:

> For my own part, I cannot consent to any abridgment of the rights of American citizens in any respect. The honor and self-respect of the nation is involved. We covet peace and shall preserve it at any cost but the loss of honor. To forbid our people to exercise their rights for fear we might be called upon to vindicate them would be a deep humiliation.... It would be a de-

liberate abdication of our hitherto proud position as spokesmen ... for the law and right.... What we are contending for in this matter is of the very essence of the things that have made America a sovereign nation.

When again American lives were lost in the submarine sinking of the allied steamer Sussex in March 1916, Wilson sent an ultimatum to Germany. "Unless the Imperial Government should now immediately declare and effect an abandonment of its present methods of submarine warfare against passenger and freight-carrying vessels, the government of the United States can have no choice but to sever diplomatic relations." Within the code of the duel established by the eastern aristocrat Wister for his cowboy hero, Woodrow Wilson, another eastern aristocrat, had drawn a line in the dust and warned the aggressive villain that one step further would lead to drawn guns and the final solution of death.

The German government responded to this warning by suspending its unrestricted submarine warfare until February 1917. Then, when it resumed submarine warfare, Wilson reacted to the German challenge by immediately breaking diplomatic relations and asking Congress for authority to arm American merchant ships carrying supplies to England. The inevitable conflict with German submarines brought the next step of asking Congress to declare war. When the United States officially declared war in April 1917, Wilson explained the meaning of American participation once again as that of a redeemer nation:

Our object ... is to vindicate the principles of peace and justice in the life of the world as against selfish and aristocratic power and to set up amongst the really free and self-governed peoples of the world such a concert of purpose and of action as will henceforth insure the observance of those principles. The present German submarine warfare against commerce is a warfare against mankind. It is a war against all nations.... The challenge is to all mankind.... The world must be made safe for democracy. ... The right is more precious than peace, and we shall fight for the things which we have always carried nearest our hearts— for democracy, for the rights and liberties of small nations, for a universal dominion of right by such a concert of free peoples as shall bring peace and safety to all nations and make the world itself at last free.

Even in his reluctance to take sides between Germany and the Allies, England and France, Wilson was acting within the dramatic framework of Wister's novel. The Virginian, as cowboy hero, was not an aggressive reformer. His philosophy was to go his own way and let other people go their own way. The cowboy fought only when challenged repeatedly by the aggressiveness of the villain. Or, to put it within the framework of John Dewey's distinction, the cowboy acted with defensive and innocent force against the threat of aggressive and corrupt violence from the villain. Now, from 1914 to 1917, the United States had been challenged repeatedly by such aggressive and corrupt violence until it must react with defensive and innocent force. But in acting in self-defense, the United States, as cowboy hero, was killing once and for all the aggressive villain who had brought chaos and conflict to the entire world community. Once more, therefore, the United States was defined as the fullest expression of the Reformation spirit which had sought for so long to purge the conspiratorial danger of medieval civilization. When Woodrow Wilson asked his nation to participate in a crusade to make the world safe for democracy, he saw the German and Austro-Hungarian empires as the last vestige of medievalism. And he believed their destruction would usher in a middle-class millennium for all men in all continents.

Wilson had taken an uncompromising stand against Germany and a compromising one against English violation of neutral rights in 1915 because, in spite of his conviction that England held corrupt war aims, he made a distinction between Germany as a potential villain and enemy and England as a potential friend and ally. In holding this clearcut distinction, Wilson represented the dramatically changing attitude of American intellectuals toward Germany between 1890 and 1914.

During the decades from 1810 to 1830 American intellectuals had turned against the outlook of Jefferson and the American Enlightenment that philosophical guidance was to be found in France. As the Enlightenment gave way to Romanticism in the United States, younger intellectuals, like the historian George Bancroft and the poet Ralph Waldo Emerson, turned violently against French influence and instead looked to Germany for such philosophical guidance. One major aspect of this change was the rejection of eighteenth-century cosmopolitanism in favor of extreme nationalism. Like the German philosophers, the Americans were rejecting the ideal of international civilization in favor of the ideal of autonomous national culture. Like the Germans, the Americans were attacking what they called soulless eighteenth-century materialism. Only in the nation, they argued, could one develop the full spiritual potential of the soul. And, again like the Germans, they attributed special spirituality to the Anglo-Saxon race. They too claimed that the Anglo-Saxons had preserved their autonomous national culture in the face of the attempt to impose universal and materialistic patterns of civilization upon them.

Beginning in the 1880s and 1890s, American scholars trained in the German universities had begun to establish social science disciplines. The academic prestige for these disciplines rested upon the authority of the method of the German seminar. The irony of the situation, however, was that these American scholars in the 1890s were beginning to turn away from the emphasis on national culture to an emphasis on international patterns. They were beginning to turn away from an emphasis on racial instinct toward an emphasis on the universal characteristics of human psychology. They were beginning to return to the eighteenth-century outlook of both internationalism and environmentalism.

In rediscovering Jefferson and the American Enlightenment, these new academics chose now to ignore the narrow nationalism and racism of American Romanticism and instead to stress the uniqueness of German hostility to the Enlightenment, to universalism and environmentalism. A significant part of the American return to the Enlightenment was to transform Marxist international doctrine into respectable middle-class terms. And the American intellectuals found particular guidance among the English Fabian socialists for this philosophic effort.

Together these two trends, one using Germany as a scapegoat for nineteenth-century racial nationalism and the other finding new intellectual links with England, began a major reorientation of American attitudes comparable to that of the period 1810–1830. Looking primarily to Germany for philosophic guidance between 1830 and 1890, Americans were now dramatically to reject such an association between 1890 and 1917, replacing it by a new philosophic friendship with England.

This trend was given further momentum by the way in which the progressive movement was defined in images of conflict between industrial democracy and feudal vestiges, against robber barons.

As German romantic nationalism was called into question, suddenly it was discovered that German political and social life was still feudal. As American intellectuals were forced to modify their nineteenth-century national identity with the physical landscape, with the pastoral tradition, they again used German Romanticism as a scapegoat to explain why the German people had not been taught to recognize the growth of industrialism and to adjust their political and social life to its democratic logic by ending political and social feudal patterns.

As war approached in the summer of 1914, American newspapers, like American intellectuals, were describing the cause of the crisis as the continued presence of feudalism in Europe: "Whatever happens," one editorial declared, "Europe—humanity—will not settle back into a position enabling these emperors . . . to give, on their individual choice or whim, the signal for destruction and massacre." And another editorial continued this theme:

> The threat of war on this unprecedented scale, its very nearness . . . are proofs of the backwardness of Europe. . . . It is medieval, it is barbarous; it is horrible that men should turn out at the behest of sovereigns. . . . If war must come, the only compensating benefit it would bring to Europe would be the crushing out of the imperial idea; the end, once for all times, in those three empires of absolute rule and the substitution for all powerful sovereigns and their titled advisors of an executive with power to carry out only the will of the people.

The beginning of the war in Europe also brought a group of books like that of John Jay Chapman, *Deutschland über Alles or Germany Speaks,* in which the author declared: "Germany then has been suffering and causing us to suffer from the fact that She . . . has been living in spiritual isolation since the dark ages. Her cure will come through her entry into the modern world." E. Ellsworth Shumaker's book *The World Crisis and the Way to Peace* concurred with Chapman, as did Owen Wister in *The Pentecost of Calamity,* where he wrote: "We have heard the wild, incoherent ring in many German voices besides the Kaiser's, and we know today that Germany's mania is analogous to those mental epidemics of the Middle Ages, when fanaticism . . . sent entire communities into various forms of madness."

Upper middle-class magazines like the *Outlook* and the *North American Review* continually defined the war in these terms and were ready in April 1917 to agree with the prophecy of Ignatius Donnelly in his *Golden Bottle* of 1892 that Americans could no longer tolerate corruption in the Old World. Donnelly had argued that, since evil men were always aggressive, they must necessarily invade the western hemisphere. He had argued that the only permanent protection of New World virtue was the total destruction of European vice. Now in 1917 the respectable *North American Review* echoed the man whom the upper middle class had ignored or despised a generation earlier:

> For three hundred years America has been striving to live its own life, apart from European intrigues and oppression. It has contented itself with being on the defensive, and with repelling European aggressions.... It has been effective with most of the European powers, but with one it has been unavailing. A large portion of the rest of Europe has been leavened with the New World spirit, but one power and its satellites still cherish the Old World spirit of despotism.... It is now incumbent upon us ... to pursue our enemy into Europe itself and crush it.

And a newspaper survey on the day of Wilson's war message reported: "Congressmen are beginning to look upon defense of our trade routes as merely incidental. The members of the House of Representatives, all fresh from home, now interpret the sentiment of their communities to mean that when the United States enters the war it will be as a great democracy aiding in the overthrow of an aristocracy of the worst sort."

The millennialism of the cranks of 1890, like Donnelly, had been transferred by 1912 and 1917 to the respectable, middle-of-the-road Presidents like Theodore Roosevelt and Woodrow Wilson. The millennialism of alienated fringe groups like the Populists of 1890 had become the millennialism of middle- and upper middle-class Americans who could call for a holy war to bring the kingdom of God on earth. In March 1917 an editorial in the *North American Review* had urged:

> ... so mighty a change cannot be wrought in a month or likely in a year,—and not at all unless and until the rulers of central Europe shall yield to a world of freemen. Wholly aside, then, from the injuries and insults which America has endured at the hands of the War Lord and which she is expected to advance as technical grounds for action, does not America's higher duty, her

greater opportunity, lie along the path of the shot heard "round the world"? Are we to permit others to finish the glorious work which we began . . . in the name of Almighty God.

Woodrow Wilson then should not be interpreted, any more than Theodore Roosevelt, as an isolated fanatic, as an unrepresentative ideologue, who by chance circumstance was in a position to define American participation in World War I as a crusade for world salvation. Steadily, but with increasing momentum, more and more of the American public had become caught up in a millennial out-look which told them that they stood at Armageddon to battle for the Lord. More and more middle-class readers turned either to the novels of Winston Churchill, in which the forces of light would de-feat the forces of blackness through the triumph of love, or to the novels of Owen Wister, in which the forces of light would defeat the forces of blackness through the triumph of violence.

If Wilson differed from his chief advisors, it was not by being less realistic, but by being more committed to love and less to violence than they were. These advisors and friends were Walter Hines Page, the American ambassador in England, Colonel Edward House, Wilson's closest friend and confidant, and Robert Lansing, who became Secretary of State in 1915.

Page had reacted immediately in 1914 by demanding war against Germany because, he wrote: "We should do for Europe on a large scale essentially what we did for Cuba on a small scale and thereby usher in a new era in human history. . . . The United States would stand, as no other nation has ever stood in the world—predominant and unselfish—on the highest ideals ever reached in human govern-ment. It is a vision as splendid as the Holy Grael."

Colonel House throughout 1915 and 1916 tried to persuade Wil-son to go to war against Germany because "we had no intention of permitting a military aristocracy to dominate the world. . . .He believed this was a fight between democracy and aristocracy and we would stand with democracy."

And Secretary of State Lansing wrote in January 1916:

It is my opinion that the military oligarchy which rules Germany is a bitter enemy to democracy in every form; that, if that oli-garchy triumphs over the liberal governments of Great Britain and France, it will then turn upon us as its next obstacle to im-perial rule over the world.

Bibliography

This bibliography will list the books that have been most important in developing my ideas about the progressive imagination. However, the attempt to interrelate artistic and philosophic expression results from my association with the American Studies Program at the University of Minnesota, and especially from the several years I spent in teaching a seminar on the 1890–1917 period in conjunction with Professor Joseph J. Kwiat of the University of Minnesota English Department.

Much of my perspective on the progressive mind also comes from the dissertations done by my students at the University of Minnesota. I am especially indebted to Gregg Campbell for his thesis on Walter Lippmann, Joseph Dubbert for his thesis on William Allen White, and Harry Stein for his thesis on Lincoln Steffens. I have borrowed explicitly most of the themes in the chapter on Theodore Roosevelt from a dissertation by Richard Fry, the ideas on the cowboy and Owen Wister from a dissertation by John Barsness, and the analysis of Thomas Dixon from a dissertation by F. Garvin Davenport which has been published as *The Myth of Southern History* (1970). The themes developed in the chapter on Norris and Churchill have been taken from a dissertation by Robert Schneider which has been published as *Five Novelists of the Progressive Era* (1965). In addition, I have learned much about American music from unpublished papers by Colleen Davidson and Charles Sigmund, about Ignatius Donnelly from a paper by Michael Passi and about Noble Drew Ali from a paper by Steven Johnson.

Chapter I
The Crisis of 1890

The interrelationship between the breakdown of medieval civilization and the simultaneous discovery of the New World that encouraged the imaginative outlook in the Renaissance and Reformation which defined America in utopian or millennial terms has received a great deal of scholarly attention in the last decade. The most important books dealing with this theme are Charles Sanford, *The Quest for Paradise* (1961) which emphasizes the way Renaissance definitions of America as a place where man could reenter paradise have continued to find expression in twentieth-century American political and literary thought, and Ernest L. Tuveson, *Redeemer Nation, The Idea of America's Millennial Role* (1968) which emphasizes the transfer of Reformation millennialism to the New World and also traces its continuity into twentieth-century America. Also important is Edmundo O'Gorman's *The Invention of America* (1961) which describes the transfer of the medieval view of Europe as the center of the World to the Renaissance view that the New World might be that center. Developing this theme is an essay by Mircea Eliade, "Paradise and Utopia: Mythical Geography and Eschatology," in *Utopias and Utopian Thought* (1967), edited by Frank Manuel. Durand Echeverria in his *Mirage in the West* (1957) describes the development of these imaginative patterns in eighteenth-century France and the way in which they were used by French intellectuals to define the American Revolution as the liberation of the New World paradise from European corruption. Cushing Strout, *The American Image of the Old World,* (1963) provides a summation of these ideas of the difference between Europe and America.

City on a Hill (1964) by Loren Baritz traces the important role of these themes from seventeenth-century New England to early nineteenth-century America in giving European settlers in America a sense of rebirth and regeneration. A. Whitney Griswold, *Farming and Democracy* (1948) and Arthur K. Moore, *The Frontier Mind*

(1957) describe the importance of physical nature to the identity of Americans at the end of the eighteenth century. Henry Nash Smith, *Virgin Land: The American West as Symbol and Myth* (1950) is the pioneering book which has emphasized the way in which nineteenth-century Americans looked to physical nature for spiritual salvation. R. W. B. Lewis, *The American Adam* (1955) explores the relationship of the religion of nature to nineteenth-century novels, and David Levin explores the same relationship in historical writing in his book, *History as Romantic Art* (1959).

Frank Kramer in his *Voices in the Valley: Mythology and Folk Belief in the Shaping of the Middle West* (1964) and Leo Marx in his *The Machine in the Garden: Technology and the Pastoral Ideal in America* (1964) discuss the growing national crisis of the nineteenth century as Americans began to realize that the factory and the city were spreading over the landscape. Frederic C. Jaher's *Doubters and Dissenters* (1964) describes the general intellectual confusion and pessimism that possessed a wide variety of Americans by the end of the nineteenth century.

More traditional intellectual histories which cover the late nineteenth and early twentieth centuries are Vernon L. Parrington, *The Beginnings of Critical Realism in America* (1930); Charles Beard, *The American Spirit* (1942); Ralph Gabriel, *The Course of American Democratic Thought* (1956); Merle Curti, *The Growth of American Thought* (1964); Stow Persons, *American Minds* (1958); and Harvey Wish, *Society and Thought in America*, Volume 2 (1962).

The context of Sumner's thinking can be found in Richard Hofstadter's *Social Darwinism in American Thought* (1944); Stow Persons, ed., *Evolutionary Thought in America* (1956); Sidney Fine's *Laissez-Faire and the General Welfare State, a Study of Conflict in American Thought, 1865–1901* (1956); Robert McCloskey's *American Conservatism in the Age of Enterprise* (1951); and Joseph Dorfman's *The Economic Mind in American Civilization*, Volume 3 (1946). See also Edith H. Parker, "William Graham Sumner and the Frontier," *Southwest Review*, 41 (Autumn, 1956): 357–365.

The intellectual history of American reform movements is described by Eric Goldman in his *Rendezvous with Destiny* (1952) and by Richard Hofstadter in *The Age of Reform from Bryan to F.D.R.* (1955). Both are critical of Populism and see it linked to provincial nineteenth-century ideology which they find disappearing by the early twentieth century. Norman Pollack has defended the

Populists against this charge in *The Populist Response to Industrial America: Midwestern Populist Thought* (1962), as has Martin Ridge in *Ignatius Donnelly* (1962) and Walter T. K. Nugent in *The Tolerant Populists: Kansas Populism and Nativism* (1963).

The most important recent studies of Bryan and the campaign of 1896 are Paul Glad, *The Trumpet Soundeth: William Jennings Bryan and His Democracy, 1896–1912* (1960) and *McKinley, Bryan and the People* (1964); Robert F. Durden, *The Climax of Populism* (1965); and Stanley Jones, *The Presidential Election of 1896* (1964).

The ideological context of American imperialism is most fully discussed in Walter LaFeber, *The New Empire, An Interpretation of American Expansion, 1860–1898* (1963). Also helpful are Albert K. Weinberg, *Manifest Destiny* (1936); Julius Pratt, *The Expansionists of 1898* (1936); and Ernest May, *Imperial Democracy* (1961). Richard Hofstadter's essay, "Manifest Destiny and the Philippines," in Daniel Aaron, ed., *America in Crisis* (1952), relates expansion to the psychological impasse of the 1890s.

The development of an overseas frontier as an answer to the crisis of the 1890s is a theme which has attracted a great deal of scholarly activity in the 1970s. Among the most significant studies are David Healy, *U.S. Expansionism: The Imperialist Urge in the 1890s* (1970); Milton Plesur, *America's Outward Thrust* (1971); Robert Beisner, *From the Old Diplomacy to the New* (1975); Charles Campbell, *The Transformation of American Foreign Relations* (1976); and John M. Dobson, *The United States Becomes a Great Power, 1880–1914* (1978).

There has been a very important reinterpretation of Populism since 1970. James Youngdale, *Populism* (1975); Robert McMath, *Populist Vanguard* (1975); and Lawrence Goodwyn, *Democratic Promise: The Populist Movement in America* (1976) argue persuasively that many Populists were attempting to create a new, more cooperative agricultural community rather than trying to conserve the old, more individualistic farmers' frontier.

Roger C. Bannister, *Social Darwinism: Science and Myth in Anglo-American Social Thought* (1979) is also critical of previous scholarship on that subject for its failure to understand the complexities and dynamics of the late nineteenth-century intellectual community as it tried to understand and use Darwin's theories.

Cecelia Tichi, *New World, New Earth: Environmental Reform in American Literature from the Puritans through Whitman* (1979) provides an excellent analysis of the belief in the strength or plenitude of nature in America from 1600 to 1870 and then the collapse of that faith between 1870 and 1914. Her book makes clear how important it was for Progressives to substitute industrialism for physical nature as the new source of plenitude and limitless abundance. In relation to that theme in Progressivism, see Daniel Fox, *The Discovery of Abundance* (1967).

Chapter II
Turner and Beard

Turner's thought is linked to the nineteenth century pastoral tradition in the concluding chapter of Henry Nash Smith's *Virgin Land* (1950). His connection to European historical and social thought is explored by Lee Benson in his book, *Turner and Beard* (1966). The most recent extensive study of Turner is by Richard Hofstadter in *The Progressive Historians: Turner, Beard, and Parrington* (1968). See also the analytical articles by Robert F. Berkhofer, Jr., "Space, Time, Culture, and the New Frontier," *Agricultural History*, 38 (January, 1964): 21–30; William Coleman, "Science and Symbol in the Turner Frontier Hypothesis," *American Historical Review*, 72 (October, 1966): 22–49; Rudolph Freund, "Turner's Theory of Social Evolution," *Agricultural History*, 19 (April, 1945): 78–87; Gene Gressley, "The Turner Thesis—A Problem in Historiography," *Agricultural History*, 32 (October, 1958): 227–244; Gilman Ostrander, "Turner and the Germ Theory," *Agricultural History*, 32 (October, 1958): 258–261; and Walter Rundell, Jr., "Concepts of the Frontier and the West," *Arizona and the West*, 1 (Spring, 1959): 13–41.

Essays on Turner and Beard appear in *The American Historian* (1960) by Harvey Wish, and Beard's place in historical writing is described by Robert Skotheim, *American Intellectual Histories and Historians* (1966). Various aspects of Beard's outlook are explored in *Charles A. Beard: An Appraisal* (1954), edited by Howard Beale. Bernard Borning has a full length study, *The Political and Social Thought of Charles A. Beard* (1962).

Cushing Strout's book, *The Pragmatic Revolt in American History: Carl Becker and Charles Beard* (1958), links Beard with another major historian of the progressive era. This relationship is also described in my book, *Historians against History: The Frontier Thesis and the National Covenant in American Historical Writing since 1830* (1965). Beard and Becker also are contrasted to Turner in this study. Beard's other fellow pioneer in "The New History,"

James Harvey Robinson, is discussed in Luther V. Hendricks' *James Harvey Robinson* (1946) and in an essay by Harry Elmer Barnes in *American Masters of Social Science* (1927), edited by Howard W. Odum. The general problem is analyzed by Charles Crowe in his article, "The Emergence of Progressive History," *The Journal of the History of Ideas,* 27 (January, 1966): 109–124.

American Historical Explanations (1973) by Gene Wise is indispensable for understanding Turner's crisis in the 1890s. Wise uses the theoretical framework of Thomas Kuhn, *The Structure of Scientific Revolutions* (1961) to analyze the way in which the disappearance of the agricultural frontier removed the economic force which Turner believed was necessary for historical progress. Wise does not clearly identify the way in which industrialism was substituted by Beard as the economic force which would drive history in a Progressive direction in the twentieth century. He does, however, clarify the difficulties experienced by Beard in the 1920s and 1930s in trying to sustain a Progressive interpretation of history. And Wise identifies the late 1930s and 1940s as the period when the stress in Beard's explanation-form became so great that it totally collapsed.

Chapter III
Harmony through Technological Order

The view of industrialism as an economic system that demanded disciplined patterns of rational and objective order is most fully analyzed in Robert H. Wiebe, *The Search for Order, 1877–1920* (1967). It is also the theme of two important books by Samuel P. Hays, *The Response to Industrialism* (1957) and *Conservation and the Gospel of Efficiency* (1958). The place of Frederick W. Taylor in the intellectual history of the early twentieth century is fully discussed by Samuel Haber, *Efficiency and Uplift: Scientific Management in the Progressive Era, 1890–1920* (1964). The most complete analyses of Ford are to be found in Keith Sward, *The Legend of Henry Ford* (1948) and Allan Nevins and Frank E. Hill, *Ford: The Times, The Man, The Company* (1954). An illuminating analysis of Ford as an exponent of a religion of nature and industrialism is to be found in Frank Kramer, *Voices in the Valley* (1964).

The most detailed study of Veblen is still Joseph Dorfman, *Thorstein Veblen and His America* (1935). Also useful are the essays in *Thorstein Veblen: A Critical Reappraisal* (1958), edited by D. F. Dowd, and *Thorstein Veblen* (1968), edited by Carlton C. Qualey. Veblen is linked to other progressives in H. S. Commager, *The*

American Mind (1950); Daniel Aaron, *Men of Good Hope* (1951); and David W. Noble, *The Paradox of Progressive Thought* (1958).

Taylor, Ford, and Veblen have received a great deal of scholarly attention in the 1970s. Significant studies are Sudhir Kakar, *Frederick Taylor* (1970); Anne Jardin, *The First Henry Ford* (1970); David E. Nye, *Henry Ford: Ignorant Idealist* (1979); Raymond Wik, *Henry Ford and Grass-Roots America* (1972); David W. Seckler, *Thorstein Veblen and the Institutionalists* (1975); and John P. Diggins, *The Bard of Savagery: Thorstein Veblen and Modern Social Theory* (1978). James Gilbert, *Work without Salvation: America's Intellectuals and Industrial Alienation, 1880-1910* (1977) and Daniel T. Rogers, *The Work Ethic in Industrial America, 1850-1920* (1978) explore the crisis which Taylor, Ford, and Veblen were trying to overcome. James Gilbert, *Designing the Industrial State* (1972) and David F. Noble, *America by Design* (1978) describe the outlook which wanted to impose greater social discipline through the use of industrial and engineering techniques. John F. Kasson, *Civilizing the Machine: Technology and Republican Values of America, 1776-1900* (1976) and Kenneth Roemer, *The Obsolete Necessity: America in Utopian Writings, 1888-1900* (1976) provide historical perspective on the replacement of the agricultural by the industrial frontier after 1900.

Chapter IV
The Social Nature of the Social Man

Interpretations of John Dewey in relationship to progressivism can be found in Morton White, *Social Thought in America: The Revolt against Formalism* (1950); Merle Curti, *The Social Thought of American Educators* (1935); Christopher Lasch, *The New Radicalism in America* (1965); Paul K. Conkin, *Puritans and Pragmatists* (1968); and C. Wright Mills, *Sociology and Pragmatism* (1966).

The most important studies of Dewey's connection to progressive education are *The Transformation of the School: Progressivism in American Education* (1961) by Laurence Cremin and *Popular Education and Democratic Thought in America* (1962) by Rush Welter. Recent studies of Dewey in the context of philosophical tradition are John E. Smith, *The Spirit of American Philosophy* (1963); *American Religious Philosophy* (1967) by Robert J. Roth, S. J.; *The Political Theory of John Dewey* (1968) by A. H. Somjee; and *The Chicago Pragmatists* (1969) by Darnell Rucker.

Charles Cooley is discussed in *An Introduction to the History of Sociology* (1948), edited by Harry Elmer Barnes; in David W. Noble, *The Paradox of Progressive Thought* (1958); and Charles H.

Page, *Class and American Sociology* (1940). Cooley's concern for community can be placed in context by relating it to the theme developed in *The Quest for Community* (1968) by R. Jackson Wilson.

The relationship of Rauschenbusch to the social gospel movement can be gathered from James Dombrowski, *The Early Days of Christian Socialism in America* (1936); Aaron I. Abell, *The Urban Impact on American Protestantism, 1865–1900* (1943); Charles H. Hopkins, *The Rise of the Social Gospel in American Protestantism, 1860–1915* (1940); and Henry F. May, *Protestant Churches and Industrial America* (1949).

The genteel tradition and its relationship to progressivism is discussed in Henry F. May, *The End of American Innocence* (1959) and in Arthur Mann, *Yankee Reformers in the Urban Age* (1954). Robert H. Bremner, *From the Depths: The Discovery of Poverty in the United States* (1956); Roy Lubove, *The Progressives and the Slums* (1962); and Allen F. Davis, *Spearheads for Reform: The Social Settlements and the Progressive Movement, 1890–1914* (1967) describe the changing attitudes toward poverty and the poor and the increasing involvement of the middle class with reform. But Roy Lubove, *The Struggle for Social Security* (1968) demonstrates how limited this philosophical change was and to what a large extent older attitudes of individual self-sufficiency continued to be dominant.

Hostile attitudes toward the Catholic and Jewish, Latin and Slavic immigrants are discussed by John Higham, *Strangers in the Land: Patterns of American Nativism, 1860–1925* (1955); Barbara M. Solomon, *Ancestors and Immigrants, A Changing New England Tradition* (1953); Edward N. Saveth, *American Historians and European Immigrants* (1948); E. Digby Baltzell, *The Protestant Establishment, Aristocracy and Caste in America* (1964); Edward G. Hartman, *The Movement to Americanize the Immigrant* (1948); and Donald L. Kinzer, *An Episode in Anti-Catholicism: The American Protective Association* (1964).

Muckraking is described by Louis Filler, *Crusaders for American Liberalism* (1939) and David M. Chalmers, *The Social and Political Ideas of the Muckrakers* (1964).

David W. Marcell, *Progress and Pragmatism: James, Dewey, Beard, and the American Idea of Progress* (1974) is one of the most important recent studies of Progressivism. Neil Coughlan, *Young John Dewey* (1975) provides a necessary perspective. Valuable studies have been made of the relationship of social theory to the rise of professionalism among academics. Some of these are Burton Bledstein, *The Culture of Professionalism* (1976); Mary O. Furner, *Advocacy and Objectivity: A Crisis in the Professionalization of American Social Science, 1865–1905* (1975); Herman and Julia Schwendinger, *The Sociologists of the Chair* (1974); Thomas Haskell, *The Emergence of Professional Social Science* (1977); and Joel Spring, *Education and the Rise of the Corporate State* (1972). William F. Fine, *Progressive Evolutionism and American Sociology, 1890–1920* (1978) analyzes the way in which most sociologists interpreted evolution to mean inevitable progress. Paul A. Carter, *The Spiritual Crisis of the Gilded Age* (1971) provides insights into the origins of the Social Gospel movement.

Chapter V
Women for Progress and Progress for Women

Ross Evans Paulson, *Women's Suffrage and Prohibition* (1973) and David Pivar, *Purity Crusade: Sexual Morality and Social Control* (1973) discuss the interrelationship of women's reform movements and the Social Gospel. The most significant studies of Jane Addams are Daniel Levine, *Jane Addams and the Liberal Tradition* (1971) and Allen F. Davis, *American Heroine: The Life and Legend of Jane Addams* (1975). Josephine Goldmark, *Impatient Crusader: Florence Kelley's Life Story* (1955) provides an analysis of one of Addams' colleagues. Important articles are James McGovern, "American Women's Pre World War I Freedom in Manners and Morals," *Journal of American History,* 55 (September, 1968); J. O. C. Phillips, "The Education of Jane Addams," *History of Education Quarterly,* 14 (Spring, 1974); John P. Rousmanière, "Cultural Hybrid in the Slum: The College Woman and the Settlement House," *American Quarterly,* 28 (Spring, 1976); and Jill Conway, "Women Reformers and American Culture, 1870–1930," *Journal of Social History,* V (Winter, 1971).

William O'Neill, *Everyone Was Brave* (1971); Peter Filene, *Him/Herself: Sex Roles in Modern America* (1974); Joseph L. Dubbert, *A Man's Place: Masculinity in Transition* (1979); and William H. Chafe, *Women and Equality* (1977) provide broad perspectives on the drama of changing relationships between women and men during the Progressive Era, as does Barbara K. Campbell, *The Liberated Women of 1914: Prominent Women in the Progressive Era* (1979).

For Charlotte Perkins Gilman, see Carl Degler, "Charlotte Perkins

Gilman and the Theory and Practice of Feminism," *American Quarterly*, 7 (Spring, 1956), and the excellent new study by Mary A. Hill, *Charlotte Perkins Gilman: The Making of a Radical Feminist, 1860–1896* (1980).

Jean B. Quandt, *From the Small Town to the Great Community: The Social Thought of Progressive Intellectuals* (1970) is very important because it illuminates the parallels between the thinking of many male and female intellectuals. It is especially useful on Mary Parker Follett, as is the article by Henry S. Kariel, "The New Order of Mary Parker Follett," *Western Political Quarterly*, VIII (September, 1955).

Chapter VI
The South

The writings of C. Vann Woodward are crucial for an understanding of the South at the beginning of the twentieth century. Most pertinent are his "Tom Watson and the Negro," *Journal of Southern History*, 4 (February, 1938): 14–33; *Tom Watson, Agrarian Rebel* (1938); *Origins of the New South, 1877–1913* (1951); and *The Strange Career of Jim Crow* (1955). Also important for the relationship of the Negro to Populism are two articles by Jack Abramowitz, "The Negro in the Agrarian Revolt," *Agricultural History*, 23 (April, 1950): 89–95, and "The Negro in the Populist Movement," *Journal of Negro History*, 38 (July, 1953): 257–289. This relationship is explored in detail in Helen G. Edmonds' *The Negro and Fusion Politics in North Carolina, 1894–1901* (1951) and Charles E. Wynes, *Race Relations in Virginia, 1870–1902* (1961). Useful in making comparisons with Watson and Georgia are the studies of Mississippi politics, *Revolt of the Rednecks* (1951) by Albert Kirwan and *Pitchford Ben Tillman* (1944) by Francis B. Simkins.

Growing anti-Negro attitudes are described by I. A. Newby in his *Jim Crow's Defense, Anti-Negro Thought in America, 1900–1930* (1965).

There is no book yet on Thomas Dixon but there are two informative articles: Raymond A. Cook, "The Man behind the Birth of a Nation," *North Carolina Historical Review*, 39 (Autumn, 1962): 519–540, and Maxwell Bloomfield, "Dixon's the Leopard's Spots: A Study in Popular Racism," *American Quarterly*, 14 (Fall, 1964): 387–401.

Three valuable studies of the interrelationship of Progressivism and racism in the South are Bruce Clayton, *The Savage Ideal: Intolerance and Intellectual Leadership in the South, 1890–1914* (1972); Jack Temple Kirby, *Darkness at the Dawning: Race and Reform in the Progressive South* (1972); and Robert L. Allen, *Reluctant Reformers: Racism and Social Reform in the United States* (1975).

Chapter VII
The Negro and Progressivism

General studies of the Negro in American culture are John Hope Franklin, *From Slavery to Freedom* (1956) and August Meier and Elliott M. Rudwick, *From Plantation to Ghetto* (1966). A description of the deteriorating position of the Negro by 1890 is to be found in Rayford W. Logan, *The Negro in American Life and Thought: The Nadir, 1877–1901* (1954). Two books which analyze Negro thought during the progressive period are August Meier, *Negro Thought in America, 1880–1915* (1963) and S. P. Fullinwider, *The Mind and Mood of Black America* (1969). The role of Booker T. Washington is discussed in Samuel Spencer, *Booker T. Washington and the Negro's Place in American Life* (1955) and *Booker T. Washington and His Critics* (1962), edited by Hugh Hawkins. Two studies of W. E. B. DuBois are Francis L. Broderick, *W. E. B. DuBois, Negro Leader in Time of Crisis* (1959) and Elliott M. Rudwick, *W. E. B. DuBois, A Study in Minority Group Leadership* (1960). Edmund D. Cronon, *Black Moses: The Story of Marcus Garvey and the U.N.I.A.* (1955); C. Eric Lincoln, *The Black Muslims in America* (1961); and E. V. Essien-Udom, *Black Nationalism, A Search for an Identity in America* (1962) are excellent analyses of the development of black nationalism.

One of the best studies of the frustrations of blacks in the Progressive Era is June Sochen, *The Unbridgeable Gap: Blacks and Their Quest for the American Dream, 1900–1930* (1972). Also useful are Rayford W. Logan, ed., *W. E. B. DuBois, A Profile* (1971) and Louis Harlan, *Booker T. Washington* (1972).

Chapter VIII
Freedom from Form

Robert H. Bremner's *From the Depths* relates art and literature to the progressive movement. An important history of painting is

John I. H. Baur, *Revolution and Tradition in Modern American Art* (1951). On the interrelationships of art, literature, and progressivism, see Joseph J. Kwiat, "Dreiser and the Graphic Artist," *American Quarterly*, 3 (Summer, 1951): 127–141; "Dreiser's 'The Genius' and Everett Shinn, the 'Ash Can' Painter," *PMLA*, 67 (March, 1952): 15–31; and "The Newspaper Experience: The 'Ash Can' Painters," *The Western Humanities Review*, 4 (Autumn, 1952): 335–341.

Norris Kelly Smith, *Frank Lloyd Wright* (1966) and Sherman Paul, *Louis Sullivan* (1962) are good analyses of the place of these two architects in American cultural history. See also Hugh Duncan, *Culture and Democracy; The struggle for Form in Society and Architecture in Chicago and the Middle West during the Life and Times of Louis B. Sullivan* (1965).

The most recent history of American music is Wilfrid Meller's *Music in a New Found Land* (1966).

There has been a great deal of interest in Charles Ives and Frank Lloyd Wright in the 1970s. Books on Wright include Charlotte Willard, *F. L. Wright* (1972); Robert C. Twombly, *Frank Lloyd Wright* (1973); and Robert Fishman, *Urban Utopias in the Twentieth Century* (1977). On Ives, see Rosalie Perry, *Charles Ives and the American Mind* (1974) and Frank Rossiter, *Charles Ives and His America* (1975). Arthur F. Wertheim, *The New York Little Renaissance: Iconoclasm, Modernism, and Nationalism in American Culture, 1908–1917* (1976) provides an overview of the ferment in the artistic world.

Chapter IX
The Novelists

The history of American literary naturalism is discussed in Lars Ahnebrink, *The Beginnings of Naturalism in American Fiction* (1950) and Charles C. Walcutt, *American Literary Naturalism, A Divided Stream* (1956). The most recent study of Norris is Donald Pizer, *The Novels of Frank Norris* (1966). See also Jay Martin, *Harvests of Change; American Literature, 1865–1914* (1967). Churchill is discussed in Warren Titus, *Winston Churchill* (1963) and in Robert Schneider, *Five Novelists of the Progressive Era* 1965). Norris and Churchill are related to progressivism in David W. Noble, *The Eternal Adam and the New World Garden: The Central Myth in the American Novel* (1968).

Cynthia E. Russett, *Darwin in America* (1976) explores the influence of Darwinian evolution on the naturalists, and Robert W. Schneider,

Novelist to a Generation: The Life and Thought of Winston Churchill (1976) has written a fine study of Churchill and his place in the Progressive Era.

Chapter X
Theodore Roosevelt and the American Paradox

George Mowry, *The Era of Theodore Roosevelt, 1900–1912* (1958) places Roosevelt within the context of progressivism, and his earlier book, *Theodore Roosevelt and the Progressive Movement* (1946), describes that important period of Roosevelt's career. Other important studies of Roosevelt are William H. Harbough, *Power and Responsibility: The Life and Times of Theodore Roosevelt* (1961) and John M. Blum, *The Republican Roosevelt* (1954). Roosevelt's connections to the national identity crisis brought about by the end of the frontier are discussed in Roderick Nash, *Wilderness and the American Mind* (1967) and G. Edward White, *The Eastern Establishment and the Western Experience: The West of Frederic Remington, Theodore Roosevelt, and Owen Wister* (1968). Roosevelt's philosophy of imperialism has been most recently described by David H. Burton, *Theodore Roosevelt, Confident Imperialist* (1968). Roosevelt's part in the development of a conservative philosophy emphasizing the need for corporate unity has been analyzed by Gabriel Kolko, *The Triumph of Conservatism* (1963) and James Weinstein, *The Corporate Ideal in the Liberal State, 1900–1918* (1968). Charles Forcey has discussed the attitudes of the major progressive philosophers, Herbert Croly, Walter Weyl, and Walter Lippmann of the *New Republic* magazine, toward Roosevelt in *The Crossroads of Liberalism* (1961). Thomas Dyer, *Theodore Roosevelt and the Idea of Race* (1980) is an excellent analysis of the centrality of Roosevelt's concern for national revitalization.

Vaudeville is analyzed by Albert F. McLean, Jr., *American Vaudeville as Ritual* (1965). The emphasis on individual success and positive thinking is described by John G. Cawelti, *Apostles of the Self-Made Man* (1965); Sigmund Diamond, *The Reputation of American Businessmen* (1955); and Donald Meyer, *The Positive Thinkers* (1965).

John R. Gillis, *Youth and History* (1974) describes the way in which the dominant cultures in Germany, England, and the United States from 1890-1914, encouraged boys and young men to become more aggressive but within the context of uniformed and disciplined sports and semimilitary activities such as the Boy Scouts. Walter Karp, *The*

Politics of War, 1890–1920 (1979) captures this spirit of dynamic militarism as do Peter Karsten, *The Naval Aristocracy: The Golden Age of Annapolis and the Emergence of Modern American Navalism* (1972) and Richard D. Challener, *Admirals, Generals, and American Foreign Policy, 1898–1914* (1973).

Chapter XI
Woodrow Wilson and World War I

Woodrow Wilson and the Progressive Era, 1910–1917 (1954) by Arthur S. Link is the most important book relating Wilson to progressivism. See also John M. Blum, *Woodrow Wilson and the Politics of Morality* (1956). The most thorough study of the intellectual context of American foreign policy is Robert E. Osgood, *Ideals and Self-Interest in America's Foreign Relations* (1953). William Appleman Williams, *The Tragedy of American Diplomacy* (1959) provides a critical analysis. Robert E. Quirk, *An Affair of Honor: Woodrow Wilson and the Occupation of Veracruz* (1962) is a biting footnote to Wilson's moralistic approach. More favorable to Wilson are Arthur S. Link, *Wilson the Diplomatist* (1957) and Ernest May, *The World War and American Isolation* (1959). A description of the American emphasis on neutral rights is Alice M. Morrissy, *The American Defense of Neutral Rights, 1914–1917* (1939). Useful articles are Richard Leopold, "The Problem of American Intervention, 1917: An Historical Retrospect," *World Politics*, 2 (April, 1950): 404–425, and Daniel M. Smith, "National Interest and American Intervention, 1917: An Historiographical Appraisal," *Journal of American History*, 52 (June, 1965): 5–24.

Sidney Bell, *Righteous Conquest: Woodrow Wilson and the Evolution of the New Diplomacy* (1972) is a good analysis of Wilson's belief in the necessity of developing an overseas frontier. *The Captain America Complex* (1973) by Robert Jewett and *The America Monomyth* (1979) by Robert Jewett and John S. Lawrence are valuable additions to our understanding of the tradition of America as a redeemer nation. George Blakey, *Historians on the Home Front* (1970) and Carol Gruber, *Mars and Minerva* (1975) describe the enthusiasm of much of the academic community for Wilson's attempt to create a new world order. Richard Pells, *Radical Visions and American Dreams* (1973) is a very important study of the failure of intellectuals between 1920 and 1940 to reestablish a coherent vision of progress after the disillusionment of 1919.

Index